Governance
in Higher Education

*Published by Economica Ltd,
9 Wimpole Street
London W1M 8LB*

© Economica Ltd, 2001

All rights reserved

First published 2001

Printed in France

*Werner Z. Hirsch and Luc E. Weber
Governance in Higher Education
The University in a State of Flux*

ISBN 2-7178-4190-3

Governance in Higher Education

The University in a State of Flux

Edited by

Werner Z. Hirsch
Luc E. Weber

ECONOMICA
London • Paris • Genève

CONTENTS

PREFACE BY *Werner Z. Hirsch and Luc E. Weber*   vii

CONTRIBUTORS   xi

PART 1   **Missions and Responsibilities of Research Universities**   1
  CHAPTER 1   The University at the Millennium: Missions and Responsibilities of Research Universities   3
  Frank H. T. Rhodes

PART 2   **Status and Recent Trends in the Governance of Universities**   15
  CHAPTER 2   Recent Changes in the Structure and Governance of American Research Universities   17
  Katharine C. Lyall
  CHAPTER 3   Fire, Ready, Aim! University Decision-Making During an Era of Rapid Change   26
  James J. Duderstadt
  CHAPTER 4   Governance, Change and the Universities in Western Europe   52
  Guy Neave
  CHAPTER 5   Governance: the Challenge of Globalization   67
  Howard Newby

PART 3   **Governance Principles**   77

CHAPTER 6   Critical University Decisions and their Appropriate Makers: Some Lessons from the Economic Theory of Federalism   79
Luc. E. Weber

CHAPTER 7   Some Thoughts about University Governance   94
Henry Rosovsky

CHAPTER 8   Setting Strategic Direction in Academic Institutions: The Planning Dilemma   105
Peter Lorange

PART 4   **Improved Governance**   123

CHAPTER 9   Universities as Organizations and their Governance   125
Peter Scott

CHAPTER 10   Initiatives for Improving Shared Governance   143
Werner Z. Hirsch

CHAPTER 11   Variety and Impact: Differences that matter
Some Thoughts on the Variety of University Governance Systems and their Impact on University Policies and Strategies   155
Hans J.A. van Ginkel

CHAPTER 12   Three Successful Modes of Research Governance: Lessons from the Past, Issues of the Present, Implications for the Future   167
Robert Dynes, Sharon E. R. Franks, Charles F. Kennel

CHAPTER 13   An Agenda for the Governing Board   182
Harold M. Williams

APPENDIX   **The Glion Declaration 2000**   193
Frank H. T. Rhodes (on behalf of the Glion Colloquium)

PREFACE

Universities share a growing concern that they will be at risk if they do not adapt more rapidly to their changing environment and to new challenges. If this concern is valid—and the participants of the Glion Colloquium in their May 1998 meeting in Glion, Switzerland, concluded that it is—the governance of universities is becoming increasingly crucial, particularly for research universities (The Glion Declaration, 1998). Therefore, the Glion Colloquium decided to devote its January 2000 meeting in Del Mar, California, to the question of governance.

The Glion Colloquium is a private initiative. The group includes a number of higher education leaders from leading research universities from Western Europe and the United States—well-known scholars in higher education (some active, some recently retired), as well as industrialists and journalists. They share the view that the big changes characterizing our period represent serious challenges for universities. They plan to meet periodically to analyze these developments and to make concrete proposals for action.

The structures, missions, and challenges of Western European and American universities have much in common. But there are also significant differences—one relating to governing boards. In the United States, these boards fulfill important functions. But, in Western Europe, they do not exist at all, or only in a weaker form. There, mechanisms applied to advise and/or control rectors, vice chancellors, or presidents vary greatly from one university to the next. Some European countries have boards similar to American boards but with less or little decision-making power. Others have no board or a board without authority; they have instead "participation councils" in which the different internal stakeholders are represented (faculty, researchers, students, administrators). Moreover, some of the roles exercised by American boards are in Europe played by the state or other groups that monitor or make some formal decisions, such as nominating the rector or professor proposed by the university. There are great differences from one country to another, even from one university to the next.

The editors of this volume are quite aware that it concentrates somewhat on the American environment characterized by powerful boards. However, they are convinced that the thoughts expressed about the role of boards are of great interest on both continents. This is obvious for readers in the United States, where the role of boards has come under significant scrutiny and, at times, criticism. This is true for the European readers because the solution of having boards assuming some of the powers that the state used to have and supporting and/or monitoring the action of the rector, vice chancellor, or president is gaining support.

The January 2000 Glion Colloquium addressed the defining issues of *governance in research universities*. Participants agreed to look upon *governance* in a university as the formal and informal exercise of authority under laws, policies and rules that articulate the rights and responsibilities of various actors, including rules by which they interact, so as to help achieve the institution's academic objectives. To be effective, a powerful governance process must be embedded in an appropriate governance structure suited to the institution's purposes and consonant with its culture. Management, in contrast, involves the responsibility for effectively operating the institution and achieving its goals. Managerial responsibilities are in the hands of the administration; it is responsible for the effective use of resources, support and performance of teaching and research, meeting the highest standards of scholarly integrity and professionalism, and assuring its accountability for the conduct and performance of the managerial tasks. In most Western European and American universities, governance is a cooperative effort, where a governing board or government department, president (or rector/vice-chancellor) and faculty (often organized into an academic senate) are the major stakeholders. They share specific rights and responsibilities in the governance of the university.

Participants also agreed on the contours of the major characteristics of the *environment* universities are likely to face in the near future. These future circumstances will have a defining bearing on the specific structure and process of governance that will enable universities to effectively carry out their mission. Thus, the papers are forward looking and factor in to their analysis future education scenarios.

The changes in the environment are manifestations of ever greater demand for education, which however is not matched by resources to meet this demand. No less important is the rapid creation of new knowledge. One implication is an increasing demand for lifelong learning opportunities. Another relates to tenure extending over a longer time. Moreover, much new knowledge will be created increasingly at the boundaries of conventional disciplines and much of it can have great value for high-tech firms. As a consequence, faculty in science departments and many professional schools will tend to spend more time outside the university and work on research outsourced to it by high-tech firms. These developments will ever more seriously challenge faculty's commitment to the university and its ability to provide a balanced academic program. A further development that is likely to have a revolutionary effect on university governance is the cyberspace revolution. Its impact on information and communication is likely to be profound, because of the speed, reach and universality with which new networks will emerge. As a consequence, information will become universally available, almost instantaneously. One result will be a flattening of the hierarchical structure of such organizations as universities. Another will be further globalization of knowledge creation and dissemination.

This volume is the result of a rigorous selection from the papers prepared for the Del Mar meeting and the fruit of the intensive discussion provoked by those papers. It tries to provide a representative survey of the views held on the complex question of university governance and of the diversity of approaches taken to this problem. We, however, realize that much more research and debate are required to provide the universities with a governance system able to allow them to adapt to their changing environment, while ensuring that universities still serve the entire society by upholding their centenary values.

The papers in this volume are organized into four parts and followed by the presentation in an appendix of the Glion Declaration II. In the first part, the missions and responsibilities of research universities in a changing world are reexamined. The second part comprises papers that review the status and recent trends in the governance of universities in both Western Europe and the United States. The focus is on the strengths and weaknesses of today's governance systems. The third part explores governance principles in an attempt to introduce some theoretical thinking into the deliberations. These papers lead in the fourth part to proposals for improving and streamlining governance structures and processes in research universities. Some of the proposed initiatives relate to a single stakeholder, while others encompass the interaction between two or even three of them.

We thank the William and Flora Hewlett Foundation, the Bren Foundation, and Swissair for their generous support. We are also indebted to the Preuss Foundation and the University of California at San Diego for organizational and secretarial support. Finally, we are particularly pleased to thank warmly Ms Mary O' Mahony, former Deputy Secretary General of the Association of European Universities, who provided editorial assistance, and Mr Christophe Weber, who effectively standardized the formatting of the texts and references.

Werner Z. Hirsch *Luc E. Weber*
University of California, Los Angeles *University of Geneva*

REFERENCES

The Glion Declaration (1998). *The University at the Millennium*, The Glion Colloquium, Geneva.

Hirsch, W. Z. & Weber, L. E. (1999). *Challenges Facing Higher Education at the Millennium*, American Council on Education/Oryx Press, Phoenix and International Association of Universities/Pergamon, Oxford.

CONTRIBUTORS

James J. Duderstadt is President Emeritus and university Professor of Science and Engineering at the University of Michigan. His teaching and research interests span a number of areas in science, engineering, and public policy, including nuclear energy, information technology, higher education, and science policy. He has held a number of senior posts in higher education (dean, provost, and president of the University of Michigan), government (chair of the National Science Board and the Nuclear Energy Research Advisory Committee), and the National Academies (executive board, policy committees). He currently chairs several national advisory committees in areas such as nuclear energy, the federal R&D budget, and the impact of information technology on society.

Robert Dynes is the sixth Chancellor of the University of California San Diego (UCSD). He has served in this position since 1996. He is also a professor of physics at UCSD and specializes in condensed matter physics. He has been at UCSD since 1991. Before that, he was at Bell Laboratories in Murray Hill New Jersey from 1968 to 1990. His most recent position at Bell Laboratories was as Director of the Chemical Physics Research Laboratory.

Sharon Franks earned her Ph.D. in oceanography from Oregon State University in 1992. Her scientific publications concern the biogeochemical fate of particles emanating from sea-floor hydrothermal vents. During the past eight years, she has focused on outreach and education, writing about the earth, ocean and atmospheric sciences for non-scientific audiences.

Hans van Ginkel is the Rector of the United Nations University (UNU), Tokyo, since September 1997. In August 2000, he was elected President of the International Association of Universities (IAU), Paris. He is Vice-chair of the Board of Trustees of the Asian Institute of Technology (AIT), Bangkok, a Member of Academia Europea, an Honorary Fellow of ITC, Enschede and the former Rector of Utrecht University. He is also a member and officer in several professional associations and organizations. In 1979, he defended his Ph.D. thesis *cum laude* at Utrecht University and in 1997 he received an honorary doctorate from Universitatea Babes-Bolyai, Cluj. His fields of interest are urban and regional development, population, housing studies, science policy, internationalization and university management. He has published widely in these areas, and has contributed extensively to the work of various international educational organizations.

Werner Z. Hirsch is Professor of Economics at the University of California, Los Angeles, after having been at UC, Berkeley, Washington University, Harvard University and Cambridge University. He has been the founding director of public policy institutes at two universities. Dr. Hirsch has served on numerous boards, committees and councils and in an advisory capacity to many Federal, State, and local governments in the United States, as well as to international agencies and to the RAND corporation. He has chaired academic senate committes both of the University of California systems and of UCLA. He received his BS in 1947 and Ph.D. in 1949 from UC, Berkeley. He is a member of Phi Beta Kappa and Sigma Xi and was awarded citations by the Senate of the State of California and City of Los Angeles, and named by Japan's Zaisei-Gaku as a Kaizuito Hitobito "Scholar Who Helped Build the Field of Public Finance".

Charles F. Kennel has been director of the Scripps Institution of Oceanography since 1998. Prior to that, he served as executive vice-chancellor of UCLA, as associate administrator at NASA (1994-1996), and as professor of physics at UCLA (1967-1993). Prof. Kennel received his A.B. from Harvard University in 1959 and his Ph.D. from Princeton University in 1964. He is a member of the National Academy of Sciences, the International Academy of Astronautics, the American Academy of Arts and Sciences and has been awarded the NASA Distinguished Service Medal, the Aurelio Peccei Prize, the James Clerk Maxwell Prize and the Hannes Alfven Prize.

Dr. Peter Lorange has been the President of IMD since July 1, 1993. He is Professor of Strategy and holds the Nestlé Chair. He was formerly President of the Norwegian School of Management in Oslo. His areas of special interest are global strategic management, strategic planning and entrepreneurship for growth.

In management education, Dr. Lorange was affiliated with the Wharton School, University of Pennsylvania, for more than a decade, in various assignments, including director of the Joseph H. Lauder Institute of Management and International Studies, and The William H. Wurster Center for International Management Studies, as well as The William H. Wurster Professor of Multinational Management. He has also taught at the Sloan School of Management (M.I.T.). He serves on the board of directors of several corporations.

Katharine C. Lyall is president of the University of Wisconsin (UW) System, a system serving 150,000 students. The UW System contains two doctoral research universities, UW-Madison and UW-Milwaukee, in addition to eleven comprehensive universities and thirteen two-year colleges. Dr. Lyall, an economist, continues to teach microeconomics and public policy.

Guy Neave is Director of Research at the International Association of Universities (IAU), Paris. Before joining the IAU, he was the Professor of Comparative Education at London University Institute of Education. A historian by training, his interests lie in higher education policy, European Integration and comparative higher education. He has written extensively on higher education in Europe and was Joint Editor in Chief with Burton R. Clark of the Encyclopedia of Higher Education (Oxford, Pergamon, 1992, 1998) and is currently Editor of Higher Education Policy, the quarterly Journal of the IAU. Amongst his recent publications are Democracy and Governance in Higher Education with Jan de Groof and Juraj Svec (Dordrecht, Kluwer Law International) and Abiding Issues, changing perspectives: Visions of the University across a half century (Paris, IAU Press). He is Foreign Associate of the National Academy of Education of the United States and Honorary Vice President of the British Society for Research into Higher Education.

Howard Newby is Chief Executive of the Higher Education Funding Council for England and Vice-Chancellor of the University of Southampton. He was President of Universities UK, the UK body which represents the university sector, from 1999-2001. From 1988-94, he was Chairman and Chief Executive of the Economic and Social Research Council. Prof. Newby was formerly Professor of Sociology at the University of Essex and has held visiting appointments in Australia and the United States. From 1980-83 he was Professor of Sociology and Rural Sociology at the University of Wisconsin, Madison. Professor Newby was awarded a CBE in 1995 for his services to social science and a knighthood in 2000 for his services to higher education.

Frank Rhodes was president of Cornell University for eighteen years before retiring in 1995, having previously served as vice president for academic affairs at the University of Michigan. A geologist by training, Rhodes was a member of President Bush's Education Policy Advisory Committee. He has also served as chairman of the National Science Board and chairman of the boards of the American Council on Education, the American Association of Universities, and the Carnegie Foundation for the Advancement of Teaching. He was chairman of the American Council on Education's task force on minority education which produced the report "One-Third of a Nation" for which former presidents Jimmy Carter and Gerald Ford served as honorary co-chairs. He is currently president of the American Philosophical Society.

Henry Rosovsky is the Lewis P. and Linda L. Geyser University Professor Emeritus at Harvard University. His fields of interest and publications concern economic history, Japanese economic growth, and higher education. Prof. Rosovsky served as Dean of the Faculty of Arts and Sciences at Harvard from 1973 to 1984 and from 1990 to 1991. From 1985 to 1997 he also served as a member of the Harvard Corporation, the executive Governing Board of the University. Most recently, he co-chaired the Task Force on Higher Education and Society sponsored by UNESCO and the World Bank that produced *Higher Education in Developing Countries: Peril and Promise* (2000).

Peter Scott is Vice-Chancellor of Kingston University and a member of the board of the Higher Education Funding Council for England. Previously, he was Pro-Vice-Chancellor and Professor of Education at the University of Leeds. From 1976 to 1992 he was Editor of The Times Higher Education Supplement. His research interests include the governance and management of higher education and new patterns of knowledge production. His most recent books are 'Re-Thinking Science: Knowledge and the Public in an Age of Uncertainty' (with Helga Nowotny and Michael Gibbons) and 'University Leadership: the role of the chief executive' (with Catherine Bargh, Jean Bocock and David Smith).

Luc Weber, educated in the fields of economics and political science, is professor of Public Economics at the University of Geneva since 1975. As an economist, he serves as an adviser to the federal as well as to cantonal governments and he has been a member of the "Swiss Council of Economic Advisers" for three years. Since 1982, Prof. Weber is strongly involved in university management and Higher Education policy in the capacity of vice-rector, then of rector of the University of Geneva, as well as Chairman of the Swiss Rectors' Conference and, later on, as Consul for international affairs of the latter, representing Swiss universities in three European Higher Education organizations. Prof. Weber is presently vice-president of the International Association of Universities and serves as an expert to various governmental and non governmental organizations (Association of European Universities, Council of Europe, World Bank).

Harold M. Williams is President Emeritus of the J. Paul Getty Trust, having served as President and Chief Executive Officer from 1981 to 1998. Trained as a lawyer, his career included fifteen years in industry, culminating as chairman of the board of a New York Stock Exchange Company, seven years as Dean of the Graduate School of Management, UCLA and four years as Chair of the United States Securities and Exchange Commission. He served twelve years as a Regent, University of California. He is Co-Chair of the California Citizens Commission on Higher Education, member of the National Center for Public Policy and Higher Education, member of President Clinton's Committee on the Arts and Humanities, and was a member of the Association of Governing Board's Committee on the Academic Presidency.

PART 1

Missions
and Responsibilities
of Research Universities

CHAPTER 1

The University at the Millennium

Missions and Responsibilities of Research Universities

Frank H. T. Rhodes

The university as we know it is the product of the second millennium. It is one of the few institutions that span almost the whole of the millennium itself. Bologna University was founded in the 11th century; others followed soon afterwards.[1] Although many universities are of much more recent origin, the university, as an institution, is a creation of the early years of the second millennium. The university is one of the most distinctive institutions of the second millennium, with a nature, membership, responsibility and autonomy that make it unique.

It is also, as Clark Kerr (1996) has reminded us, one of the most durable institutions of the millennium: "About eighty-five institutions in the Western World established by 1520 still exist in recognizable forms, with similar functions and with unbroken histories, including the Catholic church, the Parliaments of the Isle of Man, of Iceland, and of Great Britain, several Swiss cantons, and seventy universities. Kings that rule, feudal lords with vassals, and guilds with monopolies are all gone. These seventy universities, however, are still in the same locations with some of the same buildings, with professors and students doing much the same things, and with governance carried on in much the same way".

---

1 The medical school at Salerno, founded in the 9th century, remained a medical school, rather than developing into a university. The University of Paris was founded between 1150 and 1170 and Oxford by the end of the 12th century. Smaller centers of learning also existed in some other places at earlier times, such as, for example, in some mosques.

The original purpose of the university was to conserve and transmit the learning and skills of the church, by which most were founded and accredited. Their membership included chiefly ordinands and those who were to serve in offices for which the church held a special responsibility, such as law and medicine.

Growing secularization of the universities in the 19th century saw not only changes in financing and governance, but also change in mission. The curriculum was expanded and professionalized. In the United States, the Morrill Act of 1862 gave great impetus to this movement, while research and public service were increasingly seen as the responsibilities of the university.

Until the 19th century, the universities had little impact upon the professions, modest impact upon their surrounding societies, and made little contribution to the general corpus of knowledge and invention. But in a mere century, all that has been transformed.

- Universities have become the essential gateway to and foundation of every major profession. They have expanded and improved training in what were once non-professional occupations, from interior design, library science and business to nutrition, agriculture and journalism.
- Universities have become the primary agents for basic research in this country and they are having a growing impact upon applied research, in everything from medicine and bioengineering, to computer science and communications.
- Universities have had a huge impact upon their regions, from Route 128 in Massachusetts, to the Research Triangle of North Carolina, to Silicon Valley. Employment, economic development, and almost every area of public life have been influenced by this growing impact.
- Universities have become major agents of social mobility, growing in their own inclusiveness, and providing the means for economic advancement for many who had previously been denied access to traditional careers and opportunities.
- Universities have become significant providers of social services, beginning with model schools, but now embracing such things as tertiary care hospitals, health networks, legal services, technology parks, engineering research centers and athletic and other entertainment.

In this major accretion of tasks and this huge expansion of role, the university of 2000 bears only the most general resemblance to the university of 1900. The contemporary university has grown not only in size and number, but also in inclusiveness of knowledge, in variety, in complexity, in quality, in the inclusiveness of its membership, and in its intellectual, professional and social role. Paradoxically, in spite of these major changes in responsibility, membership and complexity, the university has shown almost no change in its organization, management, and governance and only modest change in its teaching style. Indeed, the responses it has made to changing social needs have been only in part planned and only in part idealistic. In part they have also been opportunistic, sometimes reluctant and sometimes absentminded.

At the close of the millennium, one must ask, whether the university, in spite of all its success, is prepared for the major growth in responsibility that it must assume in the new millennium. I believe that there are six pressing issues that the university must address if it is to play an optimum role in the development of the society its serves.

Mission, Role and Function of the University

Many in higher education are cynical of mission and value statements, perhaps justifiably, for many read as bland and self-serving. But that skepticism may also reflect uneasiness in attempting to pin down the precise purpose and function of an individual institution, as opposed to the more generic role of the university. Yet with every industrialized country now seeking to expand its educational programs, it becomes less and less credible for individual institutions simply to offer generic identities. In the future, the institutions that prosper will be those which have embraced a more specific role and a more restricted niche.

To talk in specific terms about role and function of a university is to make a statement of priorities. Just as no institution can possibly teach all languages and all literatures, so no institution, even the wealthiest, can now offer programs of the highest quality in every major area of learning. It is this very selectivity and differentiation, however, against which many academics rebel. Perhaps the most urgent and the most difficult task of both board members and rector/presidents is to identify, in appropriately refined terms, the mission, role and functions of their institutions. This will involve a responsible blend of vision and hard-headed realism, as well as patient negotiation and difficult choices, but only by making choices in this way can universities continue as strong and vigorous institutions, capable of seizing new opportunities, developing promising areas and effectively serving their communities.

Basis, Methods, Style and Effectiveness of Learning

Given the explosive growth of knowledge, to which the universities have themselves made substantial contributions, and our increasing dependence on it, we have to ask whether the existing traditional patterns of learning are adequate for the needs of the changing world. Not only is knowledge itself increasing at an ever expanding rate, but new methods of learning and new means of delivery are themselves undergoing rapid development. In contrast to this, the leading universities still employ what is essentially a medieval residential system in which youthful students are instructed by tutors and lecturers in a broad range of subjects judged to be appropriate for a baccalaureate degree.

This traditional structure has been supplemented over the years by other means of study, including especially post-graduate and professional schools, internships and other similar programs, part-time, sandwich and extra-mural arrangements, continuing professional education, both formal and informal, and most recently a major expansion in distance learning.

Unexamined among the burgeoning numbers who still participate in traditional educational schemes is the question of whether or not the format, contents and nature of a baccalaureate degree, and especially of a traditional residential experience, remain appropriate to the needs of the new millennium. In some countries, such as the U.K. for example, there has been implicit recognition that it does not, where degrees that formerly occupied three years of full-time student attendance, now typically require four. Such change, though significant, is scarcely radical and it remains easier to continue the present pattern and style than it is to challenge and modify it.

Yet our net investment in the traditional campus-based residential baccalaureate experience is enormous, and is made even more so in the United States by the professional requirement that those aspiring to practice in fields such as medicine and law should receive virtually no professional instruction in those areas until they have completed a non-professional, though frequently pre-medical, or pre-legal, baccalaureate degree.

What is surprising here is the lack of any debate, professional, national, or institutional, as to whether these ancient arrangements continue to serve society well. Nor is it clear who should address that question, for it may be argued that the universities themselves are ill-equipped to provide an impartial review and recommendation. Yet few are as well equipped as universities to address these issues, even if the ultimate decisions do not rest in their hands. With increasing demands from the higher education community for a greater investment in plant, equipment and capital needs, such a review seems both timely and important.

At another level, other questions remain unaddressed. In spite of the volume of research produced by the university, little attention has been paid to the cognitive process and to the effectiveness of various teaching methods. Nor is there any serious study of the value added to the educational experience by its residential component, together with the large and costly range of services typically associated with it. A critic might argue that unless universities can demonstrate significant value-added to the educational experience from the residential style, one should examine other alternative arrangements.

Even to raise these questions will be seen by some as an unfriendly act, but universities, if they are to prosper, need themselves to address these issues and to lead both the debate that they would generate and the reforms that may arise from such reviews.

Information Technology

Research universities are awash with information technology. Some would claim that they invented it. Certainly, they have made major contributions to its development. They use it on a massive scale, not only in the mundane world of purchasing and record keeping, but also in research and scholarship of all kinds. Furthermore, it has revolutionized practice in fields as different as medicine, law and architecture, as well as being the basis for huge improvements in information storage and retrieval systems.

Yet, strangely, the process of learning remains only marginally influenced by the extraordinary power of information technology, perhaps because those who are our students enjoy much greater skills and imaginative capacities than those who are their teachers.

How universities collectively and individually respond to the challenges and opportunities of information technology will do much to shape the future. This technology has the capacity, even in its present form, to provide vast increases in access, to provide improved quality, to create new partnerships, to reduce costs, and thus to increase the capacity of the university to serve its several audiences. The world's cyber universities are growing rapidly and some appear impressively effective. Britain's Open University, which has 157,000 students, was recently ranked 10th out of 77 traditional universities in the quality of its teaching programs, which were offered at 50% of the cost of those of the typical traditional campus. Other countries offer similar examples of success. Anadolu University in Turkey has 530,000 students, and the cost of instruction is one tenth of that at conventional Turkish universities.

I believe no institution is immune to either the competitive effects or the educational benefits of information technology. How it will be used will vary from institution to institution and in that variety will lie the seeds for future success. It is doubtful if any institution can go it alone as far as the development of off-site learning is concerned. But, just as books have expanded the capacity of a leading author to reach a wider audience, so in time must well-crafted video lectures by the world's leading authorities displace the one-time performances on local campuses, with those who had formerly served as lecturers, now serving as coaches, mentors and guides to the new learning experience. This will threaten both traditional university practices and also, perhaps, the role of the professor, but it may represent one way of making a significant reduction in costs, while at the same time allowing improvement in quality. Many questions will be involved if such a practice develops. How, for example, will questions of intellectual property be resolved? Who should produce teaching materials? Should we follow the practice of books, where independent publishers contract with the professor, or will the contract be with the university, who will then invite particular members of its faculty to contribute, or will both systems exist side-by-side? What about questions of copyright and royalties? How will credit be determined? What kinds of business partnerships and alliances will this involve? To what extent will institutional autonomy and academic freedom be influenced by any such arrangements? These and related questions are now pressing and deserve serious attention.

Patterns and Limits of Outreach

Since their earliest days, America's universities have accepted responsibility for a measure of public outreach. Nowhere is this more fully developed than in the Land-Grant universities, whose record of success in this area has been extraordinary and whose influence continues to be of major significance in regional economic development and societal well being. As the importance and impact of knowledge increases, more and more demands are made upon both the expertise and the purse of universities—public and private—to address issues of community concern. These requests range from research and professional service, to investment in community development. Increasingly, universities are seen not only as agents of economic growth, but also as sources of community renewal. What is unaddressed in these increasing demands is the larger question of coincidence between such outreach and the core responsibilities and obligations of the universities to its own members. Ideally, each would complement the other, but in practice, the total costs of outreach are rarely recovered by those providing support, and frequently the university covers part of these ventures out of its own resources. Where universities choose to do this, there is clearly no problem, but the difficult question involves the extent to which the university facilities, faculty, student time and administrative attention can satisfy the needs and demands of the local community. It would be particularly helpful to have a thoughtful review of the guidelines and benchmarks that representative institutions have developed in this important activity.

A related area concerns partnerships, for, increasingly, such outreach and public service involves partnerships with government agencies, corporations, foundations and private individuals, some of which require new protocols and procedures if they are to be successful. These partnerships may range from cooperation in field tests of new crops or clinical tests of new pharmaceutical products, to public health programs, community services or environmental projects.

The issues involved in these partnerships involve far more than the financial arrangements by which they are supported. They also involve questions of ethical norms and values, institutional autonomy and accountability, and the interests of both the public and of students, especially graduate students, who may be active participants in the programs.

Here again there is little to guide individual institutions as the number of these partnerships proliferates. A task force dealing with codes of practice, benchmarking and best practices would be of substantial value.

Scholarly Careers

Until the present decade, the traditional scholarly career has been reasonably standard across the range of various institutions. Typically, a young faculty member began as an assistant professor and, after five or six years of performance which was judged appropriate, received tenure, promotion and an indefinite appointment. Only in some cases, especially those institutions involved heavily in clinical practice, or with access to large numbers of adjunct professors and lecturers, has that pattern been supplemented by others.

More recently, in part as a result of changes in the pattern of retirement, and in part as a result of financial constraints, tenure has come under critical review and the proportion of non-tenured individuals teaching in the universities has grown substantially. The question to be confronted is whether the practice of tenure, which was developed in the United States early in the 20th century, still represents the most appropriate contractual arrangement for members of the faculty. This becomes especially acute when only a minority of all those teaching now enjoy such tenured appointments. There are strong arguments, passionately held, on both sides of this issue, but it is one that needs attention, not least because of its growing impact.

Merely raising the question of the future of tenure will be seen by many as a subversive act, but unless the universities address it themselves, it is likely that others, less devoted to the values of the institutions, and less persuaded of the values of tenure, will make the study for them. A review of tenure is long overdue.

Organization, Governance, Leadership and Management

The pattern of university organization has remained essentially unchanged for the last century. But, during that period, the university has experienced explosive growth in numbers, size and complexity, and the significance and impact of its work has multiplied.

Governance and management need to be reviewed at at least four distinct levels:

The department: Does the traditional unit of university organization—the department—still represent the most appropriate organizational unit? Departments arose in the late 19th and early 20th centuries to represent the disciplines for which they were named. These disciplines, in turn, reflected the division of the curriculum. We need to ask whether intellectually, pedagogically, and administratively, the division of a university into departments—the traditional focus of tenure decisions, curricular design and student supervision—still seems appropriate.

Intellectually, much has changed since the turn of the century. What were pursued then largely as pure disciplines are still so pursued, though in most cases the disciplines have become more professionalized and, in some cases, practical application has influenced their development. But, increasingly, intellectual interests span a variety of disciplines. Cultural, linguistic, sociological, political, historical and other studies within the humanities and social sciences are less and less frequently confined to a single discipline. Increasingly, such studies have become multi-disciplinary in their approach and sometimes in their authorship. Nor do the problems of society come in neat disciplinary packages. The traditional disciplines are therefore not wholly appropriate in terms of intellectual categories. Furthermore, they sometimes tend to weaken interest in interdisciplinary and multidisciplinary approaches, particularly when appointments and tenure are held only in traditional departments.

The transitory nature of disciplines is reflected in changes that have taken place in disciplines, and thus in departments themselves. Disciplines that were once apparently well-established—geography for example—are now less widely recognized and less highly regarded and geography departments have been closed in many universities. Other disciplines are fragmented into a host of subfields and specialties, which may enjoy little common discourse. The typical discipline of "English" is such an example. Within the sciences, new disciplines have developed and evolved, including such things as biochemistry, computer science, neuroscience, and others. The emergence of new disciplines is often cumulative, rather than substitutionary. Thus, geophysics does not obviate the need to continue to teach both geology and physics, its parent disciplines.

If one asks whether pedagogically the department still "makes sense" the answer is far from clear. Departments were established when the curriculum was relatively fixed, involving a dozen or so disciplinary courses. The departments at that time had very strong influence, not only upon the development of the curriculum, but also in their responsibility for its implementation and representation. Furthermore, they provided nurture and evaluation to students, who found in them a congenial home. The influence of departments in both these areas is now much less significant than it once was. Courses have proliferated. Department offerings have fragmented. Interdisciplinary courses abound. The oversight of the curriculum is in limbo.

Administratively, the department has been the foundation of the organization of the university, but, as the disciplines have developed, some departments have shrunk in size, being now represented by only three or four faculty members, while others—such as English and psychology—may number 100 or more faculty members in some of the larger universities. Added to this, the once strong role of department head has been replaced by department chair, and the individual appointed to this position often has little influence upon the imaginative development of the department or the creation of constructive linkages with other departments.

Taking these three aspects of the life of a typical department: its intellectual contribution, its pedagogic contribution and its administrative contribution, it is tempting to say that there must be a better method of coordination and management within the university. Unfortunately, that is far from clear. Though it is easy to suggest that the smallest departments should be merged into larger units, it is not clear that any alternative method is superior to the departmental organization we now have, even with all its admitted imperfections. The question may well become how do we take an imperfect organization—the department—and improve it? I believe that the two essential steps in bringing about improvement are to strengthen the leadership of the departmental chair and to provide periodic internal review, supplemented by external review, as appropriate, of the life and work of the department. In this way, one could retain the benefits of the department, but improve some of its present limitations.

The college or school: Universities, since their earliest days, have been created on the basis of the college or school, known in many European universities as the faculty. The characteristic feature of this grouping is that it represents a collection of departments united by broadly common intellectual interests and methods. One finds typically, therefore, a college of engineering or a school of medicine or a faculty of law. A traditional college is headed by a dean who, in the better universities, has substantial administrative and financial responsibility. In most cases, the dean is assisted by a small administrative staff and an appropriate advisory council. Perhaps the greatest variation in this traditional pattern of organization is found within the humanities, arts, social sciences and sciences. When I was dean at the University of Michigan, I presided over a college whose title was Literature, Science and the Arts; this was a mammoth grouping of some 50 departments, museums, colleges and institutes that, at that time, accounted for some 20,000 students. In many North American universities, this association still continues, with the arts, the social sciences and the sciences all unified under a single administrative leadership. In Europe, on the other hand, as well as in some North American universities, the three major divisions have been separated as individual colleges. In still other cases, particular groups of subjects, the earth sciences or the biological sciences, for example, have become separate schools or faculties. The reason for the separation of what had once been combined, extensive colleges is the unceasing intellectual growth in some areas, not least in the sciences. In universities where separation has taken place, it is argued that there is now little in common between, say, the sciences and the humanities. In those where an association is still continued within a single college, it is argued that the demands of liberal education favor the retention of the older association. There is no simple solution to this enigma, but the academic style, curricular direction, size and administrative complexity of the university will determine the most appropriate organization.

In general, the collegiate structure is still remarkably effective, intellectually and administratively, not least where a strong dean with a well-developed sense of intellectual purpose and direction is present. I believe it has proved effective largely because the colleges still define common intellectual interests and therefore are able to appeal to common standards and norms. Colleges have prospered when their deans have been willing to exercise authority in a way that current department chairs have generally not. What is needed here is for the deans to require of their chairpersons the same kind of financial responsibility and initiative that they themselves display.

Perhaps the other reason for the success of this division within the university is the fact that deans are generally carefully selected and well supported, occupying their positions for a significant period and regarding their appointment to these positions as an important career move.

Could the present collegiate system be improved? Certainly it could benefit from better strategic planning, from better cross-college linkages, with appropriate incentives for partnerships in the attainment of university-wide goals and in the advice of a standing visiting committee from outside the college itself. None of these improvements would be revolutionary, but they would take what is now one of the strongest aspects of university organization and make it even better.

The president: The president, rector, chancellor, or vice chancellor occupies an ancient office, the power of which varies greatly from country to country and even from institution to institution. In general, presidents, chancellors and vice chancellors in North America enjoy more autonomy than those in other parts of the world—in part, perhaps, because, unlike those in many industrialized countries, their universities are not wholly dependent upon the state for both financial support and direction. The presence of large numbers of independent universities in the United States makes the role of the president distinct.

I have recently written at some length on the art of the presidency (Rhodes, F. H. T., 1998) and there is also available a recently published report on renewing the academic presidency (Report of the Commission on the Academic Presidency, 1996). That report urges the delegation of more substantial authority to the president and I believe that, if universities are to prosper in the new millennium, that will prove desirable.

The board of trustees, board of regents, board of overseers: In contrast to all the organizational categories and responsibilities described above, the board exercises a governance function, rather than one of management. In essence, it exists to provide public accountability, public oversight and public support for the institution. It may be of several types. Some boards are statewide in their authority, overseeing the work of as many as 50 different institutions within a state, representing many levels of individual responsibility and intellectual and professional concern. Other boards have responsibility for only a single university. In public colleges and universities, board members may be appointed by the governor or, in a few cases, elected in statewide elections. In private universities they are invariably self-appointed, often including substantial representation from the alumni association.

In general, the concept of board governance and responsibility has proved remarkably resilient and successful. Given the public responsibility of the universities and its growth beyond that of providing higher education, the function of the board is likely to grow more, rather than less, critical in the years ahead. This is not to say, however, that the system has been without its problems. Boards of public institutions have, on occasion, become politicized and intrusive. The boards of some private institutions are so preoccupied by fund raising that they have become largely symbolic rather than being actively involved in governance. In practice, much of the work of the large boards characteristic of private institutions is done through board committees. Perhaps the two greatest hazards of any board are the dangers of too much engagement, on the one hand, leading to intrusive micro-management, especially in athletics and in the medical school, and, on the other, of disengagement from the major issues, where board meetings become show-and-tell events, in which senior university administrators present a fairly cut-and-dried agenda, leaving little room for enquiry or guidance on the part of the board. This places a heavy responsibility on the board chairman and the president to work together to ensure the maximum effectiveness of the board. Creatively used, the board provides an effective system, not only for assuring public accountability and responsibility of the university, but also in serving as a bulwark against both internal usurpation of authority, and public intrusion or control. The delicate balance between institutional autonomy, personal freedom and responsibility, and public support and oversight, is one that exists in a constant state of dynamic equilibrium. A wise board will recognize the delicacy of that equilibrium and will nurture the vitality of the various forces that contribute to it (Rhodes, F. H. T., 1999).

This list of topics leaves unaddressed several of great importance, among them future financial support for universities. But, without broad agreement on the future *role* of higher education, there can be no agreement on sources of financial support. It is the debate on role, and the related discussions of scale and scope, which should drive the discussion of methods, means, and finance. That is a public discussion that deserves urgent attention, and it is the responsibility of the universities to ensure its place on the public agenda.

Universities are one of the glories of the past millennium, one of the treasures of human vision and creativity. Arising from humankind's highest aspirations, they have made a unique and growing contribution to enlarging human understanding and advancing the human condition. In a new millennium where population continues to outstrip resources, where natural disaster compounds human mismanagement, where ancient animosities fuel new hatred and terror, where hunger, poverty and misuse still blight the lives of one quarter of our fellows, the challenge to universities will be greater still. Their products—experience shared, considered and analyzed; knowledge created, refined and applied; and skills perfected, focused and humanely used—are the essential, but frail, tools by which we fashion our collective future well-being. These skills are not given. Each must be cultivated. None is freestanding. Each requires community. None is self-sustaining. Each depends on support.

It is these three vital commodities—shared experience, demonstrable knowledge and humanely used skills—which are the business of the university: at once both its means and its products. Our successors at the Glion Colloquium in the year 2999 will look back on a planet and a people whose condition will largely reflect how responsibly, intelligently and humanely we, the leaders of the universities, have cultivated them today.

REFERENCES

Kerr, C. (1995). *The Uses of the University*, Fourth Edition, Harvard University Press, Cambridge, MA, p. 115.

Report of the Commission on the Academic Presidency (1996). *Renewing the Academic Presidency: Stronger Leadership for Tougher Times*, Association of Governing Boards of University and Colleges, Washington, D.C.

Rhodes, F. H. T. (1998). The Art of the Presidency, *The Presidency*, American Council on Education, Washington, D.C., Vol. 1, n° 1.

Rhodes, F. H. T. (1999). Speedbumps on the Road Ahead, *Trusteeship*, Association of Governing Boards of Universities and Colleges, Washington, D.C.

The Glion Declaration (1998). *The University at the Millennium*, Glion Colloquium, Geneva.

PART 2

Status and Recent Trends in the Governance of Universities

CHAPTER 2

Recent Changes in the Structure and Governance of American Research Universities

Katharine C. Lyall

The manner in which research universities in the United States and in Europe operate to achieve their missions has evolved dramatically over the past century; so must their governance structures, if they are to continue as powerful and effective contributors to knowledge and the global economy.

American research universities at the turn of the twentieth century overwhelmingly adopted the German model: internal governance mirrored the division of knowledge into disciplinary departments or colleges, each with considerable autonomy to establish its own rules and make its own hiring, tenure, and promotion decisions. The overall university then grew as a collection of departments and colleges overseen and administered collectively by a president or chancellor who, in turn, was responsible to a governing board of lay individuals. This is a model that maximizes the autonomy of disciplines and attaches the loyalty of faculty first to their discipline, second to their department or college, and only third to the collective institution—the university of which they are a part. Over the decades, this has proven to be a very powerful model for driving first-rate scholarship and the training of future researchers. Coupled with a national commitment to investing in basic and applied scientific research, it has propelled American research universities into the top ranks recognized around the world. It is a model that worked well for the first half of the twentieth century.

In the 1960s, however, the social and political environment of American universities began to change significantly. College attendance in the United

States swelled dramatically in the post-World War II years, from about 15% of the total population before the War to nearly 50% today. Propelled by the G.I. Bill, and a booming economy, states began to establish large numbers of new universities to fulfill a universal dream to go to college. The mandate of these new public universities was unabashedly pragmatic—to prepare graduates for the workforce, to expand the frontiers of knowledge, especially in the sciences, agriculture, and technology, and to provide an entry credential for their graduates into the middle class American dream of prosperity—a home, a car, and leisure time, and the expectation of a continually rising standard of living.

In this new environment, governments paid the lion's share of the bill for public higher education and expected universities to be responsive to the broader needs of society. For the most part, they were not disappointed. But as the century wore on, strains began to develop between the incentives of decentralized "shared governance" organization of universities and the expected pace of change and responsiveness desired by political and corporate stakeholders. Research universities particularly were criticized for sacrificing teaching to their research mission, for neglecting undergraduate education and for being too slow to accommodate to more rapid changes occurring in American economy and society as it moved into global competition.

This paper notes four trends in American university governance that have significantly affected our research universities in the past few decades:

1. The organization of higher education into statewide university *systems*;
2. The changing nature and role of *governing boards*;
3. The progressive weakening of the university *presidency*;
4. The waning of *traditional faculty governance* and the *expansion of shared governance* to other constituencies within the university.

ORGANIZATION INTO STATEWIDE UNIVERSITY SYSTEMS

One response to the demand for greater public responsiveness in higher education was to *create statewide higher education systems* to manage and coordinate the many individual institutions within state borders. In the United States today, 45 states have such system structures which are expected to coordinate programming, prevent unnecessary duplication of programs and missions, allocate public funding for higher education equitably, and ensure that educational needs are met statewide. About 80% of all students in higher education in the U.S. today attend an institution that is part of a statewide system (National Association of System Heads, 1994).

Public research universities have been both helped and hindered as members of multi-campus systems. To their *advantage* is that their position as the flagship institution in most systems is politically protected against the much larger numbers of comprehensive, regional universities with representation in state legislatures, and they often set academic standards for the entire system. Statewide enrollment and admissions policies often manage competition within a system so that research universities can be more selective than would otherwise be politically possible. And, in many systems, much of the lobbying for public financial support is carried by the system organization, freeing research universities, in part, to compete intensively for the private, corporate, and alumni support that underwrite the research mission.

In exchange, research universities must fit into a larger educational network—one based on geography rather than academic mission—and focus curriculum and programs more carefully. Faculty and administrators must attend more conscientiously to the needs of their state and develop habits of collaboration with unlike institutions which would probably not emerge in the absence of statewide higher education systems.

More recently, some higher education systems have begun to evolve in their missions, moving from basic regulatory and coordinating functions to functions that add value to the work of their constituent institutions (Gaither, G., Ed., 1999). The president of the University of Maryland System, Don Langenberg, has identified the functions that systems are uniquely positioned to perform as: *synergy, strategy, efficiency, accountability*, and *integrity* (Langenberg, D., March-April 1994). To these I would add: *advocacy* (for the value of sustaining educational opportunity and affordable access), and the ability to *push for reform of state government* practices that enable universities to adopt more effective and competitive administrative and operating procedures (Lyall, K. C., 1996). These trends help public research universities gain some traction in a political environment in which they might otherwise be out-voted and out-flanked by more parochial, short-term interests.

THE CHANGING ROLE OF GOVERNING BOARDS

Both public and private research universities in the U.S. have lay governing boards charged with responsibility for the oversight and long-term preservation and enhancement of the institution. Traditionally, boards of trustees (or regents) have served both to buffer the academy from direct political intervention and as advocates for the mission of the academy to the outside worlds of commerce and politics. The governing boards of public universities tend to be visible policymaking entities while the boards of private universities often function less visibly and with more direct fundraising responsibilities for their institutions.

Over the past decade, the role of public university governing boards in particular has been changing, from advocacy to a *greater emphasis on oversight and public accountability* (Association of Governing Boards, 1997). In some instances, members have been elected or appointed to a governing board with an explicit agenda to change or reform the curriculum, appoint or eliminate a particular president, eliminate or install a specific ideology in the institution at large (Smith, M., January-February 1998). It is not surprising, then, that many inside the academy see governing boards in the present day less as buffers against, than as conduits for, the importation of larger political disputes into the campus and the academy (Association of Governing Boards, December 1999). In some cases, this new political agenda militates against financial advocacy for support of the university as well.

A member of the Board of Trustees of the State University of New York expressed it this way:

"Many trustees have ceded too much of their statutory authority for overseeing public higher education to campus presidents and faculty councils... it is not necessarily in the public's or the institution's interest for trustees reflexively to press for ever-higher government subsidies for the colleges and universities they oversee, even though some administrators and faculty members see that as trustees' primary responsibility...

When properly conceived, shared governance can be very advantageous. But when it becomes, in effect, governance by multiple veto by campus groups with vested interests, it can stymie necessary reforms (de Russy, C., October 1996). *Similar views were expressed in Virginia* (Healy, P., March 1997) *and Colorado"* (Hebel, S., October 1999).

The 1990s have been a confusing mixture of diametrically opposed organizational "reforms" across the states: some states (such as New Jersey and Illinois) have *decentralized* their statewide higher education systems by eliminating or reducing the powers of statewide systems and governing boards (Snyder, J., March 1995) (Ohio State University Board of Trustees, May 1997), while other states (such as Minnesota, Pennsylvania, and Virginia) have *centralized and consolidated* their governance structures by creating or consolidating powers in a state coordinating board or a systemwide governing board (Selingo, J., July 1998) (Healy, P., March 1997). Still other states (such as Wisconsin and Maryland) have maintained their statewide system organizations but *streamlined* their functions to decentralize more powers throughout the system and delegate authority from the center to individual campuses (Schmidt, P., November 1998). A few states (such as Montana and Oklahoma) have considered eliminating lay governing boards altogether and placing the governance of higher education with a state secretary of education reporting to an elected governor (Association of Governing Boards, November-December 1995).

While this ferment about the role of governing boards may have reassured policy makers and members of the public that greater oversight and accountability is being exercised over universities, the academy itself remains unsure of the larger values for which it is to be accountable (Green, M. F. & Eckel, P. & Hill, B., July-August 1998). Are access and affordability more important than educational quality and performance? Is efficiency more important than excellence in scholarship (inherently an "inefficient" search for truth)? And how should "accountability" be construed for complex organizations like research universities, which receive *multiple* sources of support (government, corporate, foundations, student fees, patent income, gifts and grants, etc.) and have *multiple stakeholders*?

Governing board members often come to appreciate these complexities over time, but the public rhetoric has yet to catch up with the realities of modern university management.

THE CHANGING UNIVERSITY PRESIDENCY

These confusing crosscurrents are also changing the nature of the university presidency. The presidents of major research universities are CEOs of large and complex enterprises in every sense of that word (Iosue, R. V., March 1997). They are called upon to lead their institutions with vision and wisdom, at the same time they must plan strategically and raise the resources required (Winerip, M., August 1999) to do business in an increasingly competitive environment while maintaining effective political and community relations. Unlike private corporations, major research universities have extensive shared governance traditions that require consultation and, in some instances, formal action by faculty and staff governance organizations before a policy change can be implemented. In the case of public universities, every step of the decision making and implementation process is subject to public reporting, controversy, and scrutiny.

There are a number of signs that the presidency of a public research university is a less attractive and much more difficult position than it once was, and substantially less attractive than the counterpart position in a private university. The average tenure in office for public university presidents has been falling over the past twenty years and is currently only about five years, barely time to get traction on any set of enduring changes on the agenda. Increasingly, experienced university CEOs move from a public university presidency to a private one, but there is very little traffic in the opposite direction (Ross, M. & Green, M., 1998).

John Brandl, professor of public affairs at the University of Minnesota, has observed:

"Public universities have become arenas for all the big political issues of the day, but, at the same time, the automatic deference that society and politicians used to have toward public universities has eroded". (Healy, P., August 1996)

It has become a much more difficult job. In the past three years, a large number of the United States' most prominent public research universities have been in the market for new CEOs, including: the University of Michigan, Ohio State University, University of Maryland-College Park, University of Minnesota, the State University of New York, University of California-Berkley, University of Iowa, University of Colorado, University of North Carolina, and the University of Texas.

Altogether, the presidencies of 38% of the 58 AAU universities, the United States' most prominent research universities, have changed in the past four years. Increasingly, these changes reflect tensions and confusions between boards and CEOs about the legitimate roles of each. Boards with a political activist philosophy believe that public college presidents should carry out the policies that a particular governor and political party in power espouse, regardless of the president's personal vision for the university or the sentiments of the shared governance organizations on campus. Job announcements and public interviews, however, continue to stress the presidential vision for the university and leadership, not just management skills. General public and press rhetoric also underline the expectation that major university presidents will be independent leaders of their institutions and in their larger communities (Basinger, J., August 1999). This cognitive dissonance is shrinking the pool of ready leadership candidates for university presidencies.

As the Association of Governing Boards noted in its report on "Renewing the Academic Presidency": *"The concept of shared governance must be reformed and clarified to enable colleges and universities to respond more quickly and effectively to the challenges they face. Shared governance must be clarified and simplified so that those with the responsibility to act can exercise the authority to do so. Board members must remember that their allegiance and responsibility is to the institution and the public interest, not to the party that put them on the board. Presidential performance depends on board performance. The president and the board should be reviewed together for the benefit of the institution they serve".* (Association of Governing Boards, 1996)

THE WAXING AND WANING OF TRADITIONAL SHARED GOVERNANCE

Robert M. Rosenzweig, president emeritus of the American Association of Universities, has noted that shared governance is a pervasive American institution. The U.S. Constitution created a shared governance system that balances the states against the federal government and the three branches of the federal government among themselves. It is, he says, "the only kind of system that could have worked in a society that was hostile to centralized authority, that valued liberty over order, and in which efficiency in decision making had a much lower priority than the need for institutions that would mediate among competing interests without allowing any to dominate. That is (also) a fair description of a university" (Rosenzweig, R. M., 1998).

And, indeed, criticism of shared governance has grown as the larger environment brings into question whether these basic values are still properly balanced for the 21st century. Is reaching consensus still more important than efficient decision making? Is more orderly decision making necessarily a threat to academic liberty? Couldn't we have a better balance of both?

Interestingly, criticisms of the operation of shared governance come from faculty themselves, as well as from boards, administrators, and the public. The latter complain of the long time it takes faculty to decide to address, much less to come to decisions on, critical matters, and the apparent ability of faculty governance processes to obstruct decision making by other actors. Faculty complain of the time consumed in governance matters, which deflects them from their teaching and research; some faculty also complain that governance processes on their campuses have been 'captured' by a small group of activists (or in-activists) with special agendas. A national survey conducted by the National Center for Education Statistics in 1993 indicates that faculty in U.S. colleges and universities spend about 11% of their work time (about six hours per week) in committee meetings and other efforts that are part of shared governance procedures. The same survey indicates that faculty report getting less and less satisfaction from their participation in governance, as well.

A second trend on American university campuses has further complicated the structure and practice of governance: at many universities, *shared governance rights have been extended to non-faculty professional staff as well.* These include a large and growing number of computing and technical staff, student services counselors and advisors, housing directors, clinicians, and many other individuals who play essential roles in making the university run smoothly and serve students well. Indeed, it is not uncommon for the overall number of these academic staff to exceed the total number of faculty, so that what originally began as "faculty governance" is now "shared governance" much more broadly construed. Differences of opinion can and do arise between faculty and non-faculty staff, giving presidents and boards a multiplicity of advice and compounding problems of working with competing constituencies.

Finally, at a growing number of American research universities, graduate students and teaching assistants have organized themselves into collective bargaining units. At some universities, these unions have been aggressive and militant, striking for higher wages, benefits and working conditions. Apart from the merit of these claims, the mixing of collective bargaining, an essentially *adversarial* process, with shared governance, an essentially *collegial* process, further complicates the overall governance environment of research universities. In private universities, such as Yale, unionized staff bargains directly with the university administration and board, but in some public universities, unionized staff bargain with an executive unit of state government. In these instances, the board and administration employ the faculty and academic staff, but the state employs the classified staff.

Where teaching assistants are unionized, their status within the university—whether they are primarily students who are teaching to learn their trade, or primarily employees who are studying on the side—is often blurred, along with their loyalties and their vision of themselves as professional academics in a shared governance environment. Ensuring merit rewards and equitable treatment across these various categories of employees is often a substantial challenge.

CONCLUSION

Reviewing these trends—the changing roles of *systems* of higher education, the divergence in perceived roles of *governing boards*, the progressive weakening of the *presidency*, and the diffusion of traditional "faculty governance" and extension of the *shared governance* franchise to non-faculty staff—one might wonder whether American research universities will be able to maintain their eminence in scholarship nationally and internationally.

And yet, I believe these trends can lead to renewed conceptions of shared governance that will strengthen and enhance our institutions. Americans are a relentlessly inventive lot and our research universities too valuable a national asset to decline. We recognize that we must engage vigorously in the 21st century with excellent universities around the world in that unique mixture of competition and academic collaboration that so effectively pushes out the global frontiers of knowledge.

In my view, the Glion Colloquium provides the right forum for us to identify and focus on the needs to streamline, not abandon, the shared governance policies that have fostered excellence in the past and can continue to do so in the future.

REFERENCES

Association of Governing Boards (November-December 1995). "Real Threats to Lay Governance", *Trusteeship*, Vol. 3, n° 6.

Association of Governing Boards (1996). *Renewing the Academic Presidency*, Washington, D.C.

Association of Governing Boards (1997). "Transforming Public Trusteeship" AGB *Public Policy Paper Series*, n° 97-2, Washington, D.C.

Association of Governing Boards (December 1999). "Composition of Governing Boards of Public Colleges and Universities, *AGB Occasional Paper*, n° 37, Washington, D.C.
Basinger, J. (August 1999). "In Evaluating the College President, Governing Boards Assert More Authority", *The Chronicle of Higher Education*, pp. A39-40.
Gaither, G., Ed. (1999). *The Multicampus System: Perspectives on Practice and Prospects*, Sterling, Stylus Pub., VA.
Green, M. F. & Eckel, P. & Hill, B. (July-August 1998). "Core Values and the Road to Change", Association of Governing Boards, *Trusteeship*, pp. 11-20.
Healy, P. (August 1996). "Activist Republican Trustees Change the Way Public Universities Seek Presidents" *The Chronicle of Higher Education*, pp. A19-20.
Healy, P. (March 1997). "Virginia Board Members Urged to Become Activists", *The Chronicle of Higher Education*, pp. A-35-36.
Hebel, S. (October 1999). "A New Governor's Approach Rankles Colleges in Colorado", *The Chronicle of Higher Education*, pp. A44.
Iosue, R. V. (March 1997). "Crossing Cultures—from college president to CEO" *AAHE Bulletin*, pp. 10-12.
Langenberg, D. (March-April 1994). "Why a System?", *Change*.
Lyall, K. C. (1996). "The Role of Governance in Systems", *Journal for Higher Education Management*, Vol. 11, n° 2, pp. 39-46.
National Association of System Heads (1994). *Multi-Campus Systems of Public Higher Education in the United States*.
Ohio State University Board of Trustees (May 1997). "Focusing on Priority Roles and Supporting Initiatives: Next Step Toward a New Governance Plan", Board presentation.
Rosenzweig, R. M. (1998). "University Governance: Why It Matters and What To Do About It", *National CrossTalk*, National Center for Public Policy and Higher Education, Vol. 6, n° 1, pp. 11-12.
Ross, M. & Green, M. (1998). *The American College President 1998 Edition*, Washington, D.C.
de Russy, C. (October 1996). "Public Universities Need Rigorous Oversight by 'Activist' Trustees", *The Chronicle of Higher Education*, pp. B3-4.
Schmidt, P. (November 1998). "Some Campuses Want to Leave University of Maryland System", *The Chronicle of Higher Education*, pp. A26-28.
Selingo, J. (July 1998). "Pennsylvania Weighs How to Coordinate a Sprawling Higher Education System", *The Chronicle of Higher Education*, pp. A37-40.
Smith, M. (January-February 1998). "Governing Well: Is the Process Keeping Away Qualified Regents Candidates? Could Alumni Suggestions for Reform Make a Difference?", *Minnesota*, pp. 37-40.
Snyder, J. (March 1995). "Illinois Legislature Approves Bill to Decentralize Seven Public Colleges", *The Chronicle of Higher Education*, pp. A24.
Winerip, M. (August 1999). "Making the Ask", *New York Times Magazine*, pp. 22-41.

CHAPTER 3

Fire, Ready, Aim!
University Decision-Making During an Era of Rapid Change

James J. Duderstadt

INTRODUCTION

"There is no more delicate matter to take in hand, nor more dangerous to conduct, nor more doubtful of success, than to step up as a leader in the introduction of change. For he who innovates will have for his enemies all those who are well off under the existing order of things, and only lukewarm support in those who might be better off under the new."

Niccolo Machiavelli, The Prince

The contemporary university is one of the most complex social institutions of our times. The importance of this institution to our society, its myriad activities and stakeholders, and the changing nature of the society it serves, all suggest the importance of experienced, responsible, and enlightened university leadership, governance, and management. American universities have long embraced the concept of *shared governance* involving public oversight and trusteeship, collegial faculty governance, and experienced but generally short-term administrative and usually amateur leadership. While this system of shared governance engages a variety of stakeholders in the decisions concerning the university, it does so with an awkwardness that tends to inhibit change and responsiveness.

The politics swirling about governing boards, particularly in public universities, not only distracts them from their important responsibilities and stewardship, but also discourages many of our most experienced, talented, and dedicated citizens from serving on these bodies. The increasing intrusion of state and federal government in the affairs of the university, in the name of performance and public accountability, but all too frequently driven by political opportunism can trample on academic values and micromanage many institutions into mediocrity. Furthermore, while the public expects its institutions to be managed effectively and efficiently, it weaves a web of constraints through public laws that makes this difficult indeed. Sunshine laws demand that even the most sensitive business of the university must be conducted in the public arena, including the search for a president. State and federal laws entangle all aspects of the university in rules and regulations, from student admissions to financial accounting to environmental impact.

Efforts to include the faculty in shared governance also encounter obstacles. To be sure, faculty governance continues to be both effective and essential for academic matters such as faculty hiring and tenure evaluation. But it is increasingly difficult to achieve true faculty participation in broader university matters such as finance, capital facilities, or external relations. The faculty traditions of debate and consensus building, along with the highly compartmentalized organization of academic departments and disciplines, seem incompatible with the breadth and rapid pace required in today's high momentum university-wide decision environment. Most difficult and critical of all are those decisions that concern change in the university.

A rapidly evolving world has demanded profound and permanent change in most, if not all, social institutions. Corporations have undergone restructuring and reengineering. Governments and other public bodies are being overhauled, streamlined, and made more responsive. Individuals are increasingly facing a future of impermanence in their employment, in their homes, and even in their families. The nation-state itself has become less relevant and permanent in an ever more interconnected world.

Yet, while most colleges and universities have grappled with change at the pragmatic level, few have contemplated the more fundamental transformations in mission and character that may be required by our changing world. For the most part, our institutions still have not grappled with the extraordinary implications of an age of knowledge, a society of learning, which will likely be our future. Most institutions continue to approach change by reacting to the necessities and opportunities of the moment rather than adopting a more strategic approach to their future.

The glacial pace of university decision making and academic change simply may not be sufficiently responsive to allow the university to control its own destiny. There is a risk that the tidal wave of societal forces could sweep over the academy, both transforming higher education in unforeseen and unacceptable ways while creating new institutional forms to challenge both our experience and our concept of the university.

This time of great change, of shifting paradigms, provides the appropriate context within which to consider the decision process of the university. Like other social institutions, the university needs strong leadership, particularly during a time of great change, challenge, and opportunity. In this paper, we will explore the specific topic of decision making in the university–the issues, the players, the process, and the many challenges–within the broader context of university leadership, governance, and management.

THE ISSUES

There is a seemingly endless array of decisions bubbling up, swirling through and about the contemporary university. At the core are those *academic decisions* that affect most directly the academic process: Whom do we select as students (admissions)? Who should teach them (faculty hiring, promotion, and tenure)? What should they be taught (curriculum and degree requirements)? How should they be taught (pedagogy)? There is a long-standing tradition that the decisions most directly affecting the activities of teaching and scholarship are best left to the academy itself. Yet in many institutions, particularly those characterized by overly intrusive government controls or adversarial labor-management relationships between faculty and administration, this academic autonomy can be compromised.

Since most universities are large, complex organizations, enrolling tens of thousands of students, employing thousands of faculty and staff, and involving the expenditures of hundreds of millions or even billions of dollars, there is also an array of important *administrative decisions*. Where do we get the funds necessary to support our programs and how do we spend them (resource acquisition and allocation, budgets)? How do we build and maintain the campus environment necessary for quality teaching and research (capital facilities)? How do we honor our responsibilities and accountability to broader society (financial audits, compliance with state and federal regulations)? How do we manage our relationships with the multiple stakeholders of the university (public relations, government relations, and development)?

In addition to the ongoing academic and administrative decisions necessary to keep the university moving ahead, there are always an array of unforeseen events–challenges or opportunities–that require immediate attention and rapid decisions. For example, when student activism explodes on the campus, an athletic violation is uncovered, or the university is attacked by politicians or the media, *crisis management* becomes critical. While the handling of such matters requires the time and attention of many senior university administrators, from deans to executive officers and governing boards, all too frequently, crisis management becomes the responsibility of the university president. At any meeting of university presidents, the frequent disruption of pagers, faxes, or phone calls provides evidence of just how tightly contemporary university leaders are coupled to the issues of the day. A carefully developed strategy is necessary for handling such crises, both to prevent universities from lapsing into a reactive mode, as well as to take advance of the occasional possibility of transforming a crisis into an opportunity.

More generally, universities need to develop a more strategic context for decision making during a period of rapid change. Yet *strategic planning* in higher education has had mixed success, particularly in institutions of the size, breadth, and complexity of the research university. Planning exercises are all too frequently attacked by faculty and staff alike as bureaucratic. In fact, many universities have traditionally focused planning efforts on the gathering of data for supporting the routine decision process rather than providing a context for longer-term considerations. As a result, all too often universities tend to react to—or even resist—external pressures and opportunities rather than take strong, decisive actions to determine and pursue their own goals. They frequently become preoccupied with process rather than objectives, with "how" rather than "what."

The final class of decisions consists of those involving more fundamental or even radical transformations of the university. The major paradigm shifts that will likely characterize higher education in the years ahead will require a more strategic approach to *institutional transformation*, capable of staying the course until the desired changes have occurred. Many institutions already have embarked on transformation agendas similar to those characterizing the private sector (Gumport, P. J. & Pusser, B., 1998). Some even use similar language, as they refer to their efforts to "transform" "restructure" or even "reinvent" their institutions. But, herein lies one of the great challenges to universities, since our various missions and our diverse array of constituencies give us a complexity far beyond that encountered in business or government. For universities, the process of institutional transformation is necessarily more complex and possibly more hazardous. It must be approached strategically rather than reactively, with a deep understanding of the role and character of our institutions, their important traditions and values from the past, and a clear and compelling vision for their future.

THE PLAYERS

The decision process in a university interacts with a diverse array of internal and external constituencies that depend on the university in one way or another, just as our educational institutions depend upon each of them. Internally, the key players include students, faculty, staff, and governing boards.

Externally, the stakeholders include parents, the public and their elected leaders in government, business and labor, industry and foundations, the press and other media, and the full range of other public and private institutions in our society. The management of the complex roles and relationships between the university and these many constituencies is one of the most important challenges facing higher education, particularly when these relationships are rapidly changing.

The Internal Stakeholders: The contemporary university is much like a city, comprised of a sometimes bewildering array of neighborhoods and communities. To the faculty, it has almost a Balkan structure, divided up into highly specialized academic units, frequently with little interaction even with disciplinary neighbors, much less with the rest of the campus. To the student body, the university is an exciting, confusing, and sometimes frustrating complexity of challenges and opportunities, rules and regulations, drawing them together only in cosmic events such as football games or campus protests. To the staff, the university has a more subtle character, with the parts woven together by policies, procedures, and practices evolving over decades, all too frequently invisible to, or ignored by, the students and faculty. In some ways, the modern university is so complex, so multifaceted, that it seems that the closer one is to it, the more intimately one is involved with its activities, the harder it is to perceive and understand its entirety.

The Students: Of course, the key stakeholders in the university should be its students. These are our principal clients, customers, and increasingly, consumers of our educational services. Although students pressed in the 1960s for more direct involvement in university decisions ranging from student life to presidential selection, today's students seem more detached. Many students sometimes feel that they are only tourists visiting the university, traveling through the many adventures—or hurdles—of their university education, entering as raw material and being stamped and molded into graduates during their brief experience on campus. Their primary concerns appear to be the cost of their education and their employability following graduation, not in participating in the myriad decisions affecting their education and their university.

The Faculty: Probably the most important internal constituency of a university is its faculty, since the quality and achievements of this body, more than any other factor, determine the quality of the institution. From the perspective of the academy, any great university should be "run by the faculty for the faculty" (an objective that would be contested by students or elements of broader society, of course). The involvement of faculty in the governance of the modern university in a meaningful and effective fashion is both an important goal and a major challenge. While the faculty plays the key role in the academic matters of most universities, its ability to become directly involved in the detailed management of the institution has long since disappeared as issues have become more complex and the time-scale of the decision process has shortened. Little wonder that the faculty frequently feels powerless, buffeted by forces only dimly understood, and thwarted by bureaucracy at every turn.

The Staff: Although frequently invisible to faculty and students, the operation of the university requires a large, professional, and dedicated staff. From accountants to receptionists, investment officers to janitors, computer programmers to nurses, the contemporary university would rapidly grind to a halt without the efforts of thousands of staff members who perform critical services in support of its academic mission. While many faculty members view their appointments at a particular institution as simply another step up the academic ladder, many staff members spend their entire career at the same university. As a result, they frequently exhibit not only a greater institutional loyalty than faculty or students, but they also sustain the continuity, the corporate memory, and the momentum of the university. Ironically, they also sometimes develop a far broader view of the university, its array of activities, and even its history than do the relative short-timers among the faculty and the students. Needless to say, their understanding and support is essential in university efforts to respond to change. Although staff members make many of the routine decisions affecting academic life, from admissions to counseling to financial aid, they frequently view themselves as only a small cog in a gigantic machine, working long and hard for an institution that sometimes does not even appear to recognize or appreciate their existence or loyalty.

Governing Boards: American higher education is unique in its use of lay boards to govern its colleges and universities. In the case of private institutions, governing boards are typically elected by alumni of the institution or self-perpetuated by the board itself. In public institutions, board members are generally either appointed by governors or elected in public elections, usually with highly political overtones. While the primary responsibility of such lay boards is at the policy level, they also frequently find themselves drawn into detailed management decisions. Boards are expected first and foremost to act as trustees, responsible for the welfare of their institution. But, in many public institutions, politically selected board members tend to view themselves more as governors or legislators rather than trustees, responsible to particular political constituencies rather than simply for the welfare of their institution. Instead of buffering the university from various political forces, they sometimes bring their politics into the boardroom and focus it on the activities of the institution (National Commission on the Academic Presidency, 1996).

The External Constituencies: The contemporary university is accountable to many constituencies: students and parents, clients of university services such as patients of our hospitals and spectators at our athletic events; federal, state, and local governments; business and industry; the public and the media. The university is not only accountable to present stakeholders, but it also must accept a stewardship to the past and a responsibility for future stakeholders. In many ways, the increasing complexity and diversity of the modern university and its many missions reflect the character of American and global society. Yet this diversity—indeed, incompatibility—of the values, needs, and expectations of the various constituencies served by higher education poses a major challenge.

Government: Compared with higher education in other nations, American higher education has been relatively free from government interference. Yet, while we have never had a national ministry of education, the impact of the state and federal government on higher education in America has been profound. With federal support, however, has also come federal intrusion. Universities have been forced to build large administrative bureaucracies to manage their interactions with those in Washington. From occupational safety to control of hazardous substances to health-care regulations to accounting requirements to campus crime reporting, federal regulations reach into every part of the university. Furthermore, universities tend to be whipsawed by the unpredictable changes in Washington's policies with regard to regulation, taxation, and funding, shifting with the political winds each election cycle.

Despite this strong federal role, it has been left to the states and the private sector to provide the majority of the resources necessary to support and sustain the contemporary university. The relationship between public universities and state government is a particularly complex one, and it varies significantly from state to state. Some universities are structurally organized as components of state government, subject to the same hiring and business practices as other state agencies. Others possess a certain autonomy from state government through constitutional or legislative provision. All are influenced by the power of the public purse—by the strings attached to appropriations from state tax revenues.

Local Communities: The relationship between a university and its surrounding community is usually a complex one, particularly in cities dominated by major universities. On the plus side is the fact that the university provides the community with an extraordinary quality of life and economic stability. It stimulates strong primary and secondary schools, provides rich cultural opportunities, and generates an exciting and cosmopolitan community. But there are also drawbacks, since the presence of such large, nonprofit institutions takes a great amount of property off the tax rolls. The impact of these universities, whether it is through parking, crowds, or student behavior, can create inevitable tensions between town and gown.

The Public: The public's perception of higher education is ever changing. Public opinion surveys reveal that, at the most general level, the public strongly supports high-quality education in our colleges and universities (Immerwahr, J., 1998). But, when we probe public attitudes more deeply, we find many concerns, about cost, improper student behavior (alcohol, drugs, political activism), and intercollegiate athletics. Perhaps more significantly, there has been an erosion in the priority that the public places on higher education relative to other social needs. This is particularly true on the part of our elected officials, who generally rank health care, welfare, K–12 education, and even prison systems higher on the funding priority list than higher education. This parallels a growing spirit of cynicism toward higher education and its efforts to achieve excellence.

The Press: In today's world, where all societal institutions have come under attack by the media, universities prove to be no exception. Part of this is no doubt due to an increasingly adversarial approach taken by journalists toward all of society, embracing a certain distrust of everything and everyone as a necessary component of investigative journalism. Partly to blame is the arrogance of many members of the academy, university leaders among them, in assuming that the university is somehow less accountable to society than other social institutions. And it is in part due to the increasingly market-driven nature of contemporary journalism as it merges with, or is acquired by, the entertainment industry and trades off journalistic values and integrity for market share and quarterly earnings statements.

The issue of sunshine laws is a particular concern for public institutions. Although laws requiring open meetings and freedom of information were created to ensure the accountability of government, they have been extended and broadened through court decisions to apply to constrain the operation of all public institutions including public universities. They prevent governing boards from discussing sensitive policy matters. They allow the press to go on fishing expeditions through all manner of university documents. They have also been used to hamstring the searches for senior leadership, such as university presidents.

A Growing Tension: Higher education today faces greater pressure than ever to establish its relevance to its various stakeholders in our society. The diversity—indeed, incompatibility—of the values, needs, and expectations of the various constituencies served by higher education poses one of its most serious challenges. The future of our colleges and universities will be determined in many cases by their success in linking together the many concerns and values of these diverse groups, even while the relationships with these constituencies continue to change.

THE PROCESS

Throughout its long history, the American university has been granted special governance status because of the unique character of the academic process. The university has been able to sustain an understanding that its activities of teaching and scholarship could best be judged and guided by the academy itself, rather than by external bodies such as governments or the public opinion that govern other social institutions. Key in this effort was the evolution of a tradition of shared governance involving several major constituencies: a governing board of lay trustees or regents as both stewards for the institution and protectors of broader public interest, the faculty as those most knowledgeable about teaching and scholarship, and the university administration as leaders and managers of the institution.

Institutional Autonomy: The relationship between the university and the broader society it serves is a particularly delicate one, because the university has a role not only as a servant to society but as a critic as well. It serves not merely to create and disseminate knowledge, but to assume an independent questioning stance toward accepted judgments and values. To facilitate this role as critic, universities have been allowed a certain autonomy as a part of a social contract between the university and society. To this end, universities have enjoyed three important traditions: academic freedom, tenure, and institutional autonomy (Shapiro, H. T., 1987). Although there is a considerable degree of diversity in practice—as well as a good deal of myth—there is general agreement about the importance of these traditions. No matter how formal the autonomy of a public university, whether constitutional or statutory, many factors can lead to the erosion of its independence (MacTaggart, T. J., 1997). In practice, government, through its legislative, executive, and judicial activities, can easily intrude on university matters. The autonomy of the university, whether constitutional or statutory, depends both on the attitudes of the public and the degree to which it serves a civic purpose. If the public or its voices in the media lose confidence in the university, in its accountability, its costs, or its quality, it will ask "autonomy for what purpose and for whom." In the long run, institutional autonomy rests primarily on the amount of trust that exists between state government and institutions of higher education.

The Influence of Governments: The federal government plays a significant role in shaping the directions of higher education. For example, the federal land-grant acts of the nineteenth century created many of our great public universities. The GI Bill following World War II broadened educational opportunity and expanded the number and size of educational institutions. Federal funding for campus-based research in support of national security and health care shaped the contemporary research university. Federal programs for key professional programs such as medicine, public health, and engineering have shaped our curriculum. Federal financial aid programs involving grants, loans, and work-study have provided the opportunity of a college education to millions of students from lower- and middleclass families. And federal tax policies have not only provided colleges and universities with tax-exempt status, but they have also provided strong incentives for private giving.

State governments have historically been assigned the primary role for supporting and governing public higher education in the United States. At the most basic level, the principles embodied in the Constitution make matters of education an explicit state assignment. Public colleges and universities are largely creatures of the state. Through both constitution and statute, the states have distributed the responsibility and authority for the governance of public universities through a hierarchy of governing bodies: the legislature, state executive branch agencies or coordinating boards, institutional governing boards, and institutional executive administrations. In recent years there has been a trend toward expanding the role of state governments in shaping the course of higher education, thereby lessening the institutional autonomy of universities. Few outside of this hierarchy are brought into the formal decision process, although they may have strong interests at stake, for example, students, patients of university health clinics, corporate clients.

As state entities, public universities must usually comply with the rules and regulations governing other state agencies. These vary widely, from contracting to personnel requirements to purchasing to even limitations on out-of-state travel. Although regulation is probably the most ubiquitous of the policy tools employed by state government to influence institutional behavior, policies governing the allocation and use of state funds are probably ultimately the most powerful, and these decisions are generally controlled by governors and legislatures.

Governing Boards: The lay board has been the distinctive American device for "public" authority in connection with universities (Houle, C. O., 1989).

The function of the lay board in American higher education is simple, at least in theory. The governing board has final authority for key policy decisions and accepts both fiduciary and legal responsibility for the welfare of the institution. But because of its very limited expertise, it is expected to delegate the responsibility for policy development, academic programs, and administration to professionals with the necessary training and experience. For example, essentially all governing boards share their authority over academic matters with the faculty, generally awarding to the academy the control of academic programs. Furthermore, the day-to-day management of the university is delegated to the president and the administration of the university, since these provide the necessary experience in academic, financial, and legal matters.

While most governing boards of private institutions do approach their roles in this spirit, governing boards of public institutions frequently fall victim to politics, focusing instead on narrow forms of accountability to the particular political constituencies represented by their various members. Political considerations are frequently a major factor in appointing or electing board members and often an important element in their actions and decisions (Ingram, R. T., 1998; Trow, M., 1997). Many public board members view themselves as "governors" rather that as "trustees" of their institutions and are more concerned with their personal agendas or accountability to a particular political constituency than with the welfare of their university. They are further constrained in meeting their responsibilities by sunshine laws in many states that require that their meetings, their deliberations, and their written materials all be open and available to the public, a situation that makes candid discussion and considered deliberation all but impossible.

Faculty Governance: There has long been an acceptance of the premise that faculty members should govern themselves in academic matters, making key decisions about what should be taught, whom should be hired, and other key academic issues. There are actually two levels of faculty governance in the contemporary university. The heart of the governance of the academic mission of the university is actually not at the level of the governing board or the administration, but rather at the level of the academic unit, typically at the department or school level. At the level of the individual academic unit, a department or school, the faculty generally has a very significant role in most of the key decisions concerning who gets hired, who gets promoted, what gets taught, how funds are allocated and spent, and so on. The mechanism for faculty governance at this level usually involves committee structures, for example, promotion committees, curriculum committees, and executive committees. Although the administrative leader, a department chair or dean, may have considerable authority, he or she is generally tolerated and sustained only with the support of the faculty leaders within the unit.

The second level of faculty governance occurs at the university level and usually involves an elected body of faculty representatives, such as an academic senate, that serves to debate institution-wide issues and advise the university administration. Faculties have long cherished and defended the tradition of being consulted in other institutional matters, of "sharing governance" with the governing board and university officers. In sharp contrast to faculty governance at the unit level that has considerable power and influence, the university-wide faculty governance bodies are generally advisory on most issues, without true power. Although they may be consulted on important university matters, they rarely have any executive role. Most key decisions are made by the university administration or governing board.

Beyond the fact that it is frequently difficult to get faculty commitment to—or even interest in—broad institutional goals that are not necessarily congruent with personal goals, there is an even more important characteristic that prevents true faculty governance at the institution level. Authority is always accompanied by responsibility and accountability. Deans and presidents can be fired. Trustees can be sued or forced off governing boards. Yet faculty members, through important academic traditions such as academic freedom and tenure, are largely insulated from the consequences of their debates and recommendations. It would be difficult if not impossible, either legally or operationally, to ascribe to faculty bodies the necessary level of accountability that would have to accompany executive authority.

Many universities follow the spirit of shared governance by selecting their senior leadership, their deans, directors, and executive officers, from the faculty ranks. These academic administrators can be held accountable for their decisions and their actions, although, of course, even if they should be removed from their administrative assignments their positions on the faculty are still protected. However, even for the most distinguished faculty members, the moment they are selected for administrative roles, they immediately become suspect to their faculty colleagues, contaminated by these new assignments.

The Academic Administration: Universities, like other institutions, depend increasingly on strong leadership and effective management if they are to face the challenges and opportunities posed by a changing world. Yet in many–if not most–universities, the concept of management is held in very low regard, particularly by the faculty. Of course, most among the faculty are offended by any suggestion that the university can be compared to other institutional forms such as corporations and governments. Pity the poor administrator who mistakenly refers to the university as a corporation, or to its students or the public at large as customers, or to its faculty as staff. The academy takes great pride in functioning as a creative anarchy. Indeed, the faculty generally looks down upon those who get mired in the swamp of academic administration. Even their own colleagues tapped for leadership roles become somehow tainted, unfit, no longer a part of the true academy, no matter how distinguished their earlier academic accomplishments, once they succumb to the pressures of administration.

Yet all large, complex organizations require not only leadership at the helm, but also effective management at each level where important decisions occur. All presidents, provosts, and deans have heard the suggestion that any one on the faculty, chosen at random, could be an adequate administrator. After all, if you can be a strong teacher and scholar, these skills should be easily transferable to other areas such as administration. Yet, in reality, talent in management is probably as rare a human attribute as the ability to contribute original scholarship. And there is little reason to suspect that talent in one characteristic implies the presence of talent in the other.

One of the great myths concerning higher education in America, particularly appealing to faculty members and trustees alike, is that university administrations are bloated and excessive. To be sure, organizations in business, industry, and government are finding it important to flatten administrative structures by removing layers of management. Yet most universities have rather lean management organizations, inherited from earlier times when academic life was far simpler and institutions were far smaller, particularly when compared to the increasing complexity and accountability of these institutions.

The Presidential Role: The American university presidency is both distinctive and complex. In Europe and Asia, the role of institutional leadership–a rector, vice-chancellor, or president–is frequently a temporary assignment to a faculty member, sometimes elected, and generally without true executive authority, serving instead as a representative of collegial faculty views. In contrast, the American presidency has more of the character of a chief executive officer, with ultimate executive authority for all decisions made within the institution. Although today's university presidents are less visible and authoritative than in earlier times, they are clearly of great importance to higher education in America. Their leadership can be essential, particularly during times of change (Bowen, W. G. and Shapiro, H. T., 1998).

American university presidents are expected to develop, articulate, and implement visions for their institution that sustain and enhance its quality. This includes a broad array of intellectual, social, financial, human, and physical resources, and political issues that envelop the university. Through their roles as the chief executive officers of their institutions, they also have significant management responsibilities for a diverse collection of activities, ranging from education to health care to public entertainment (e.g., intercollegiate athletics). Since these generally require the expertise and experience of talented specialists, the president is the university's leading recruiter, identifying talented people, recruiting them into key university positions, and directing and supporting their activities. Furthermore, unlike most corporate CEOs, the president is expected to play an active role generating the resources needed by the university, whether by lobbying state and federal governments, seeking gifts and bequests from alumni and friends, or clever entrepreneurial efforts. There is an implicit expectation on most campuses that the president's job is to raise money for the provost and deans to spend, while the chief financial officer and administrative staff watch over their shoulders to make certain they all do it wisely.

The university president also has a broad range of important responsibilities that might best be termed symbolic leadership. In the role as head of the university, the president has a responsibility for the complex array of relationships with both internal and external constituencies. These include students, faculty, and staff on the campus. The myriad external constituencies include alumni and parents, local, state, and federal government, business and labor, foundations, the higher education community, the media, and the public at large. The president has become a defender of the university and its fundamental qualities of knowledge and wisdom, truth and freedom, academic excellence and public service against the forces of darkness that rage outside its ivy-covered walls. Needless to say, the diverse perspectives and often-conflicting needs and expectations of these various groups make the management of relationships an extremely complex and time-consuming task.

Yet the presidency of a major university is an unusual leadership position from another interesting perspective. Although the responsibility for everything involving the university usually floats up to the president's desk, direct authority for university activities almost invariably rests elsewhere. There is a mismatch between responsibility and authority that is unparalleled in other social institutions. As a result, there are many, including many university presidents, who have become quite convinced that the contemporary public university is basically unmanageable and unleadable.

THE CHALLENGES

The Complexity of the University: The modern university is comprised of many activities, some nonprofit, some publicly regulated, and some operating in intensely competitive marketplaces. We teach students; we conduct research for various clients; we provide health care; we engage in economic development; we stimulate social change; and we provide mass entertainment (athletics). The organization of the contemporary university would compare in both scale and complexity with many major global corporations. Yet at the same time, the intellectual demands of scholarship have focused faculty increasingly within their particular disciplines, with little opportunity for involvement in the far broader array of activities characterizing their university. While faculty members are—and should always remain—the cornerstone of the university's academic activities, they rarely have deep understanding or will accept the accountability necessary for the many other missions of the university in modern society.

Faculties have been quite influential and effective within the narrow domain of their academic programs. However, the very complexity of their institutions has made substantive involvement in the broader governance of the university problematic. The current disciplinary-driven governance structure makes it very difficult to deal with broader, strategic issues. Since universities are highly fragmented and decentralized, one frequently finds a chimney organization structure, with little coordination or even concern about university-wide needs or priorities. The broader concerns of the university are always someone else's problem.

Bureaucracy: The increased complexity, financial pressures, and accountability of universities demanded by government, the media, and the public at large has required far stronger management than in the past (Balderston, F. E., 1995). Recent furors over issues such as federal research policy, labor relations, financial aid and tuition agreements, and state funding models, all involve complex policy, financial, and political issues. While perhaps long ago universities were treated by our society—and its various government bodies—as largely well-intentioned and benign stewards of education and learning, today we find the university faces the same pressures, standards, and demands for accountability of any other billion-dollar corporation. Yet as universities have developed the administrative staffs, policies, and procedures to handle such issues, they have also created a thicket of paperwork, regulations, and bureaucracy that has eroded the authority and attractiveness of academic leadership.

More specifically, it is increasingly difficulty to attract faculty members into key leadership positions such as department chairs, deans, and project directors. The traditional anarchy of faculty committee and consensus decision making have long made these jobs difficult, but today's additional demands for accountability imposed by university management structures have eroded the authority to manage, much less lead academic programs. Perhaps because of the critical nature of academic disciplines, universities suffer from an inability to allocate decisions to the most appropriate level of the organization and then to lodge trust in the individuals with this responsibility. The lack of career paths and adequate mechanisms for leadership development for junior faculty and staff has also decimated much of the strength of mid-level management. Many of our most talented faculty leaders have concluded that becoming a chair, director, or dean is just not worth the effort and the frustration any longer.

Part of the challenge is to clear the administrative underbrush cluttering our institutions. Both decision-making and leadership is hampered by bureaucratic policies and procedures and practices, along with the anarchy of committee and consensus decision making. Our best people feel quite constrained by the university, constrained by their colleagues, constrained by the "administration", and constrained by bureaucracy. Yet, leadership is important. If higher education is to keep pace with the extraordinary changes and challenges in our society, someone in academe must eventually be given the authority to make certain that the good ideas that rise up from the faculty and staff are actually put into practice. We need to devise a system that releases the creativity of faculty members while strengthening the authority of responsible leaders.

The Pace of Change: Both the pace and nature of the changes occurring in our world today have become so rapid and so profound that our present social institutions—in government, education, and the private sector—are having increasing difficulty in even sensing the changes (although they certainly feel the consequences), much less understanding them sufficiently to respond and adapt. It could well be that our present institutions, such as universities and government agencies, which have been the traditional structures for intellectual pursuits, may turn out to be as obsolete and irrelevant to our future as the American corporation in the 1950s. There is clearly a need to explore new social structures capable of sensing and understanding the change, as well as capable of engaging in the strategic processes necessary to adapt or control change. The glacial pace of academic change simply may not be sufficiently responsive to allow the university to control its own destiny.

As the time scale for decisions and actions compresses, during an era of ever more rapid change, authority tends to concentrate so that the institution can become more flexible and responsive. The academic tradition of extensive consultation, debate, and consensus building before any substantial decision is made or action taken will be one of our greatest challenges, since this process is simply incapable of keeping pace with the profound changes swirling about higher education. A quick look at the remarkable pace of change required in the private sector—usually measured in months, not years—suggests that universities must develop more capacity to move rapidly. This will require a willingness by leaders throughout the university to occasionally make difficult decisions and take strong action without the traditional consensus-building process.

The Resistance to Change: In business, management approaches change in a highly strategic fashion, launching a comprehensive process of planning and transformation. In political circles, sometimes a strong leader with a big idea can captivate the electorate, building a movement for change. The creative anarchy arising from a faculty culture that prizes individual freedom and consensual decision making poses quite a different challenge to the university. Most big ideas from top administrators are treated with either disdain (this too shall pass…) or ridicule. The same usually occurs for formal strategic planning efforts, unless, of course, they are attached to clearly perceived and immediately implementable budget consequences or faculty rewards. As Don Kennedy, former president of Stanford, noted, "The academic culture nurtures a set of policies and practices that favor the present state of affairs over any possible future. It is a portrait of conservatism, perhaps even of senescence." (Kennedy, D., 1993)

This same resistance to change characterizes the response of the academy to external forces. The American higher education establishment has tended to oppose most changes proposed or imposed from beyond the campus, including the GI Bill (the veterans will overrun our campuses), the Pell Grant program (it will open our gates to poor, unqualified students), and the direct lending program (we will be unable to handle all the paperwork). Yet in each case, higher education eventually changed its stance, adapted to, and even embraced the new programs.

Change occurs in the university through a more tenuous, sometimes tedious, process. Ideas are first floated as trial balloons, all the better if they can be perceived to have originated at the grassroots level. After what often seems like years of endless debate, challenging basic assumptions and hypotheses, decisions are made and the first small steps are taken. For change to affect the highly entrepreneurial culture of the faculty, it must address the core issues of incentives and rewards. Change does not happen because of presidential proclamations or committee reports, but instead it occurs at the grassroots level of faculty, students, and staff. Rarely is major change motivated by excitement, opportunity, and hope; it more frequently is in response to some perceived crisis. As one of my colleagues put it, if you believe change is needed, and you do not have a convenient wolf at the front door, then you had better invent one.

Of course, the efforts to achieve change following the time-honored traditions of collegiality and consensus can sometimes be self-defeating, since the process can lead all too frequently right back to the status quo. As one of my exasperated presidential colleagues once noted, the university faculty may be the last constituency on Earth that believes the status quo is still an option. To some degree, this strong resistance to change is both understandable and appropriate. After all, the university is one of the longest enduring social institutions of our civilization in part because its ancient traditions and values have been protected and sustained.

Cultural Issues: There are many factors that mitigate against faculty involvement in the decision process. The fragmentation of the faculty into academic disciplines and professional schools, coupled with the strong market pressures on faculty in many areas, has created an academic culture in which faculty loyalties are generally first to their scholarly discipline, then to their academic unit, and only last to their institution. Many faculty members move from institution to institution, swept along by market pressures and opportunities. The university reward structure—salary, promotion, and tenure–is clearly a meritocracy in which there are clear "haves" and "have-nots." The former generally are too busy to become heavily involved in institutional issues. The latter are increasingly frustrated and vocal in their complaints. Yet they are also all too often the squeaky wheels that drown out others and capture attention. The increasing specialization of faculty, the pressure of the marketplace for their skills, and the degree to which the university has become simply a way station for faculty careers have destroyed institutional loyalty and stimulated more of a "what's in it for me" attitude on the part of many faculty members.

In sharp contrast, many non-academic staff remain with a single university throughout their careers, developing not only a strong institutional loyalty but in many cases a somewhat broader view and understanding of the nature of the institution. Although faculty decry the increased influence of administrative staff, to some degree this is due to their own market- and discipline-driven academic culture, their abdication of institution loyalty, coupled with the complexity of the contemporary university, that has led to this situation.

There many signs of a widening gap between faculty and administration on many campuses. The rank-and-file faculty sees the world quite differently from campus administrators (Government-University-Industry Research Roundtable and National Science Board, 1997). There are significant differences in perceptions and understandings of the challenges and opportunities before higher education. It is clear that such a gap, and the corresponding absence of a spirit of trust and confidence by the faculty in their university leadership, could seriously undercut the ability of universities to make difficult yet important decisions and move ahead.

Politics: Most of America's colleges and universities have more than once suffered the consequences of ill-informed efforts by politicians to influence everything from what subjects can be taught, to who is fit to teach, and whom should be allowed to study. As universities have grown in importance and influence, more political groups are tempted to use them to achieve some purpose in broader society. To some degree, the changing political environment of the university reflects a more fundamental shift from issue-oriented to image-dominated politics at all levels–federal, state, and local. Public opinion drives political contributions, and vice-versa, and these determine successful candidates and eventually legislation. Policy is largely an aftermath exercise, since the agenda is really set by polling and political contributions. Issues, strategy, and "the vision thing" are largely left on the sidelines. And since higher education has never been particularly influential either in determining public opinion or in making campaign contributions, the university is frequently left with only the option of reacting as best it can to the agenda set by others.

The Particular Challenges faced by Public Universities: All colleges and universities, public and private alike, face today the challenge of change as they struggle to adapt and to serve a changing world. Yet there is a significant difference in the capacity that public and private institutions have to change. The term "independent" used to describe private universities has considerable significance in this regard. Private universities are generally more nimble, both because of their smaller size and the more limited number of constituencies that has to be consulted—and convinced—before change can occur. Whether driven by market pressures, resource constraints, or intellectual opportunity, private universities usually need to convince only trustees, campus communities (faculty, students, and staff) and perhaps alumni before moving ahead with a change agenda. Of course, this can be a formidable task, but it is a far cry from the broader political challenges facing public universities.

The public university must always function in an intensely political environment. Public university governing boards are generally political in nature, frequently viewing their primary responsibilities as being to various political constituencies rather than confined to the university itself. Changes that might threaten these constituencies are frequently resisted, even if they might enable the institution to serve broader society better. The public university also must operate within a complex array of government regulations and relationships at the local, state, and federal level, most of which tend to be highly reactive and supportive of the status quo. Furthermore, the press itself is generally far more intrusive in the affairs of public universities, viewing itself as the guardian of the public interest and using powerful tools such as sunshine laws to hold public universities accountable.

As a result, actions that would be straightforward for private universities, such as enrollment adjustments, tuition increases, program reductions or elimination, or campus modifications, can be formidable for public institutions. For example, the actions taken by many public universities to adjust to eroding state support through tuition increases or program restructuring have triggered major political upheavals that threaten to constrain further efforts to balance activities with resources (Gumport, P. J. & Pusser, B., 1997). Sometimes, the reactive nature of the political forces swirling about and within the institution is not apparent until an action is taken. Many a public university administration has been undermined by an about-face by their governing board, when political pressures force board members to switch from support to opposition on a controversial issue.

Little wonder that administrators sometimes conclude that the only way to get anything accomplished within the political environment of the public university is by heeding the old adage, "It is simpler to ask forgiveness than to seek permission." Yet even this hazardous approach may not be effective for the long term. It could well be that many public universities will simply not be able to respond adequately during periods of great change in our society.

SOME OBSERVATIONS

Fire, Ready, Aim! Traditional planning and decision-making processes are frequently found to be inadequate during times of rapid or even discontinuous change (Porter, M. E., 1998). Tactical efforts such as total quality management, process reengineering, and planning techniques such as preparing mission and vision statements, while important for refining status quo operations, may actually distract an institution from more substantive issues during more volatile periods. Furthermore, incremental change based on traditional, well-understood paradigms may be the most dangerous course of all, because those paradigms may simply not be adequate to adapt to a future of change. If the status quo is no longer an option, if the existing paradigms are no longer viable, then more radical transformation becomes the wisest course. Furthermore, during times of very rapid change and uncertainty, it is sometimes necessary to launch the actions associated with a preliminary strategy long before it is carefully thought through and completely developed.

Here, a personal observation may be appropriate. As a scientist-engineer, it was not surprising that my own leadership style tended to be comfortable with strategic processes. Yet, it should also be acknowledged that my particular style of planning and decision-making was rather unorthodox, sometimes baffling both our formal university planning staff and my executive officer colleagues alike. Once, I overheard a colleague describe my style as "fire, ready, aim" as I would launch yet another salvo of agendas and initiatives.

This was not a consequence of impatience or lack of discipline. Rather, it grew from my increasing sense that traditional planning approaches were simply ineffective during times of great change. Far too many leaders, when confronted with uncertainty, tend to fall into a "ready, aim… ready, aim… ready, aim…" mode and never make a decision. By the time they are finally forced to pull the trigger, the target has moved out of sight. Hence, there was logic to my "anticipatory, scattershot" approach to planning and decision-making (Downs, L. & Mui, C., 1998).

Note that this viewpoint suggests that one of the greatest challenges for universities is to learn to encourage more people to participate in the high-risk, unpredictable, but ultimately very productive confrontations of stagnant paradigms. We must jar as many people as possible out of their comfortable ruts of conventional wisdom, fostering experiments, recruiting restive faculty, turning people loose to "cause trouble" and simply making conventionality more trouble than unconventionality.

University Transformation: The most difficult decisions are those concerning institutional transformation. Experience suggests that major change in higher education is usually driven by forces from outside the academy. Certainly, earlier examples of change, such as the evolution of the land-grant university, the growth of higher education following World War II, and the evolution of the research university all represented responses to powerful external forces and major policies at the national level. The examples of major institutional transformation driven by strategic decisions and plans from within are relatively rare. Yet, the fact that reactive change has been far more common than strategic change in higher education should not lead us to conclude that the university is incapable of controlling its own destiny. Self-driven strategic transformation is possible and probably necessary to cope with the challenges of our times.

Universities need to consider a broad array of transformation areas that go far beyond simply restructuring finances in order to face a future of change (Dolence, M. G. & Norris, D. M., 1995). The transformation process must encompass every aspect of our institutions, including the mission of the university, financial restructuring, organization and governance, the general characteristics of the university (e.g., enrollment size and program breadth), relationships with external constituencies, intellectual transformation, and cultural change. While such a broad, almost scattershot approach is complex to design and challenging to lead, it has the advantage of engaging a large number of participants at the grassroots level.

The most important objective of any broad effort at institutional transformation is not so much to achieve a specific set of goals, but rather to build the capacity, the energy, the excitement, and the commitment to move toward bold visions of the university's future. The real aims include removing the constraints that prevent the institution from responding to the needs of a rapidly changing society; removing unnecessary processes and administrative structures; questioning existing premises and arrangements; and challenging, exciting, and emboldening the members of the university community to view institutional transformation as a great adventure.

Structural Issues: The modern university functions as a loosely coupled adaptive system, evolving in a highly reactive fashion to its changing environment through the individual or small group efforts of faculty entrepreneurs. While this has allowed the university to adapt quite successfully to its changing environment, it has also created an institution of growing size and complexity. The ever growing, myriad activities of the university can sometimes distract from or even conflict with its core mission of learning.

While it is certainly impolitic to be so blunt, the simple fact of life is that the contemporary university is a *public corporation* that must be governed, led, and managed like other corporations to benefit its stakeholders. The interests of its many stakeholders can only be served by a governing board that is comprised and functions as a true board of directors. Like the boards of directors of publicly held corporations, the university's governing board should consist of members selected for their expertise and experience. They should govern the university in way that serves the interests of its various constituencies. This, of course, means that the board should function with a structure and a process that reflect the best practices of corporate boards.

Again, although it may be politically incorrect within the academy to say so, the leadership of the university must be provided with the authority commensurate with its responsibilities. The president and other executive officers should have the same degree of authority to take actions, to select leadership, to take risks and move with deliberate speed, that their counterparts in the corporate world enjoy. The challenges and pace of change faced by the modern university no longer allow the luxury of "consensus" leadership, at least to the degree that "building consensus" means seeking the approval of all concerned communities. Nor do our times allow the reactive nature of special interest politics to rigidly moor the university to an obsolete status quo, thwarting efforts to provide strategic leadership and direction.

Yet a third controversial observation: while academic administrations generally can be drawn as conventional hierarchical trees, in reality the connecting lines of authority are extremely weak. In fact, one of the reasons for cost escalation is the presence of a deeply ingrained academic culture in which leaders are expected to "purchase the cooperation" of subordinates, to provide them with positive incentives to carry out decisions. For example, deans expect the provost to offer additional resources in order to gain their cooperation on various institution-wide efforts. Needless to say, this "bribery culture" is quite incompatible with the trend toward increasing decentralization of resources. As the central administration relinquishes greater control of resource and cost accountability to the units, it will lose the pool of resources that in the past was used to provide incentives to deans, directors, and other leaders to cooperate and support university-wide goals.

Hence, it is logical to expect that both the leadership and management of universities will need increasingly to rely on lines of real authority, just as their corporate counterparts. That is, presidents, executive officers, and deans will almost certainly have to become comfortable with issuing clear orders or directives, from time to time. So, too, throughout the organization, subordinates will need to recognize that failure to execute these directives will likely have significant consequences, including possible removal from their positions. While collegiality will continue to be valued and honored, the modern university simply must accept a more realistic balance between responsibility and authority.

The Need to Restructure University Governance: Many universities find that the most formidable forces controlling their destiny are political in nature— from governments, governing boards, or perhaps even public opinion. Unfortunately, these bodies are not only usually highly reactive in nature, but they frequently either constrain the institution or drive it away from strategic objectives that would better serve society as a whole. Many university presidents—particularly those associated with public universities—believe that the greatest barrier to change in their institutions lies in the manner in which their institutions are governed, both from within and from without. Universities have a style of governance that is more adept at protecting the past than preparing for the future.

The 1996 report of the National Commission on the Academic Presidency (1996) reinforced these concerns when it concluded that the governance structure at most colleges and universities is inadequate. "At a time when higher education should be alert and nimble, it is slow and cautious instead, hindered by traditions and mechanisms of governing that do not allow the responsiveness and decisiveness the times require." The Commission went on to note its belief that university presidents were currently unable to lead their institutions effectively, since they were forced to operate from "one of the most anemic power bases of any of the major institutions in American society."

This view was also voiced in a study (Dionne, J. L. & Kean, T., 1997) performed by the RAND Corporation, which noted, "The main reason why institutions have not taken more effective action (to increase productivity) is their outmoded governance structure—i.e., the decision-making units, policies, and practices that control resource allocation have remained largely unchanged since the structure's establishment in the 19th century. Designed for an era of growth, the current structure is cumbersome and even dysfunctional in an environment of scare resources."

It is simply unrealistic to expect that the governance mechanisms developed decades or, in some cases, even centuries ago can serve well either the contemporary university or the society it serves. It seems clear that the university of the twenty-first century will require new patterns of governance and leadership capable of responding to the changing needs and emerging challenges of our society and its educational institutions. The contemporary university has many activities, many responsibilities, many constituencies, and many overlapping lines of authority. From this perspective, shared governance models still have much to recommend them: a tradition of public oversight and trusteeship, shared collegial internal governance of academic matters, and, experienced administrative leadership.

Yet shared governance is, in reality, an ever-changing balance of forces involving faculty, trustees, staff, and administration. The increasing politicization of public governing boards, the ability of faculty councils to use their powers to promote special interests, delay action, and prevent reforms; and weak, ineffectual, and usually short-term administrative leadership all pose risks to the university. Clearly it is time to take a fresh look at the governance of our institutions.

Governing boards should focus on policy development rather than management issues. Their role is to provide the strategic, supportive, and critical stewardship for their institution. Faculty governance should become a true participant in the academic decision process rather than simply watchdogs of the administration or defenders of the status quo. Faculties also need to accept and acknowledge that strong leadership, whether from chairs, deans, or presidents, is important if their institution is to flourish during a time of significant change.

The contemporary American university presidency also merits a candid reappraisal and likely a thorough overhaul. The presidency of the university may indeed be one of the more anemic in our society, because of the imbalance between responsibility and authority. Yet, it is nevertheless a position of great importance. Governing boards, faculty, students, alumni, and the press tend to judge a university president on the issue of the day. Their true impact on the institution is usually not apparent for many years after their tenure. Decisions and actions must always be taken within the perspective of the long-standing history and traditions of the university and for the benefit of not only those currently served by the institution, but on behalf of future generations.

CONCLUSION

We have entered a period of significant change in higher education as our universities attempt to respond to the challenges, opportunities, and responsibilities before them (The Glion Declaration, 1998). This time of great change, of shifting paradigms, provides the context in which we must consider the changing nature of the university (Duderstadt, J. J., 2000).

From this perspective, it is important to understand that the most critical challenge facing most institutions will be to develop the capacity for change. As we noted earlier, universities must seek to remove the constraints that prevent them from responding to the needs of a rapidly changing society. They should strive to challenge, excite, and embolden all members of their academic communities to embark on what should be a great adventure for higher education. The successful adaptation of universities to the revolutionary challenges they face will depend a great deal on an institution's collective ability to learn and to continuously improve its decision making process. It is critical that higher education give thoughtful attention to the design of institutional processes for planning, management, and governance. Only a concerted effort to understand the important traditions of the past, the challenges of the present, and the possibilities for the future can enable institutions to thrive during a time of such change.

As the quote from Machiavelli at the beginning of this paper suggests, leading in the introduction of change can be both a challenging and a risky proposition. The resistance can be intense, and the political backlash threatening. To be sure, it is sometimes difficult to act for the future when the demands of the present can be so powerful and the traditions of the past so difficult to challenge. Yet, perhaps this is the most important role of university leadership and the greatest challenge for the university decision process in the years ahead.

REFERENCES

Balderston, F. E. (1995). *Managing Today's University: Strategies for Viability, Change, and Excellence*, Jossey-Bass, San Francisco, p. 398.

Bowen, W. G. & Shapiro, H. T. (1998). eds., *Universities and Their Leadership*, Princeton University Press, Princeton.

Dionne, J. L. & Kean, T. (1997). *Breaking the Social Contract: The Fiscal Crisis in Higher Education*, report of the Commission on National Investment in Higher Education, Council for Aid to Education, New York.

Dolence, M. G. & Norris, D. M. (1995). *Transforming Higher Education: A Vision for Learning in the 21st century*, Society for College and University Planning, Ann Arbor.

Downs, L. & Mui, C. (1998). *Killer App*, Harvard Business School Press, Cambridge.

Duderstadt, J. J. (2000). *A University for the 21st century*, University of Michigan Press, Ann Arbor.

Government-University-Industry Research Roundtable and National Science Board (1997). "Convocation on Stresses on Research and Education at Colleges and Universities", <http://www.2.nas.edu/guirrcon>.

Gumport, P. J. & Pusser, B. (1997). "Academic Restructuring: Contemporary Adaptation in Higher Education", in *Planning and Management for a Changing Environment: A Handbook on Redesigning Post-Secondary Institutions*, ed. M. Petersen, D. Dill, & L. Mets, Jossey-Bass, San Francisco.

Gumport, P. J. & Pusser, B. (1998). *Academic Restructuring in Public Higher Education: A Framework and Research Agenda*, National Center for Postsecondary Improvement, Stanford, p. 111.

Houle, C. O. (1989). *Governing Boards*, Jossey-Bass, San Francisco, p. 223.

Immerwahr, J. (1998). *The Price of Admission: The Growing Importance of Higher Education*, National Center for Public Policy and Higher Education, Washington, D.C.

Ingram, R. T. (1998). *Transforming Public Trusteeship*, Public Policy Paper Series, Association of Governing Boards, Washington, D.C.

Kennedy, D. (1993). "Making Choices in the Research University" the American Research University, *Daedelus*, 122, n° 4, pp. 127–56.

MacTaggart, T. J. (1997). ed., *Seeking Excellence through Independence*, Jossey-Bass, San Francisco.

National Commission on the Academic Presidency (1996). *Renewing the Academic Presidency: Stronger Leadership for Tougher Times*, Association of Governing Boards of Universities and Colleges, Washington, D.C.

Porter, M. E. (1998). *Competitive Strategy: Techniques for Analyzing Industries and Competitiveness*, Free Press, Boston.

Shapiro, H. T. (1987). *Tradition and Change: Perspectives on Education and Public Policy*, University of Michigan Press, Ann Arbor.

The Glion Declaration (1998). "The University at the Millennium", *The Presidency*, American Council on Education, Washington, D.C., pp. 27-31.

Trow, M. (1997). "The Chiefs of Public Universities Should be Civil Servants, Not Political Actors" *Chronicle of Higher Education*.

CHAPTER 4

Governance, Change and the Universities in Western Europe

Guy Neave

INTRODUCTION

For nigh on three decades in Western Europe, what Anglo Saxon terminology calls 'governance' has tried the ingenuity of leaders and the patience of governments. Indeed, it has been the object of unremitting concern - of political parties, Ministries and, last but very far from least, of the legislator. From a long-term perspective, the issue of governance—that is the organization, control and distribution of responsibility for teaching, learning and research at the level of the individual university—is both enduring and vexatious. It is also highly political. In Europe, it tends also to engage a very different discourse and evokes a very different mental landscape from its counterpart in those other 'referential systems'[1] of higher education, Britain and the United States.

Precisely because the context, historical, political and organizational, is so very different from either Britain or the United States, I want to mark out some of these differences, beginning first of all with the notion of governance itself. There is some merit in doing this. It should remind us that if our dialogue has reached a point where meaningful lessons may be exchanged, we should not lose sight of the fact that the paths which bring us together today themselves started from very different premises and in very different circumstances. Nor does it exclude the possibility that they could diverge later.

---

1 Guy Neave [1998] "Quatre modèles pour l'Université", *Courrier de l'UNESCO*, septembre 1998.

Governance: a far from Universal Term

That "governance" is increasingly used as coterminous with 'la gestion interne de l'université', 'Bestuursorganisatie', 'Universitaetsverwaltung' is not simply a reflection of the convenience that various forms of English have as the *lingua franca* of our domain. The concept of governance in Britain and the United States assumes that the individual university possesses very real and substantial powers for determining the use of the resources assigned to it and in the decision to raise other resources. It also presumes that the individual university controls independently and on its own, the appointment, promotion, recognition and reward of academic excellence amongst both students and academic staff. Thus, the supposedly plain and straightforward concept of governance makes certain presumptions about the 'proper' relationship between public authorities, their representatives and the universities in which the latter posses a high degree of self-government (De Groof, J. & Neave, G. & Svec, J., 1998).

Fifteen years ago, few of these assumptions applied in the same way in Western Europe. The assumptions contained in the Anglo-American usage of the term implied a type of relationship between government and universities that did not then exist. Much has changed in the intervening period. If today we can debate the notion of governance within the Western European context, it is precisely because the relationship between university and government evolved beyond its classic—and long enduring—mode of 'State control'. Beneath the unfolding patterns of institutional self-regulation in Western Europe lies a very radical change in relationship between central national administration and university. This particular dynamic which, if sometimes deriving from and inspired by, American practice, sets 'governance' within a very different political and cultural environment and has imparted to it a very different evolutionary path.

The centrality of governance in today's university world reflects a particular thrust in the higher education policy of Western European States. To the adepts of Public Administration, this development is seen as part of a wider trend, permeating into higher education from other sectors of public life. Often described as the 'new public management', it entails on the one hand a reduction in the range of activities coming under the oversight of central national administration, together with greater efficiency and public accountability in the use of public resources on the other (Bliekle, I., 1998) (Maassen, P. A. M. & Van Vught, F. A, 1994). An extension of this perspective concentrates on the relationship between state and university. It involves a shift from detailed scrutiny and central direction, which parades under the short hand of 'State control', before a more accommodating and more flexible concept of 'State supervision' (Van Vught, F. A., 1997) (Neave, G. & Van Vught, F. A.,

1991). Functions hitherto vested in a central Ministry have, in the course of the past fifteen years or so, been delegated to the individual university and, with them, an enhanced degree of 'self regulation'. In most European systems, academic appointments at senior level, self-validation of the curriculum or a diminution in the degree of formal central control exercised over the latter (Askling, B. & Bauer, M. & Marton, S., 1999) figure amongst these 'repatriated' functions (Neave, G., 1999).

Two Reforms for the Price of One

Changes in governance come from re-considering both the location and weight of historic systems of control and regulation, which, by and large, have been in place for the best part of a century or more. However, current debate in Western Europe over forms of governance does not take place in an historical vacuum. And whilst it would be exaggerated to argue that what is happening today is an attempt to correct earlier developments, this interpretation is not wholly unfounded. If we dismiss the first wave of reform in governance that took place during the late Sixties to the late Seventies, we risk being less sensitive to some aspects that arose in the course of the second.

Most denizens of British and American academia, aged 50 plus, are in the case of the former, engaged in putting in place the idea of the entrepreneurial university or, in the case of the latter, involved in adjusting it to economic or technological change. Many of their fellows in mainland Europe have, however, been through *two* reforms in governance. Of these, the present challenge of the 'new economy' is probably less traumatic, though more radical in its consequences for the distribution of authority.

Le Grand Soir of the Ordinarienuniversitaet: 1968 and its Aftermath

The significance of the reforms that from 1968 onwards rolled in upon the university in Western Europe lies in several areas. [2] First, it was a highly political affair and treated as such by both its protagonists and its adversaries. From the standpoint of its adepts, the pressure for overhauling 'university governance' drew justification from the notion of 'participant democracy'. Participant democracy extended 'democracy' beyond the issue of who should have access to knowledge. It focused specifically on the organization, decision-making, participation and thus the distribution of authority, which accompanied the dissemination of knowledge inside the university itself. In this scheme of things, the 'Gruppenuniversitaet" (The University of Repre-

---

[2] For an irascible and testy account of these developments, see Shils E. & Daalder H., (eds), (1982), *Universities, Politicians and Bureaucrats*: Cambridge University Press.

sentative Groups) was erected as counter example to the dysfunctional and supposedly 'non democratic' Ordenarienuniversitaet–the University of the Senior Professors.

The pressure to found the 'inner life' of universities upon the transparency of 'collective representation' of interests–junior staff, non academic personnel and students (Neave, G. & Rhoades, G., 1987)–in both central university decision-making and in individual faculties generated a number of developments which have direct bearing on the present debate. First, the principle of Tripartite representation (*Drittelparitaet*) set aside one third of seats on university and faculty Councils to each constituency - academic staff, university personnel and students. The number of officially recognized 'constituencies' inside academia increased. Their relative weighting altered profoundly (De Boer, H. & Denters, B. & Goedegebuure, L., 1998b). Second, and beginning with the Dutch law of 1970, the principle of 'corporate representation'— the representation of formally constituted groups within the university— became the Ark of Covenant which, in the course of the Seventies laid the basis of institutional governance in mainland Europe. Enshrined in the fundamental legislation of Germany and Austria in 1976 [3], the system of 'electoral colleges' embraced Sweden the following year, with similar measures introduced in Greece and Spain during the early Eighties.

Fragmentation and Shifts in Basic Units

What might, perhaps mischievously, be called 'Mode One' [4] in the reform of decision-making structures in Continental Europe, formally strengthened internal accountability in the university sector [5] and supposedly counter-balanced professorial power by a system of checks and balances. From the standpoint of those less enthused by collective decision-making, 'electoral collegi-

---

3 Respectively, in the shape of the Hochschulrahmengesetz of 1976 and the Universitaetsorganizationsgesetz of the same year, in Sweden a year later with the 1977 reforms.
4 Honour paid where honour is due. This term was first coined by Michael Gibbons and applied to developments in science policy and research. It has, to the best of my belief, not as yet been applied to the historical development of governance. The logic of so doing becomes, however, unstoppable, once we change our perspective on the university qua institution to that of being a sub-set of the 'knowledge production process' (sic)—see Gibbons, M. & Limoges, C. & Nowotny, H. & Schwartzmann, S. & Scott, P. & Trow, M. (1994), *The new production of knowledge: the dynamics of science and research in contemporary societies*, London/Thousand Oaks/New Delhi, SAGE Publications, p. 179.
5 To call this process accountability is both an inaccuracy and an anachronism, but convenient nevertheless. Accountability, like governance, is a concept almost impossible to translate directly into other European languages. Responsabilité, imputabilité in French do not carry the same connotations of rendering accounts to those to whom the establishment has a moral obligation so to do.

ality' served both to fragment and to politicize the inner life of the university (Shils, E. & Daalder, H., 1982). Fragmentation, however, was not confined to the shifting alignments of the various groups inside either university or faculty councils. It also emerged in the shape of new 'basic units' below Faculty level. The creation of sub faculty groupings—the so called Unites d'Enseignement et de Recherche—in the wake of the French Loi d'Orientation of 1968 and their counterparts in the Netherlands and Germany—the Vakgroep and the Fachbereiche—the first introduced by the law on University Governance of 1970 (Wet op de Universitaire Bestuurshervorming) and the second by the Higher Education Guideline Law of 1976, are interesting from several points of view. They reflected, at a time of massive student growth, the need for a teaching unit below the faculty level, less remote from either students or staff. They also reflected the conviction that a student body, of increasing diversity, required a closer, pedagogic 'encadrement'. In truth, the faculty had literally outgrown its functions, both as the main administrative and as a teaching unit. In terms of relationship between teaching staff, 'Department' equivalents were cast 'as the very model of a modern' collegiality. In the Netherlands, following the promulgation of the 1970 Law on University Governance, Departmental Boards, with a majority of teaching staff, but also including non academic personnel and students, elected their Chairmen on a one year mandate from amongst full professors (De Boer, H. & Denters, B. & Goedegebuure, L., 1998a).

Change and Continuity

Radical though changes in the basic units for knowledge delivery and the strengthening of 'corporate participation' were—the latter to be understood in its original meaning of a guild or medieval corporation—they remained reforms *internal* to the university. In terms of co-ordination and authority, neither the relationship with the State, nor with the market, were objects of revision. The impact fell within the 'academic oligarchy'. Certainly, the apparent demise of the Ordinarienuniversitaet was radical in itself. But, the way in which change was carried out and the basic principles that underlay it, from an administrative and legal standpoint, in no way departed from well-established practice. Instruments of change remained, in effect, the traditional armory of national legislation. They applied in a homogeneous fashion across the whole of the university sector throughout the breadth and depth of the land. In France and Germany, re-definition of participant constituencies and 'knowledge delivery systems' formed a sub-set within broader, framework legislation which set down the overall operating frame for the university, whilst reserving the right of the Ministry to elaborate on those aspects—finance or curriculum development, for instance,—which might require attention later.

Thus, inner change was balanced by continuity in the instrumentality that implemented it. Though agendas naturally varied from university to university, the composition, size and remit of committees and councils—university, faculty or department—did not. They reflected the 'national' nature and status of the university. In short, the principle of 'legal homogeneity' both symbolic of, and as a means of upholding national unity, survived intact.[6] So, also, did established boundaries of national regulation over such domains as degree validation, control over curriculum, length of courses, creation of posts—and in some instances, nomination to posts—areas which, with certain exceptions, fell firmly under the oversight of national authority and were subject to national legal stipulation, remained set in that mould.

Despite internal reform, the distinction Trow drew a quarter of a century ago between the 'public' and 'private' lives of academia in Britain and the United States (Trow, M., 1975) remained less clearly delineated in Europe. National regulation still penetrated into and set norms for those functions, which in both Britain and the United States, stood as quintessential features of institutional self-regulation.

Mode One of Governance Reform: a Retrospective View

What were the lasting achievements of Mode One reform? Given the passions, heat and energy aroused, the outcomes were remarkably modest. By the same token, given the very radical changes Mode 2 reform introduced to the inner decision-making machinery of universities in Western Europe, how little effervescence it generated amongst the student estate is just as astounding. If there was much heart-searching amongst academia, it found little echo amongst society at large—a phenomenon which itself deserves closer scrutiny. Mode One reform focused on a political agenda. In the long run, neither the relationship with State nor with Society, still less the instruments of national policymaking, were altered.

The same cannot be said of the second wave of reform, which since the mid Eighties in Western Europe has been urged on by economic and industrial considerations—though these are no less ideologically powerful. Though not always couched in such terms, 'de-regulation' and 'marketisation' (Dill, D. &

---

6 For the notion of legal homogeneity, see Neave, G. & Van Vught, F. A., (1991), *Prometheus Bound: the changing relationship between higher education and government in Western Europe*, Oxford, Pergamon; Neave, G. & Van Vught, F. A., (1994), *Government and Higher Education across Three Continents: the winds of change*, Oxford, Pergamon; for a more historic account of this value set in its importance in shaping the development of universities in Europe see Neave, G., (2001), "The European Dimension in higher education: the use of historical analogues" in Huisman, Maassen, P. A. M. & Neave, G., (eds), *Higher Education and the Nation State*, Oxford/Paris, Elsevier Science for IAU Press.

Sporn, B., 1996) began to unravel the financial nexus between university and central government. Sometimes, part of the budgetary burden was transferred to regional and local government—Spain (Garcia Garrido, J.-L., 1992) and France (Merrien, F.-X. & Musselin, C., 1999) being particular examples of this partial 'diversification'. The more modest role now attributed to central national administration in running higher education, a development variously described as 'remote steering' (Van Vught, F. A., 1988) or as the 'off-loading state', was accompanied by radical overhaul to the instrumentality employed and to its point of application.

The Radicalism of Mode 2 Reform in Governance

Viewed from outside mainland Europe, the shift from 'national regulation' to 'self-regulation' may appear both just and natural, the equivalent of those who have sinned by over reliance on State protection against the chill winds of the market, coming to repentance and admitting, at last, the error of their ways. It is a view, which, if understandable, tends to underplay the theories of political and social development that such a relationship once underpinned.[7] With central administration now defined as 'strategic' or 'remote', so the instrumentality of policy underwent revision. Revision involved adding national systems of qualitative evaluation, indicators of performance with the possibility of moving towards 'benchmarking' (Scheele, J. P. & Maassen, P. A. M. & Westerhijden, D. J., 1998) as the prime means for assessing outcomes. With higher education policy concentrating on outcomes and relying on individual institutions setting their own objectives for the attainment of national priorities, the formal legal fiction, long defended in many Western European countries, that all universities were equal in status, could no longer be sustained.[8]

---

7 For a more extensive development of this problematique and the political assumptions which underpin the notion of the university serving the 'national' – as opposed to the 'local' community, see Neave, G., (1997), "The European Dimension in Higher Education", *op. cit.*, also Brinckmann, H., (1998) *Neue Freiheit der Universitaeten: operative Autonomie der Lehre und Forschung an Hochschulen*, Sigma, Berlin.

8 A minor parenthesis, but nevertheless an important one. It is only during the Nineties in Europe that the term 'Research University' began to gather credence. To European ears, it is an oxymoron. Universities were research universities to the extent that all trained students to the Ph.D or its equivalent level and had the right to award the doctoral degree. If research was not undertaken, the formal obligation was nevertheless incumbent on academic staff. Interestingly, the term 'research university' only began to assume extended usage when the principle of externally defined competition became an integral instrument for the 'steering' of higher education policy in Western Europe.

The Drive to Convergence

De-regulation expanded the area of institutional discretion—and responsibility. Instead of being concerned primarily with verifying the application of national legislation, governance now extended to such areas as income generation, the negotiation of paid services to the external community[9], the internal attribution of resources, financial and human. The second wave of governance reform began with the French Higher Education Guideline laws of 1984 and 1989. It assumed further momentum with the 1993 reforms in Sweden (Askling, B. & Bauer, M. & Marton, S., 1999) Denmark (Rasmussen, 1999) and Austria (Pechar, H. & Pellert, A., 1998), reached Norway in 1996 and the Netherlands with the 1997 University Modernisation Act (De Boer, H. & Denters, B. & Goedegebuure, L., 1998a). The salient feature of the second wave lies in governance *a l'européenne* taking on a substantial discretionary dimension with which it is usually associated in the Anglo-American literature (Harmon, G., 1992).

Changing Focus, Changing Instrumentalities

The rationale beneath 'Mode 2' governance reform differed markedly and radically from its predecessor. Whilst 'Mode One' rested on a political interpretation—extending internal democracy by bringing the joys of participation to new constituencies—the second drew its strength from the imperatives of economic progress. As the decade unfolded, so did government priorities. What began as exercises in cost containment and a quest for new ways to enforce and to ascertain institutional efficiency acquired its own dynamic, which moved towards adjusting the internal workings of universities as key institutions in a 'knowledge-based economy'.

Within the individual university, reform of governance focused upon strengthening executive authority, upon closer internal scrutiny of the cost, output and performance of individual components—be they faculties, departments or research units—, upon developing explicit ties with the *local* and/or the *regional* community in contrast to previous concentration upon the university's place in the *national* community. Certainly, legislation aimed at strengthening institutional autonomy. But, it was an autonomy which, if more extensive, was tempered by a no less extensive system of institutional accountability and by the setting up of 'agencies of public purpose', sometimes sited inside the Ministry of Education or its counterpart, sometimes occupying a formal independence from the Ministry, but located within the purlieu of central administration. Amongst examples of the former arrangement are Ireland

---

9 In France, for example, until 1980, individual universities required formal clearance from the Ministry to engage in contract work with the private sector.

and Sweden, whereas the latter are to be found in France (Staropoli, A., 1987) and in the British Quality Assessment Agency (Scheele, J. & Maassen, P. A. M. & Westerheijden, D. J., 1998).

The controlling framework itself shifted focus from input to output and from a predominantly legislative basis through ministerial decrees and circulars to a more complex, sophisticated and certainly more inquisitive instrumentality, specifically conceived for and focused on, higher education. This new instrumentality grew up in addition to its juridically based predecessor (De Groof, J. Neave, G. & Svec, J., 1998).

Changes in Leadership Legitimacy

This was not the only change that followed in the wake of overhauling patterns of governance in mainland Europe. As much symbolic as substantive has been the re-seating of the source of authority and legitimacy, which now attaches to the Rector, Vice Chancellor or University President. Three decades ago, Mode One reform, if anything underlined Rectoral legitimacy as deriving directly from the extended collegiality it had established [10] (CRE, 1986, 1987). Since one of the explicit purposes of contemporary governance reform is to make the university more sensitive to economic change, more efficient and more business-like, it is not greatly surprising that such shifts in purpose are also accompanied by shifts in the basis of legitimacy on which leadership itself resides. Indeed, that Presidential authority is increasingly interpreted in terms of positive 'leadership' rather than in its traditional responsibility of collective institutional representation which befell university Presidents as 'primi inter pares'. This change in interpretative context is itself of more than passing interest, since it is symbolic of those deep changes contained in the underlying values of quality, efficiency and enterprise that current reforms in governance seek to embed in Europe's universities. At this point, we need to return to a rather less explored aspect of the long historic relationship between universities in Europe and the notion of public service. It is a tie that deserves some attention, if only for the fact that it stands as a major contextual difference between universities in Europe and in the United States.

Irrespective of how the withdrawal of the State is interpreted, whether in terms of 'de-regulation', 'marketisation' or (to use an awful French neologism) 'contractualisation', it is a process which involves a fundamental displacement of what is best described as the 'referential institution'—that is, the

---

[10] In the aftermath of 1968, certain universities saw rectoral candidates no longer drawn exclusively from the senior professoriate, but also included representatives of the Assistant estate. Some in France and Germany even elected Rectors from amongst their ranks, an enthusiasm since corrected!

prime source of 'good practice'—effectively, a referential model from which standards are set and procedures taken over and emulated. Since the foundation of the Nation State in Europe, the major referential institution for the universities has been the national civil service, in terms of conditions of employment, formal status of individual academics. Seen from this standpoint, one of the outstanding strategic thrusts behind Mode 2 governance reforms involves detaching the university from the national civil service as referential institution and putting the private sector in its stead. The new referential institution is the business enterprise.

Clearly, the implications of this change in referential perspective deserve closer exploration *per se*, though obviously this is not the place to do so. But, one area where its impact is already evident is in the source of presidential legitimacy and authority. In contemporary Europe, Presidential authority currently is in process of moving from its historic base grounded in collegiality to authority grounded on managerial rationality, a move encapsulated in the redefinition of presidential authority along the lines of being the Chief Executive Officer or deriving from the role of president *qua* 'corporate leader' (Askling, B. & Bauer, M. & Marton, S., 1999).

Stakeholders, Governors or Trustees

Strengthening of presidential and executive authority, a more formally identified 'chain of responsibility', are the central purposes of much recent legislation in Western Europe. There is, however, a further dimension involved in Mode 2 reform of governance, which sets it off from its predecessor. As we have seen, the reforms of the Sixties and Seventies turned around extending the 'participant constituencies' *inside* the university. Those of the Eighties and Nineties place particular stress, however, on reinforcing the weight of '*external* constituencies' and of outside interests—of 'civil', 'lay' or 'stakeholder' society (Rasmussen, J. G., 1998).

Not surprisingly, the ways in which 'external' society is represented are subject to considerable variation. The Consejo Social in Spanish universities is one variant. Essentially, it brings together representatives of employers, unions and the local community, acting in an advisory capacity and as a forum for consulting local opinion (Garcia Garrido, J.-L., 1992). Bereft of executive powers, the Consejo Social harks back an earlier tradition of 'constituency collegiality'. More radical are the changes introduced in recent Dutch legislation and, more particularly, the 1997 Act on Modernizing the University (De Boer, H. & Denters, B. & Goedegebuure, L., 1998b). Here, the representation of external interests is set at the highest level. The Act split leadership between Rector and President of the Executive Board, an arrangement not dissimilar to the American model of University President and Chairman of the Board of Trustees. The Rector assumes the executive responsibility for university affairs, whilst the President of the Executive Board is drawn from outside the university. Another variation, though this time putting a slightly different interpretation on the *duplex ordo*, was enacted with the 1996 Norwegian Act on Universities and Colleges. The 1996 Act placed further emphasis on strong academic and administrative leadership and set down clear responsibility between academic and administrative leaders (Dimmen, A & Kyvik, S., 1998).

France provides a further example of tipping the balance more clearly in favor of external interests, though it remains exceptional and limited to new universities, mainly technological in bias, founded in the course of the Eighties. Here, the Governing Board (Comité d'Orientation) is made up of a majority of representatives from business, industry and regional authorities. Conceived as an interface between university and the outside world, the Governing Board is chaired by a 'external personality' (Merrien, F.-X. & Musselin, C., 1999).

These few examples show the way current reforms in the governance structures of Europe's universities seek to accommodate 'stakeholder society'. They also display certain common features. The first is the evident and increasing centrality of 'external interests'. No longer are they confined to a suspicious 'marginality' as ill-defined constituencies in a large and amorphous body, which tended to be their fate under the regime of 'participant democracy'. Second, theirs is a position of strategic significance, firmly rooted at leadership level and exercising leadership responsibility rather than maintaining a merely representative presence. Third, external interests are seated in key executive bodies which, compared to those created to meet the press of 'participant democracy' a quarter of a century or more ago, are relatively restricted in size - a feature which is shared by the 'new universities' in the United Kingdom, in contrast to their more venerable colleagues.

The Ghost of Reform Past

Yet, the rationalization of responsibility and the concentration of executive authority, which are the heart of current reforms in the governance of Western Europe's universities, do not take place in a vacuum. New patterns of institutional co-ordination, management and decision-making have settled upon others already in place. These other arrangements are themselves the heartland of an earlier, perhaps less efficient form of governance, grounded in the notion of collegiality, whose strength lies at departmental level. In short, the current state of institutional governance is split between two very different organizational and organized value systems, which, in this essay for sake of convenience, we have labeled Mode One, and Mode Two. This de facto 'mixed model', combining central executive authority and peripherally-based strongholds of collegiality may indeed be transitory, just as it may also possess high innovative potential (Clark, B. R., 1998). Nevertheless, it is no less a source of potential conflict. Recent research into the impact of governance reforms at the institutional level suggests that it is not without its downside (Dimmen, A. & Kyvik, S., 1998) (Askling, B. & Bauer, M. & Marton, S., 1999) (Rasmussen, J. G., 1998). The burden of self-regulation and expanded accountability procedures are often construed as a threat to their influence and authority by departments and basic units (Askling, B. & Bauer, M. & Marton, S., 1999).

That said, the issue of boundary between central managerialism and what some may see as the apparent imperviousness of departments remains intact. What is no less intact is the paradox that policies of self-regulation and decentralization become themselves subject to bitter dispute as managerial authority in the self-regulating institution begins to bite. It is a situation fraught with peril since, ultimately, it bids fair to drive a wedge between institutional leadership and academic staff.[11]

CONCLUSION

From the *de facto* co-existence of two conflicting interpretations of self-regulation, one operating in the institution at central level based on executive authority, backed by the weight of law, the other, collegial and representative, based on established practice, a number of conclusions may be drawn.

First, that the move from governance based on a participatory ethic to one grounded in management rationality—from Mode One to Mode Two—in Western Europe is far from being complete, though clearly some countries will be more advanced along this path than others. Nor has the drive to strengthen institutional efficiency been universally successful in terms of exchanging old governance patterns for new (Pechar, H. & Pellert, A., 1998).

Second, introducing change in governance systems reflects a very old adage: "Legislate in haste and dispute at leisure." As we penetrate behind legislative enactment into its consequences at institutional level, so the task of transformation appears both protracted and delicate. It is, moreover, a task the

---

11 Nor is this situation confined to Europe. Commenting on the discrepancy between the values, objectives and agenda of management and of the devolved units - Faculties and Departments - in Australian universities, Wood & Meek noted: "the increased conflict and alienation amongst rank and file staff as institutions become more corporate -like and managerial in orientation. The executive appears in danger of increasingly distancing itself from the collegial needs and philosophical outlook of most academic staff while itself lacking confidence in the institution's peak governing body." (Wood & Lynn Meek 1998, "Higher education governance and management: Australia", Higher Education Policy, Vol. 11, No 2-3)

success of which is dependent on the weight—or its absence—of informal traditions and values contained in an organizational ethic that still retains a very particular strength in Western Europe. That strength derives very especially from the fact that the first step in modernizing governance systems in Europe entailed the State's earlier underwriting, extending and endorsing that very principle of academic collegiality that appears increasingly at odds with the drive towards the concentration of executive responsibility around key individuals and key posts which is the essence of contemporary reform in the governance of Europe's universities. It is from such a context that the thesis of the 'confiscated revolution' has drawn inspiration. Simply stated, this view interprets enhanced institutional autonomy as advancing less the authority of the academic estate so much as the power of its administrative counterpart.

The third conclusion must be that in Western Europe the issue of governance is, at present, in a state of considerable flux and transition. The burden of reform may indeed have shifted to the individual university. But as attention comes to focus on the institutional level, so we become aware of the presence of deeply-laid centrifugal forces acting on the periphery, obeying their own interpretation of self-regulation in defense of identity, territory and internal coherence. True, the priorities of what has been described as Academic Tribes (Becher, A., 1989), the disciplinary fields, subdividing, splitting off, each seeking a new identity and means to uphold it, may indeed be seen by some as a source of potential fragmentation. Against the tidiness of the new managerialism, this situation bids fair to perpetuate a multi-layered and complex model of decision-making which may well nullify whatever gains have been already been made in efficiency (Braun, D. & Merrien, F.-X., 1999).

It remains to be seen whether the new executive bodies are powerful enough to complete what some see as a half-finished managerial revolution, or, whether they will be brought up short by those interests that have been long in place. That the issue still hangs in the balance should give cause for thought to those who believe that direct intervention by government is a thing of the past. In Europe, de-regulation and non-intervention are far from being acquired rights. And even in those instances where they once were, there is no reason why they should remain so. Rather both are conditional. They are conditional on the successful outcome of a reform, which more than any other in recent times has direct impact on the nature and the way academic work is carried out.

REFERENCES

Askling, B. & Bauer, M. & Marton, S. (1999). "Swedish universities views' towards self-regulation: a new look at institutional autonomy", *Tertiary Education and Management*, Vol. 5., n° 2, pp. 175-195.

Becher, A. (1989). *Academic Tribes and Territories*, Milton Keynes, Open University Press for SRHE.

Bliekle, I. (1994). "Norwegian and Swedish graduate reform policy", *Higher Education Policy*, Vol. 7, n° 1.

Braun, D. & Merrien, F.-X. (1999). *Towards a new model of governance for universities: a comparative view*, Jessica Kingsley, London, pp. 259ff.

Brinckmann, H. (1998). *Neue Freiheit der Universitaeten: operative Autonomie der Lehre und Forschung an Hochschulen*, Sigma, Berlin.

Clark, B. R. (1998). *Creating Entrepreneurial Universities: organizational pathways of transformation*, Pergamon Press for IAU Press, Oxford, p. 154.

CRE (1986). "European University systems: part I", *CRE Bulletin*, No. 75, 3rd Quarter, Geneva, p. 140.

CRE (1987). "European University systems: part II", *CRE Bulletin*, No. 77, 1st Quarter, Geneva, p. 136.

De Boer, H. & Denters, B. & Goedegebuure, L. (1998a). "On Boards and Councils: shaky balances considered. The governance of Dutch Universities", *Higher Education Policy*, Vol. 11, n° 2-3.

De Boer, H. & Denters, B. & Goedegebuure, L. (1998b). "Dutch disease or Dutch model: an evaluation of the pre-1998 system of democratic university government in the Netherlands", *Policy Studies Review*, Vol. 15, n° 4, pp. 37–50.

De Groof, J. & Neave, G. & Svec, J. (1998). *Democracy and Governance in higher education*, Kluwer International Law Series, Dordrecht, pp. 8-9.

Dill, D. & Sporn, B., (eds) (1996). *Emerging Patterns of Social Demand and University Reform: through a glass darkly*, Pergamon Press, Oxford.

Dimmen, A. & Kyvik, S. (1998). "Recent changes in the governance of higher education institutions in Norway", *Higher Education Policy*, Vol. 11, n° 2-3, p. 218.

Garcia Garrido, J.-L. (1992). "Spain" in Burton Clark R. & Neave G., (eds), *The Encyclopedia of Higher Education*, Pergamon Press, Oxford, Vol. 1, pp. 663–676.

Harmon, G. (1992). "Introduction to Vol. 2, part 2, Governance, Administration and Finance" of Clark & Neave (eds), *The Encyclopedia of Higher Education*, Pergamon, Oxford.

Maassen, P. A. M. & van Vught, F.A. (1994). "Alternative models of governmental steering in higher education: an analysis of steering models and policy instruments in five countries", *Comparative Policy Studies in higher education*, Utrecht, Lemma, pp. 35–63.

Merrien, F.-X. & Musselin, C. (1999). "Are French universities finally emerging? Path dependency phenomena and innovative reforms in France", in Braun, D. & Merrien, F.-X., *Towards a new model of governance for universities: a comparative view*, Jessica Kingsley, London, pp. 220-239.

Neave, G. (1999). "Some thoughts on the fin de siècle university", *Address to the 5th ALFA-BRACARA Conference "Higher Education: the last 5 years and the challenges for the future"*, Universidade Federal do Ceará, Fortaleza (Brazil), (Xerox) p. 23.

Neave, G. (2001). "The European Dimension in higher education: the use of historical analogues" in Huisman & Maassen & Neave, *Higher Education and the Nation State*, Elsevier Science for IAU Press, Oxford/Paris.

Neave, G. & van Vught, F.A. (1991). *Prometheus Bound: the changing relationship between government and higher education in Western Europe*, Pergamon Books, Oxford.

Neave, G. & Rhoades, G. (1987). "The academic estate in Western Europe", in Burton R. Clark, *The Academic Profession: national, disciplinary & institutional settings*, University of California Press, Berkeley/Los Angeles, pp. 211-270.

Pechar, H. & Pellert, A. (1998). "Managing change: organization reform in Austrian Universities", *Higher Education Policy*, Vol. 11, n° 2-3, p. 148.

Rasmussen, J. G. (1998). "New Rules of university governance in Denmark", *Higher Education Policy*, Vol. 11, n° 2-3.

Scheele, J. P. & Maassen. P. A. M. & Westerheijden, Don J., (eds) (1988). *To Be Continued... follow up of Quality Assurance in Higher Education*, The Hague, Elsevier/De Tijdstroom.

Shils, E. & Daalder, H. (1982). *Politicians, Universities and Bureaucrats*, Cambridge University Press.

Staropoli, A. (1987). "The French National Evaluation Committee", *European Journal of Education*.

Trow, M. (1975). "The Public and private lives of higher education", *Daedalus*, Vol. 2, pp. 113-127.

Van Vught, F.A. (1988). *Governmental Strategies and Innovation in higher education*, Jessica Kingsley, London.

Van Vught, F.A. (1997). "Combining planning and the market: an analysis of the Government strategy towards higher education in the Netherlands", *Higher Education Policy*, Vol. 10, n° 3-4, pp. 211-224.

CHAPTER 5

Governance: the Challenges of Globalization

Howard J. Newby

GLOBALIZATION

Higher education is not immune to the forces of globalization so visible in the world of business and commerce. This is already particularly apparent on the research side of most universities. Top-quality researchers have long had their own international network of peers who take on the roles, variously, of deadly rivals and friendly collaborators. In areas of so-called "big science", this has long been a necessity due to the very high cost of equipment and infrastructure. However, in recent decades this trend has also been apparent in most areas of academic activity, including the arts and social sciences. In Europe, it is being encouraged by the European Union and successive Framework Programmes, which have taken forward quite remarkably the degree of cooperation across national boundaries. Moreover, the nature of recently emergent scientific problems – global environmental change, the human genome project, etc. – has also demanded scientific analysis, organization and cooperation on a truly global scale.

The globalization of research has been both a cause and a consequence of two major innovations. The first, and most obvious, is the growth of information and communication technologies, which have allowed fast, cheap and user-friendly means of communication between research groups. In the UK, for example, probably the single biggest impact upon the daily lives of most academics was the introduction of the joint academic network (JANET) in the 1970s. The growth of the Internet was therefore something that most academics found relatively unproblematic. Now there is the promise of digital broadcasting to open up a whole new era of global communications which, as we shall see below, will begin to feed into the teaching, and not just the research, side of university life.

The second innovation is less commented upon but, in my view, it is equally decisive. This is the growth of English as the *de facto* global language. This is particularly true of science and it is being fostered by the growth of the information technologies (IT) described in the previous paragraph. The emergence of English as the global language has provided a competitive advantage to Higher Education in the UK, but one which is, of course, not unique to the UK: the United States, Canada, Australia and other English-speaking countries have also used this advantage to foster their international links, not least to recruit overseas students to their universities.

While globalization is well advanced on the research side of most universities, it is less prominent so far in teaching and learning. However, the global spread of IT and the English language are now providing the conditions for the development of a truly global market in teaching and learning in higher education. It is possible, for example, to set a terminal anywhere in the world and undertake an MBA Course mounted by any one of a number of leading North American and European institutions. The market for higher education through distance learning has been estimated at $300 billion worldwide—and this is growing. As we move more and more into a knowledge-driven economy, there is no reason to believe that the higher education market will not rapidly become globalized.

In the United States some of these tendencies are already well advanced. There has been a range of responses amongst higher education institutions in the USA, many of which give an indication of how matters may develop in Europe, ranging from for-profit organizations like the University of Phoenix to the launch of a combined on-line course catalogue by a number of leading established US universities, some of whom have enlisted private sector support for their courseware development. Knowledge-providers in the private sector are also lining up to attack the global market in higher education in the twenty-first century, sometimes on their own, more often in conjunction with existing universities. While the universities provide most of the academic expertise and crucially the "branding" necessary for market credibility, the partners provide production facilities, distribution, marketing, etc, as well as much of the underlying technology, in order for the operation to proceed on a truly global basis. The universities have access to the necessarily large amounts of funding needed to invest in the development and maintenance of courseware, while the private sector partners have access to the quality control procedures, accreditation and status of established universities.

In the UK there are few signs that these kinds of partnerships are being brought together, despite the high quality of British higher education and the high quality of creative talent in the UK media sector. Higher education, of course, remains a social, and not just a cognitive, experience. Students want more than to sit in front of VDU screens. Nevertheless for certain, and growing, parts of the market, such as distance learning, provided it can be of high quality, IT-based education fulfils an important need. This particularly applies to what one might call the continuing professional development end of the market. This also happens to be a rather profitable area of higher education in the UK.

These possibilities will also be assisted by changing patterns of student demand for teaching and learning. The conventional three-year, fulltime, residential course was based upon what might be called a "just in case" philosophy of learning. We have all known that in the vast majority of subjects most of the knowledge gained in a university course is not used directly during the lifetime of a student's career. Nevertheless we have continued to teach it, "just in case" it is needed. Or, recently, the increasing flexibility of access to higher education in the UK has provoked a discernible shift to more "just in time" forms of delivery – lifelong learning and all that. In the future, however, the trends outlined at birth may well produce a further shift towards "just for you" forms of learning, in which students can access from a vast array of courseware the elements required to meet their particular needs at a particular time. While there will undoubtedly remain a market for the conventional three-year, full-time, residential degree, it may well be smaller than at present and institutions may increasingly have to choose their niche in the market.

CHANGING MISSION OF HIGHER EDUCATION

One of the reasons why these trends have largely escaped our attention in the UK is that we have been consumed recently by internally derived changes in the structure and function of higher education. The very rapid shift from an elite to a mass system of higher education need hardly be labored here – this shift is now widely acknowledged even if some of its implications still need to be worked through. Certainly the shift towards mass, or even "comprehensive", higher education has challenged traditional conceptions of the university. In particular, the old Humboldt ideal of a university – essentially that of an ivory tower separate from society at large and therefore not contaminated by pressures of everyday life – is now virtually dead. While most governments in both the developed and developing world have well understood the need to expand higher education in order to attain global competitiveness in a knowledge-driven world, they have been equally reluctant to fund higher education at a level that would simultaneously sustain mass Higher Education *and* the Humboldt ideal. This is even more true when it comes to research. Thus, as the higher education sector has grown in size, so has it become more diverse both in terms of function and institutionally. Coming to terms with this diversity is one of the major challenges for higher education in the twenty-first century.

It should also be noted that this shift from an elite to a mass system of higher education has been accompanied by a shift in public policy with regard to universities. University education is no longer funded publicly as an end in itself. Rather it is funded for more ulterior, even utilitarian, purposes. In other words, higher education is a means rather than an end. The expansion of public funding has not taken place on the basis of cultivating young minds for their own sake; rather, it has taken place on the basis of promoting societal, and not just individual, values. Universities have therefore been given a mission, one that is moreover set by those from outside the university world— principally government. In the UK at the present time, for example the mission is quite clear; it is to aid economic competitiveness and promote social inclusion. While universities remain dependent upon the public purse this is inevitable, but this also implies a degree of flexibility to change in relation to externally defined goals with which universities have felt it uncomfortable to come to terms. A good example of this is the promotion of lifelong learning. This is seen as increasingly necessary in order to fulfill the mission of universities relating to both economic competitiveness and social inclusion. But it also implies a quite radical adjustment of the structure and functioning of universities, changes which universities have, on the whole, been *responding to* rather than controlling. Thus, the delivery of lifelong learning has quite profound implications for the structure and function of higher education; it implies a set of qualitative and not just quantitative changes in the nature of teaching and learning.

GOVERNANCE AND STAKEHOLDERS

Taken together, the changes have gathered around the university sector a group of stakeholders whose roles have been subtly changing. Students, for example, see themselves less as pupils and more as customers—a trend accelerated in the UK by the recent introduction of substantial fees for undergraduate students. Moreover, the student body itself has become more diverse, whether measured in terms, of age, gender, ethnicity, modes of study, social background, etc. This in turn has created a demand for more flexible forms of delivery. Access to higher education has come to be seen less as a privilege for which students are grateful, and more as a right which carries with it attendant expectations. And this change in the culture of learning has led our students to make comparisons, not always flattering, between standards of service that they receive in universities and the standards they receive from other knowledge providers in the private sector and elsewhere. This not only applies to the quality of teaching and learning (including the quality of coursework), but also to other facets of university life, where services ranging from catering to computing are increasingly compared with standards applicable in the private sector.

As the investment of public funds in higher education has increased, so too have governments taken a closer interest in university affairs. The ulterior, and sometimes utilitarian, nature of government policies towards higher education has seen universities become more and more closely intertwined with policy delivery outside the narrowly defined educational sphere—for example, economic competitiveness, regional economic development, urban regeneration, social inclusion, technological innovation. Public funding of universities is increasingly targeted, sometimes quite specifically, towards the encouragement or achievement of particular policy goals. But overarching all of this is the government's demand for increasing value for money and hence, in the UK at least, a much more interventionist system of quality assurance, quality control and relentless evaluation.

The growth of external evaluation of our affairs has accompanied, and in part been caused by, a decline in professional trust relationships. This is being brought about because governments have, rightly or wrongly, observed that the culture of the academic profession has, on the whole, lagged behind changes in the structure, organization and—crucially—culture of other organizations in the private sector, most notably the business corporation. To use A H Halsey's well-known aphorism, "the decline of donnish dominion" is now well advanced. This is not only reflected in declining comparative salary levels and increase in staff: student ratios, but also in the decline of institutional loyalty and even manifest casualisation, especially of research staff. Any attempt to remedy these trends clearly has to take account of the strong pressures towards outsourcing which the new Internet technology and digital broadcasting technology permit. This, of course, is by no means unique to the university world, though how far universities will simply become commissioning agents for courseware the quality of which they control, but which they do not produce or distribute, remains to be seen. At this extreme, it will strike at the very heart of the Humboldt ideal – the academic profession no longer has the solitude and increasingly has less autonomy to control both the content and the assessment of the learning for which it is responsible. In the UK at the present time, this is an area of major public controversy as what are assumed by the academic profession as increasingly intrusive and bureaucratic forms of control are being promoted by quasi-governmental agencies tasked with ensuring what elsewhere might be termed trading standards.

However, these new technologies are by no means used solely to support highly centralized systems of control, quite the contrary. Internet technology has allowed self-governing communities of academics to come together in ways that quite transcend national boundaries and institutional loyalties. There is very little that senior management in universities can, or should, do to restrict this process. Indeed, in many respects, it is a development to be very much welcomed, for not only is the speed of communication enhanced by the new communication technologies, but also academic colleagues come, quite voluntaristically, to benchmark the standards and quality of their research and teaching against each other through a loosely organized, but sometimes, quite vicious, system of peer assessment and review.

In many respects these trends summarize the contradictory characteristics of present changes in governance in universities. On the one hand, a group of increasingly vocal and articulate external stakeholders make demands that drive universities towards more centralized, and certainly more bureaucratic, forms of quality control with outputs that can be measured and demonstrated to our external audiences. On the other hand, the new technologies have also empowered our colleagues as individuals in ways that are not amenable to orthodox forms of management and governance. It is little wonder that exasperated university leaders have occasionally been heard to mutter that the modern university verges upon the ungovernable.

GOVERNANCE AND GLOBAL PARTNERSHIPS

The implications of all these changes are potentially very far-reaching for traditional systems of governance in higher education. In particular, the collegial system of decision making with which we are all familiar in both Europe and North America has found it very difficult to come to terms with the accelerating rate of change. Equally, there is no evidence that a shift towards a more clearly defined system of line management, with a "command and control" style of institutional leadership, has been any more successful. In comparable knowledge-based organizations in the private sector, the shift has been in the other direction, towards flatter management structures with more participative decision-making. Nevertheless, most members of the academic profession have found it difficult to come to terms with the existence of other management techniques imported from the private sector – most notably management according to outputs rather than inputs and, especially, management by objectives. This has not been helped by some of the more arcane aspects of the performance indicator industry imported into higher education. Nevertheless, we still struggle to develop appropriate systems of governance, which can simultaneously be collegial and participative, whilst also decisive and agile. All of this has placed a very high premium on the quality of institutional leadership.

CONCLUSION

In my concluding comments, however, I do not wish to concentrate on these internal aspects of governance, important though they are. Instead, I wish to concentrate on a more emergent, and certainly little noticed, problem: the emergence of global, or at least transnational, systems of collaboration between universities, on the one hand, and the essentially national systems of accountability and evaluation which pertain, on the other.

Viewed from a European perspective, the move towards international collaboration between universities has been fuelled by two quite separate sets of initiatives. The first concerns the European Union itself, for since the Treaty of Maastricht, the Commission has possessed the legislative power to include education amongst its activities and in recent years it has been a very active player in the university world, developing programs in both teaching and research which lie alongside those developed at the national and regional levels. There has been a burgeoning of both teaching and research collaboration among the European Union member states, but also there has been a startling rise in student mobility across Europe. In this sense, higher education is being used as a vehicle for European integration, and in this respect it has been very successful. This recently culminated in both the Sorbonne declaration and its successor, the Bologna declaration, which seek to harmonize the "architecture" of higher education qualifications systems in Europe.

Meanwhile, universities themselves have been coming together quite outside the formal structures of collaboration within Europe. In part these have been quite loose partnerships of European universities aimed at influencing the Commission's Higher Education's policies and practices (e.g., the Santander Group). But, more recently, these collaborations have become more global in scope and more than just talking shops. There is a marked tendency now for quite formal collaborative structures to emerge spanning not only Europe, but also North America, Asia and Australasia. Groupings as varied as Universitas 21 and unext.com have emerged as ways in which individual universities can come together to form global alliances and partnerships which can engage in a wide range of activities: benchmarking quality in teaching and research; joint marketing (especially to attract graduate students); research collaboration; students and staff exchanges; joint coursework development; credit accumulation and transfer; and even joint ventures with private sector partners. The analogy here is rather like that of the alliances which have emerged amongst airlines, which proceed from joint marketing through to building a global brand and on into code sharing (the academic equivalent being credit accumulation and transfer). None of these groupings have—yet—proceeded far along the pathway towards full legal incorporation and trading. But, I suspect that alliances of this kind will be needed in order to service a developing global market for students and courseware that would be attractive to both the students themselves and to private sector investors. In addition, students in the future are likely to be even more mobile across national boundaries as they seek to make themselves more employable in a global market place.

These kinds of transnational alliances, then, are proceeding both top-down and bottom-up. As Haug (1999) has pointed out in a recent review, top-down and bottom-up moves towards transnational collaboration have been a response to the new environment marked by globalization, new communication technologies, English as a lingua franca, increased competition and growing commercialization. For example, he points out:

- Foreign/overseas universities increasingly recruit paying students in Europe; it has not been sufficiently noticed that in the early nineteen nineties for the first time the number of Europeans studying in the USA exceeded the number of American students in Europe.
- Foreign universities increasingly are opening branch campuses in European countries either in their own name or via a franchising agreement with a local institution in Europe; in this type of transnational education students may sometimes earn the foreign degree without leaving their country although most move abroad to finish their studies and earn the degree; the same is also true, of course, both of European universities setting up campuses, predominantly in Asia and Latin America.
- Transnational distance education originating overseas is increasing rapidly; most is produced by established, accredited universities but there are accreditation bodies at home who have in the past paid little attention to inspecting their overseas operations; the example of the University of Phoenix also indicates the development of lifelong learning delivered in modules through small, private institutions in many countries in Europe.

Overall, as Haug points out, the recent and potential growth of offshore, franchise and open transnational education has been largely ignored by universities and governments alike in Europe, or perceived as a vague threat to national higher education. However, not only is governmental interest in these operations increasing, but one can also discern a degree of ambivalence towards them: on the one hand, such competition represents a useful stimulus to change in existing national systems, but on the other hand it undermines the university sector's traditional role as guardians of national and regional cultures.

Thus, while the development of global alliances has created fears of cultural homogeneity and uniformity, many individual universities have embraced such partnerships as a means of strengthening their market position (and sometimes their status) in a potentially global market place. It is not easy, to say the least, how this fits happily into the burgeoning systems of quality control and evaluation which have been resolutely national in character throughout the world. One can immediately see a tension between the trend towards voluntary alliances among participating universities as a means of collectively strengthening their autonomy and, on the other hand, national governments' increasing insistence upon elaborate forms of quality assurance, accountability and evaluation at the national level.

As a result, there is much talk in Europe now of quality standards for transnational education. At its worst, this could involve another layer of bureaucracy introduced at the European level, which would be superimposed upon existing national schemes. All of this, of course, would be under the banner of harmonizing higher education qualifications across Europe and ensuring quality and standard and thus "student mobility". As Haug points out "next to national systems dealing mainly with institutional recognition, evaluation and accreditation, independent subject-based evaluation across borders could emerge as an essential part of the European Higher Education landscape" (Haug, G., 1999). I am not at all convinced that this is the right way forward, even though it is the line of least resistance in European thinking, accustomed as we are to very tightly State-controlled university systems. Instead, I foresee a more market-based approach, in which the bottom-up system of international collaboration outlined above will find its own level in the market place, based upon the ability of alliances to build and sustain brands, to operate their own internal rigorous forms of quality control, and to achieve a level of educational innovation which top-down systems of accreditation and quality control will only stultify. This, however, will be a battle to be fought out politically and I have to confess that, at present, it is very evenly balanced. The Bologna declaration alone indicates the degree of political interest in these issues. In the UK, a slow and hesitant move towards a more market-based approach in the form of student fees has continued to provoke widespread political resistance. Perhaps we should not be surprised at this. From the Middle Ages onwards, the universities have been the cornerstone of civic society, both in Europe and elsewhere. Universities have in many parts of the world symbolized nationhood and while the nation may be in decline as an economic and even cultural unit, those whose positions of political power rest upon the nation state will be reluctant to give up their control over the university sector. We live in interesting times.

REFERENCE

Haug, G. (1999). "Trends and Issues in Learning Structures in Higher Education in Europe", CRE, Geneva.

PART 3

Governance Principles

CHAPTER 6

Critical University Decisions and their Appropriate Makers:

Some Lessons from the Economic Theory of Federalism

Luc E. Weber

INTRODUCTION

To cope both with the rapidly changing environment and with the dilemma between being *responsive* to societal, political and economic needs and, at the same time, *responsible* towards society, universities should not only dispose of first quality staff, but be well governed (Grin, F. & Co, 2000). However, it appears that while most firms have been carried away in a strong current of restructuring and reorganization measures, universities are in general slow to adapt their organization and decision processes: in other words, they are more or less making and implementing decisions in the same way that they have been doing for decades, even centuries.

The participants in the first Glion Colloquium (Hirsch, W. Z., & Weber, L. E., 1999) agreed that the governance of universities makes it in general too difficult for them to make the important decisions that they should make if they are to adapt to the changing environment. In other words, the decision-making system is not responsive enough and thus does not allow the institution to assume in an optimal way its responsibility towards society.

The identification of the most critical decisions to be taken and of the best-placed potential decision makers is a crucial analytical step towards the improvement of university governance. This is the purpose of this contribution, which will be more strongly influenced by the European environment, at least with regard to the decision makers.

First, I shall identify the most important internal and external decisions and describe the potential decision makers. Then, I shall refer to the theory of federalism, as well to principles of management (private and public), to try to propose by induction who, in theory, is best placed to make the different important decisions. Finally, I shall use these theoretical principles to suggest for which decisions the different decision makers should be made responsible.

CRITICAL INTERNAL AND EXTERNAL DECISIONS

In a university, as in any other institution, numerous decisions have to be made. The scope, the target circles and the frequency of these decisions differ enormously. In other words, some decisions are crucial, or at least very important, for the future of the institution and others are minor and repetitive. Moreover, some decisions are focused mainly on the institution itself, whereas others concern the outside world, dealing mainly with the relationship between the institution and its social environment. Finally, some decisions are regular and very frequent (daily, weekly or monthly) or regular and less frequent (every term, semester or year), whereas some decisions are quite irregular.

In working on the details of the ideal governance system, one should obviously pay attention to all these different types of decisions. However, I shall concentrate on identifying the crucial or important decisions, distinguishing between internal and external ones.

Critical Internal Decisions

In my opinion, the most important or crucial decisions concern the following issues.

Infrastructure (buildings and heavy equipment): These are by definition long term decisions which take a long time to mature, are irregular and have an enormous impact on the governance of the university, year after year. In particular, they create great rigidities in many respects, in particular if their capacity is insufficient to accommodate new students and staff or because their characteristics do not correspond to needs 10, 20 or 50 years later. Consequently, buildings might constitute a serious constraint to a reorganization of the university structure internally or regionally. This constraint is particularly damaging in those European countries that have still the tradition to build for at least a century. Moreover, these investments in physical capital induce indirect costs to be covered every year by the ordinary budget, which may eventually lead to the crowding out of equally necessary investments in human capital. Unfortunately, decisions regarding the construction of new buildings and those regarding the development of human capital within the university are generally made separately; moreover, the growing impact of the systematic introduction of information technologies in teaching and research has not yet seriously been taken into account in the planning process.

Faculty: Recruiting professors is also a crucial decision, due to the importance of selecting the best-qualified persons and the time span of the decision (25 to 30 years). It is nevertheless inevitable to make wrong decisions from time to time; therefore, not only should faculty be accountable towards their institution, but also disciplinary measures against faculty who do not fulfill their tasks correctly should be more systematic. Moreover, the increased necessity to adapt to changing needs may require closing departments and/or programs, which may impose modifying the terms of reference or even dismissing tenured staff members. There are other related challenging decisions: in particular, it is important to employ faculty according to their best capacity and to make sure they perform according to the institution's goals; moreover, it is equally important to create a favorable study and research environment and to make sure that the brightest students write a Ph.D. and go on doing research afterwards.

University structure: Universities should be able to change their structure, that is their organization into subdivisions, to serve their teaching, research and extension missions better. If buildings and heavy equipment are a source of rigidity, so is the structure of the university, that is, its rigid division into faculties [1], schools, sections, institutes, laboratories or departments. The largest subdivisions, like faculties and schools, should not be "states within states", preventing the reallocation of resources between developing or badly funded sectors and stagnating or rich sectors. Moreover, it should be easier to move smaller sectors, like institutes or departments, into other faculties, schools and even other universities, or to close them in order to liberate the financial resources necessary to develop another activity that has greater priority. Finally, even the concept of organized and fixed subdivisions should be reexamined, as more and more, the potential of new discoveries or learning needs lie in-between traditional disciplines.

Institutional culture: Universities should be institutions where people – faculty, researchers and students – are pleased and proud to work. In particular, faculty should spontaneously be more faithful to their university than to their discipline and be able to operate in an environment conducive to this.

---

1 According to the European use of the word.

Study programs: Universities should make a constant effort to update their study programs in order to offer their students an education in line with the latest developments in science and in the needs of society. This implies that the teaching staff for each discipline has critical mass, that study programs are flexible and open to allow students to participate in the planning of their education, that interdisciplinary education is promoted (without neglecting disciplinary education) and that there is sufficient coordination between the different courses, which implies that academic freedom in teaching should be subject to the higher needs of the programs.

Teaching: Universities should pay more attention to the renewal of pedagogical methods. In particular, they should actively promote the more active participation of students in their education and the intensive use of new technologies.

Research: Universities should promote quality research (basic and applied, as well as free and contractual) in order to keep their leading position as producers of new knowledge and to assume their responsibility to have an independent and well-founded view about key societal issues. For the latter, a proactive policy on the part of the leadership of the university is necessary.

Finance: Budgetary decisions with regard both to expenditure and revenues are of great importance. On the expenditure side, the budget gives a unique opportunity to implement priorities and posteriorities. However, budgetary decisions are also at the epicenter of the conflicts of interest. On the income side, universities should try to get political support for an increased financial participation of the students and make a greater effort to reduce their dependency on State financing by searching for donations and exploiting more systematically possible collaboration and joint ventures with private firms and with the public sector.

Critical External Decisions

Due to the necessity to be more responsive without neglecting their responsibilities, universities should fight much harder against their natural tendency to behave like ivory towers or closed, protected institutions. They have to make constant efforts to open up on many fronts.

Openness and competition: To secure a good standard in teaching and research, universities should be very open. In particular, they should be truly international, accept students and faculty from different countries, promote exchange of students and faculty with other institutions, the world over, and take full advantage of the competitive climate that reigns in the world of higher education.

Integration in their regional and national environment: The societal responsibilities of universities force them to be involved in the daily life of the community, whether they like it or not. Therefore, they have to participate more intensively in the search for solutions to social problems.

Relationship with the political authorities: European universities are in general State institutions. Therefore, their most challenging external issue is to secure true political, cultural and scientific autonomy; in other words, to avoid undue intervention by the State. However, as the State is, at least in Europe, also their main provider of funds, universities have to be transparent and accountable towards it, in order to secure the support of the politicians and the citizens.

Networking: Universities should conclude alliances with other universities to run common teaching programs and research, promote the exchange of students and faculty and develop new courseware. European universities are supported in this effort by the European Union, which has presently taken a leading role in this respect. More than that, the Sorbonne and later the Bologna processes aimed at creating a European higher education space covering approximately thirty countries (Bologna Declaration, 1999), as well as the ambition of the European Union Commission to create a European research space, are enhancing this necessity (Communication from the European Commission, 2000).

Relationship with the private sector: Last but not least, the teaching and research initiatives recently undertaken by firms, as well as the necessity to find alternative financing solutions, should induce universities to develop joint ventures with them, while, however, paying great attention to preserving their independence.

POTENTIAL DECISION MAKERS

The potential decision makers are more numerous in a university than in any other institution. Some decision makers are of course more important than others; however, it appears that no one has the professional competence and the power to impose an important decision alone. This explains why universities have a secular tradition of shared governance.

I am trying to identify in this chapter all the potential decision makers, as well as their strengths and weaknesses regarding their ability to make the crucial decisions exposed above. Due to the extreme diversity that characterizes the European higher education sector, it is difficult to pay tribute to all the decision makers and decision-making bodies that are in place according to national, regional or local rules. I shall limit myself to proposing a schematic list of the different generic types of decision makers. In this way, I have identified nine specific leaders or bodies, two of them being clearly situated outside of the institution.

The students: The students may be considered as the "clients" of the institution, looking for a good education as a starting point for a good career. However, they are also stakeholders, as they spend most of their time within the institution and interact with it during the length of their studies. This specific relationship between the clients and their suppliers is a unique one, which is not to be found in any other supplier-client relationship. Moreover, in Europe too, students are increasingly invited to participate directly in the financing of their studies. It is, therefore, not only understandable, but also good policy, to involve them in the decision process. In particular, they should be made more responsible for planning their education and be able to participate in decisions regarding the quality of the education provided to them and the social environment within the institution. However, as students lack a general view and cannot have a sense of continuity for the university, they should not have any decision power regarding strategic issues.

The Faculty: Faculty have a key role to play as they empower all the accumulated knowledge within the institution. Therefore, their involvement in their professional activity and their commitment to the institution are crucial. However, faculty in their collective behavior have a tendency to be individualistic, self-centered and shortsighted; therefore, they should not have any decision power regarding strategic issues.

The Department's director and/or the department's college of faculty [2]: They clearly offer a high concentration of knowledge in their field; however, they have little overview of the institution and are very active in protecting the interests of their subdivision. This means that their views should be taken into account regarding new developments in their disciplines, but they should not play an important role in determining priorities.

The Faculty [3] *(or School) dean (or Director) and/or College*: Deans (or Directors), as well as a college of professors, are presently key players in the decision process, as they are at an intermediate level of the pyramid, not too near the

---

2 Any committee of professors at the department level.
3 "Faculty" in the European sense, meaning the main subdivision of a university.

teachers and researchers, but not too far also. However, it appears that they find themselves generally too near to their colleagues and are themselves too involved to be able to participate actively in a dynamic university policy.

The presidential level [4]: The president and/or the presidential team is by definition the executive person or body responsible for making all the important executive decisions. However, at least in Europe, it is an illusion to believe that a president (or rector) can impose important decisions against the will of the faculties and departments, as well as of the academic staff, one reason being that there is such a high professional competence at these levels.

The senate [5]: It used to be the symbol of shared governance at a time when the number of faculty was small and there were few difficult decisions to make. It has become much too large today to have any positive influence, apart from ethical considerations regarding the profession.

A participation body at the Faculty (School) and/or University levels [6]: Such a body, bringing together faculty, researchers, students and administrative staff, can obviously be useful to facilitate the dialogue between the different stakeholders and discuss student questions. However, it is certainly not the right place to make important and forward-looking decisions, as it behaves more like a Parliament than an Executive.

An external board [7]: An external board bringing together excellent representatives of the regional community is capable of creating a good relationship between the university and its environment, helping the university to be responsive and supporting the leadership in difficult decisions. However, an external board may also be composed of mediocre persons, who may be tempted to take over the leadership of the institution or micro-manage it.

The State: Whatever the size and the political organization of the country (unitary or federalist), the State inevitably plays an important role. In Europe, it is certainly the main provider of funds and the main supervisor. Regarding this second role, the State can be supportive, encouraging or even helping the institution to fulfill its missions. However, the State can also introduce many unnecessary or contradictory constraints, which makes it even more difficult for universities to fulfill them.

---

4 Rector, Vice-chancellor, president and team.
5 Defined here as the council to which all or most of the faculty belong.
6 With representatives of the main stakeholders.
7 With a majority or a totality of external members.

PRINCIPLES OF EFFECTIVE DECISION MAKING

Due to the great number and extreme diversity of the potential decision makers, it is crystal clear that a governance system, where the power to decide is shared more or less equally between all the potential decision makers, can only be cumbersome and slow and produce only small, incremental changes. If we consider the high standard the European university sector has in general reached today, one cannot say that the system was really bad, even if it is poor for making decisions. This positive point is certainly due to the fact that important decisions, in particular the choice of research subjects and the content of courses, are taken continuously by the academic staff within the scope of their academic freedom. This situation looks like a symphony orchestra with one notable difference: faculty, like musicians, know what to play; however, in addition to that, faculty "write the music".

However, many observers of university life, including the participants in the first Glion colloquium (Hirsch, W. Z., & Weber, L. E., 1999), believe that the environment is now changing too rapidly and some external constraints, like the financial constraint, have become too strong to maintain the present decision process. Universities are seen as facing a dilemma: to make a greater effort in adapting their decision process according to the requirements of the epoch or to be condemned to become obsolete and replaced by other forms of higher education institutions.

The way to successfully improve university governance is straightforward: on the one hand, to secure or even improve the ability of faculty to be at the top in their research and to provide their students with up to date knowledge and, on the other hand, to make possibly difficult and unpopular decisions, which imply discontinuous changes, without destroying the faculty's potential creativity and commitment to the institution.

This dilemma is not unique to universities. It is also an acute challenge in private firms, though the bulk of professional competence is there located higher in the hierarchy. It is also a challenge in a holding company or a federal country: in both cases, it is important to clarify which decisions have to be made at the top of the organization and which should be made in the subsidiary companies or in the states (cantons).

Other papers in this volume develop what we can learn from the theory of business management to improve governance in a university. It appears to me quite useful for this contribution to extract a few basic principles from the economic theory of federalism.

Schematically, the economic theory of federalism teaches us that the optimal hierarchical level at which a decision should be made depends on four elements:

- *The subsidiarity principle*: This principle states that all decisions should be made at the lowest level possible; in other words, the competence to make a decision should not be given to a higher ranked body if a lower one is perfectly able to make it. In a university, the justification of this principle is at least twofold. First, it helps to take into account diverse needs and constraints and it contributes to let people feel involved and responsible, which stimulates their creativity. In other words, it prevents the appearance of bureaucratic uniformity. Second, it promotes competition within the institution, which is favorable to initiatives for change and to a better use of the available means. This is principle is nevertheless constrained by the three following dimensions.
- *The realm of the consequences of a decision*: We have learned from economists that there is an externality when the benefits (or costs) of a decision accrue not only to the members of the community that makes it, but also to a broader community. When the possible positive or negative external effects of a decision are not taken into account, the decision is not optimal. In order to take these external effects into account, it is necessary that all those who are concerned by the consequences of the decision participate in it or to make it at a higher hierarchical level, which permits to internalize these external effects.
- *Search for economies of scale*: Universities are "labor intensive". This means that a high proportion of their budget serves to finance salaries and that their total current expenses grow in line with their output. Since the beginning of the nineties, most European universities are financially hard-pressed, which forces them to do more with less money. Moreover, the ICT revolution offers hopefully great opportunities to decrease the unit cost of running research or teaching programs. However, great investments have to be made to exploit this potential, which in turn requires setting up joint ventures with other organizations. Therefore, I foresee a tendency in favor of a greater concentration of efforts in order to better exploit these potential economies of scale.
- *Equal treatment of equals*: The negative side effect of too much freedom of decision is that people on an equal position will be treated differently. European universities are in general very – I might say too – sensitive to that question, in particular with regard to salaries and student admission and graduation. This is a cultural and political question. If there is a high preference for equality, the hierarchical level at which the rules must be conceived should be high, which provokes greater rigidities.

What can we infer from these four principles drawn from the economic theory of federalism? The simplest way to reply is to state that, in principle, considering the subsidiarity principle, decisions should be made at the lowest possible level (Department, Faculty or School), as long as this is not in contradiction with the other three criteria, that is, as long as there are no wide ranging externalities, there is no potential for economies of scale and that this does not produce an unacceptable inequality of treatment. In other words, as there is a lot of professional competence at the level of faculty and researchers and a great potential enthusiasm at the level of students, universities should, much more than any other organization, give a lot of freedom to these stakeholders. This is the best environment within which to promote their creativity and to secure their commitment to the institution and to their activity.

However, such a completely decentralized decision process would neglect the other aspects of a good decision structure, which all plead for a more centralized or hierarchical decision process. I shall illustrate the necessity to take into account these other elements with a few examples.

First, many decisions (or non decisions) have external effects for the university. For example, the international recognition of the excellence of a research group has positive effects not only on the group itself, but also for the whole university: it improves the image of the university within the community and the business world; it attracts students and possibly firms into the area. If these positive external effects are neglected, this research group benefits from less financial support on the part of the institution than what it should have considering the external economies. The same is true if a research group or a department concludes an important teaching or research contract with a firm. On the contrary, if the university has no system of quality evaluation in place or does not follow up on a bad evaluation report, the poor professional quality of a subdivision or of a teaching program gives a bad image to the whole institution, which has certainly a negative impact on its funding. The quasi incapacity of a subdivision (Faculty or School) to fix priorities as well as posteriorities puts a heavy burden upon the whole institution, as scarce resources are frozen on activities that have lost their priority, at the cost of new projects.

Second, decentralized decisions cannot take into account and exploit potential economies of scale, which could be realized if the activity were to be run at a higher level. Today, it is for example obvious that it is more efficient to use one single computer software for student administration than to have each subdivision running a different one. At present, and increasingly in the future, there are important economies of scale to realize in developing tools or running activities at a higher level, the university level, or even at the level of a group of universities or jointly with other organizations. This is particularly true for promising long term projects like the development of a digital library or of courseware. The new information technologies are going to modify significantly the cost function of many university activities.

Third, the equal treatment argument leads to two diametrically opposed conclusions according to the intensity of preference of the community for equality. On the one hand, the conflict of objectives with the subsidiarity principle is strong, if the community has a strong preference for equality: the latter requires more centralization and consequently greater bureaucratic rigidity, which is of great harm to the creativity and even the willingness of the faculty to involve themselves in the university goals. On the other hand, if the preference for equality is rather weak and the institution accepts a certain degree of unequal treatment, many rules or judgements can be set at a relatively decentralized level. As mentioned above, this question is critical for faculty salaries, student admission and graduation, as well as for the liberty given to the faculty to be involved in activities outside of the university. As there is a strong preference for equality in Europe, it is not surprising that many decisions are very bureaucratic and, to put it mildly, faculty are not encouraged to take too many initiatives outside of the university, apart from those which benefit the university directly.

THE IDEAL DISTRIBUTION OF RESPONSIBILITIES AMONG THE DIFFERENT DECISION MAKERS

The above developments show that the ideal system of governance must allow for an adequate combination of decentralized and centralized decisions, the latter being replaceable by strongly coordinated decisions. I shall try in this chapter to propose which decision makers should be made responsible for taking the different crucial decisions. Basically, there are two possibilities to respond to this question: 1) take the different decision makers and examine which decisions they should be responsible for; 2) take the different decisions and see which decision maker is best able to make them. I shall follow the first approach, as it focuses the attention on the decision makers, which is more relevant than to put it on the decisions to make.

The following developments are schematic and more work should be done to deepen the role of each decision maker regarding each important decision. Moreover, this essay concentrates on the role each decision maker should have, without paying much attention to how the decision-making competencies should be shared between the different potential decision makers.

Previously, we identified very schematically who are the most important potential decision makers. We are going now to go through the same list and propose what should be their main area of competencies according to the criteria developed in the preceding section.

Students: They should have a more important role in defining their education and in participating in the improvement of all social aspects of the university life. The former implies that they should be invited to evaluate the teachers and the coherence of the study programs and be offered to plan a greater part of their study program, including semesters taken in other universities, and be encouraged to do so. Regarding the latter, they should be more strongly involved in setting up and running all social aspects of university life (cultural and sport activities, food and lodging, grants and insurance, work opportunities on the campus, etc.).

Faculty: Faculty constitutes, as I mentioned above, the key human asset, as the members have the professional knowledge on which the quality of research and teaching depends. They should benefit from a working environment favorable to their creativity and commitment towards their students. However, they should not have a final say about strategic policy issues. They should have ample opportunities to express their views about the future development of their discipline and propose the creation of new study programs or research areas, but they should not take part in the decision, as this would introduce a strong bias in favor of the status quo. However, if a faculty receives financial resources to support an activity that is no longer a priority, it should be let free to work for it, but should be invited to participate in the financing of the infrastructure. More precisely, faculty should mainly be:

- responsible for the content and methodology of teaching as long as the coherence of the program is assured;
- free to choose their research topics, but responsible for getting financial support, all the more so when this is not a priority of the university;
- responsible for selecting, encouraging and training future researchers and teachers.

Colleges of faculty at Department or Faculty (School) level: The responsibilities given to any faculty committee arise from those which should be given to a faculty and entail more or less the same restrictions. It is obvious that a group of faculty belonging to the same discipline acts as a cartel, particularly inclined to defend its own interests without paying much attention to the interests of the whole organization. In addition to the competencies given to each of their members, colleges of faculty should:

- be made responsible for the coherence of study programs (in collaboration with the students);
- be invited to give their professional opinion when recruiting new faculty;

- when requested, alert the university authorities about recent developments and trends in their disciplines;
- make proposals for new programs or structures, essentially in the framework of the preparation of the strategic plan.

Deans (Faculty) or Directors (Schools): In most European universities, faculties or schools are the most important subdivisions. They hold an intermediate position between the university and the departments or institutes. In many respects, they allow for a compromise between the respect of the subsidiarity principle and the necessity to take into account the external effects, as well as the search for economies of scale and a reasonable equality of treatment. Therefore, if it is good policy to decentralize towards the faculty and the students most decisions concerning, for the former, what they bring to and, for the latter, what they can expect from the university, it is also good policy to involve Faculty (Schools) in the conception and application of policies. Looking at the world of business, one observes that some corporations are very centralized and decide most policies at headquarters, whereas others are organized as holding companies, where each member company has a broad degree of freedom. There is no single right solution as such. For companies, the right solution depends mainly on the type of business they are in, the size of the company and of each of its member firms, as well as on "the spirit of the day". In universities, the degree of decentralization towards faculties should also depend on the type of university (full, universal university or specialized one?) and on its size (5 000 or 100 000 students?). In deciding the executive competencies to give to Deans (Directors), one should have clearly in mind that if the subsidiarity principle pleads in favor of a strong decentralization towards these important university subdivisions, faculties (schools) are also the source of important externalities and the search for economies of scale pleads for increasingly greater organizations. Moreover, Deans (Directors) are so near the faculty that they can easily be their hostages, which would once again create a bias in favor of the *status quo*.

Whatever the level of decentralization, Deans (Directors) should be made responsible for the management of the subdivision regarding teaching and research. In particular, they should:

- contribute to setting the priorities at the university level;
- implement the broadly defined priorities set by the university;
- set the criteria of promotion for the study programs;
- be responsible for the functioning of the subdivision (coherence of programs, involvement of faculty in university activities, disciplinary questions, etc.).

The President and team: The President (and team) should obviously be the executive leader of the institution and therefore make all the strategic decisions. However, the preparation of decisions and their implementation should be, at least partly, delegated. For example, faculty, deans and colleges of faculty should be invited to analyze future developments in the scientific disciplines and future education needs. The elaboration of the strategic plan should also be a collective and iterative process. Moreover, many decisions have to be implemented by faculties, schools or departments. However, the President should be free to make the final decision on the basis of the documents prepared collectively. Other papers in this volume comment on how the President can make decisions. I just want to stress that it is useless to have the competence to decide, if one does not have the power to impose one's decisions; therefore, the question of how to implement decisions is to me the greatest challenge for the improvement of university governance. I personally believe that the president should use as much as possible incentives and disincentives, mainly financial, and avoid as much as possible to impose views by rules.

Senate: It is obvious that any assembly of faculty, as we still have them in many European universities, is incapable of making executive decisions. They nevertheless serve to discuss questions of general interest, among others, questions of ethics.

Participation bodies: Committees with representation from all the stakeholders within the university (students, researchers, faculty and administrative staff), as we have them in some European universities at the level of the university and/or the faculty (school), should be given ample opportunities to comment and make proposals regarding student affairs and general welfare within the university. However, they should not have any executive decision power, as they have a strong tendency to spend a lot of time on questions that have not a great priority, which slows down the decision process enormously.

External Boards: Thanks to their intermediate position between the community, the State and the University, external boards can be useful to encourage the President to make changes and to support action. To prevent them behaving like a discussion club, they should be given real competencies, like adopting the strategic plan, the budget, the creation or suppression of subdivisions and programs, the construction of new buildings, as well as to nominate professors or elect the rector.

The State: As long as the State supplies the majority of the financial resources, it should have an important supervisory role, encouraging the institution to be accountable. However, the State should not have any decision competencies and refrain from intervening in the choices made by the institution.

CONCLUSION

I have tried in this essay to identify the most critical university decisions and the appropriate decision makers that are at the core of university governance. Then, I have drawn from the theory of federalism and from some principles of management some key elements helping to define why some decisions can be decentralized and others should be centralized. Finally, I have tried to apply these principles to propose what should be the main decision competencies of the different potential decision makers.

This was clearly a first attempt for me. I nevertheless believe that this line of argument is solid, therefore capable of enlightening this most complex challenge of university governance. The effort should be deepened and refined to take into account the diverse institutional and cultural characteristics of the European as well as the American universities. However, we have to keep in mind that the best model is of no use if one is unable to implement it without creating serious trouble within the institution. I believe it is possible. If not, universities as we know and love them may have great difficulties to maintain the privileged position that they have been able to gain and secure over centuries.

REFERENCES

Commission of the European Communities (2000). *Communication from the Commission to the Council, the European Parliament, the Economic and Social Committee and the Committee of the Region, Towards a European research area*, Brussels.

Grin, F. & Harayama, Y. & Weber L. (2000). *Responsiveness, Responsibility and Accountability: an Evaluation of University Governance in Switzerland*, Federal Office for Education and Science, Berne.

Hirsch, W. Z. & Weber, L. E. (1999). *Challenges Facing Higher Education at the Millennium*, The American Council on Education and Oryx Press.

Joint declaration of the European Ministers of Education (1999). *The European Higher Education Area*, Bologna.

Weber, L. E. (2000 a). "Financial Management and Planning; or How to Implement Changes More Smoothly", in (pp. 71-79) *Higher Education Reform for Quality Higher Education Management in the 21st century*, Research Institute of Higher Education, Hiroshima University.

Weber, L. E. (2000 b). "University Financial Management at a Crossroads: some Thoughts from a Swiss Point of View" in (pp. 109-125) Xue Peijian (ed.) *Socialization of Rear Services in Institutions of Higher Education from the World Perspective*, Shanghai.

CHAPTER 7

Some Thoughts About University Governance

Henry Rosovsky

RENDER UNTO CAESAR

The student rebellion started at Berkeley in the fall of 1964. It was the beginning of a movement that eventually engulfed many of America's finest campuses. The rebellion resulted in many actions and counteractions: demonstrations and sit-ins, followed by police, tear gas, and helicopters. But the most typical manifestations were mass meetings. Some of these, strange to say, were faculty meetings. Under normal circumstances, faculty meetings were poorly attended. Once the student rebellion erupted, however, formerly quiet professorial gatherings concentrating on academic arcana became events best described many years ago in Gustave Le Bon's classic *La Foule*: "Given to exaggeration in its feelings, a crowd is only impressed by excessive sentiments. An orator wishing to move a crowd must make an abusive use of violent affirmations. To exaggerate, to affirm, to resort to repetitions, and never to attempt to prove anything by reasoning are methods of arguments well known to speakers at public meetings."

At such an assembly, one unusually calm speech made an indelible impression on me. The orator was Carl Landauer, an elderly German-Jewish refugee, a social-democrat, and a distinguished political scientist. As I recall, the debate centered on relations between the University and the State Government of California, where our reputation—in view of the recent unrest—had reached absolute bottom. Some professors wanted to challenge the Governor; others wanted to meet with him in order to prevent further misunderstandings. In the midst of the debate, Landauer gave a warning. He said: "the issue is not to render unto Caesar the things which are Caesar's; the issue is to keep Caesar at bay".

Here we have a basic principle of university governance. It is not the whole story by any means, but it surely is of great general importance. Institutions of higher education, and especially research universities, differ from private businesses and governmental organizations in important ways. In universities, individual initiative and creativity must be given full opportunities to develop; a bottom line is difficult to define and measure; collegiality needs to be cultivated; and time horizons are longer than for most other organizations. Furthermore, university administrators have the unusual challenge of contending with large numbers of tenured professors. None of this makes governance less important: on the contrary, it would be difficult to exaggerate its importance.

Following Hirsch and Weber, I take the term governance to mean the formal and informal arrangements in institutions of higher education that set the terms for the distribution of legitimate power and authority for the purposes of making decisions and taking actions. External governance refers primarily to relations between individual institutions and the state or other segments of society that have a supervisory role in higher education. Internal governance refers to the lines of authority within institutions, such as those between supervisory boards, rectors or presidents and deans, departmental chairs, faculty and students.

Governance sets the parameters for management, and no mismanaged enterprise will flourish. Higher education is no exception. However, higher education does require its own special forms of governance, and should always place a premium on reasonable *but* minimal interference from the outside.

This is not to suggest that institutional accountability to the public or to private trustees is unnecessary or undesirable. On the contrary, public and private trustee rights have to be preserved, but this does not include interference in the inner workings of institutions. (What is to be avoided is usually called "micro-management.") In my view it does include the vital obligation of "hiring and firing" the school's chief executive (president) as circumstances dictate.

Caesar represents the extra-mural authorities, i.e. issues of external governance. The other side of the coin is internal governance: the intra-mural arrangements, and they are the primary focus of these few pages. My aim is to describe a set of principles that—if adopted—would improve the governance and therefore the management of universities. They are neither new nor surprising, and may well be unduly influenced by looking at the topic through American lenses. I know that even when we confine ourselves to Europe and North America, culture and traditions differ and both have a strong influence on the way in which governance is practiced in frequently ancient institutions. Nevertheless, I have tried to achieve a level of generalization above that of an individual institution or country.

PRINCIPLES

Not Everything is Improved by Making it More Democratic

University governance often suffers from excess democracy—especially from participatory democracy. At worst, this can lead to chaos; more frequently, excess democracy slows down or prevents change. Preventing change may be a good thing when proposals are hurried or ill-considered, but that is not the normal condition in higher education. Indeed, I would argue that, generally, we suffer from an excess of checks and balances. Why else, for example, has curricular reform been compared to moving a cemetery? Or, to take another example, why has it proved so difficult to bring the academic calendar, originally designed for agricultural societies, into the twentieth century—a century that has already terminated!

The attractions of democracy as a political system are obvious: as citizens we all have the same rights, provided we are of age and have not been convicted of a serious crime. For most people, citizenship and its privileges come as a birthright. When citizenship is acquired voluntarily through naturalization, certain limitations may exist. Being a naturalized American citizen, I cannot, for example, become President of the United States. No great sacrifice for me, but my former colleague Henry Kissinger might—with reason—have different feelings.

The point is that becoming a member of a higher learning community in any capacity is also a voluntary act. It is obtained through application or invitation, and that legitimizes some—though not all—constraints. Students are invited to study, and not to govern. Faculty are invited to teach, do research, and—in a well-run institution—to set educational policy within their spheres of competence. Faculty do not, however, set salary policy for themselves or have final authority with respect to appointments. Both would create serious conflicts of interest.

What are reasonable, desirable, and legitimate constraints on institutional citizenship in higher education? To begin with, I suggest that rights and responsibilities in universities should reflect the length of commitment to the institution. Many years ago, I made a statement to a group of Harvard undergraduates that elicited their deep disapproval. This is what I said: "You are here for four years; I (a tenured professor) am here for life; and the institution is here forever." They understood my meaning all too well: control over policies and practices has to bear some relation to time-horizon. Students are transients; non-tenured faculty may be in the same category; non-academic staff vary enormously in terms of commitment. These differences are ignored at the peril of institutions in which long-term planning is critical.

It is not only a matter of long-term commitment. In the governance of universities—in contrast to the rights of citizenship—those with knowledge are entitled to a greater say. Obviously this does not apply to all issues. Student or office clerk opinions concerning the relative virtues of Republicans and Democrats are as valid as those of Nobel laureates. But the principle does apply to expert knowledge about the basic missions of universities: teaching and research. Students in particular are associated with the university because they lack knowledge and desire to acquire it. They also want their knowledge certified in the form of degrees. For these purposes, individuals with expert knowledge are to be found almost entirely among the academic staff—junior, senior and technical. None of this is meant to discourage discussion and the vigorous expression of opinion by all constituencies, but the ultimate responsibility requires qualifications not achieved merely by joining the community.

By their very nature, all universities known to me are hierarchical organizations, but the authority vested in various groups or individuals differs greatly across institutions and countries. I tend to favor stronger executive powers than is customary in universities where chairmen, deans, and rectors are elected. (I am strongly opposed to experiments with "parity.") Whatever the specific system, effective governance requires close cooperation and compatibility between different levels of institutional administration. A useful rule would state that for significant appointments, the individual in a supervisory position, (say) a dean, would have a formal role—more than merely a "voice"—in the selection of (say) a chairperson. This could prevent counterproductive, adversarial situations, a special problem where the tradition of election prevails. I know of cases where deans are completely excluded in the choice of departmental chairpersons, and where rectors are similarly excluded in the choice of deans. I know of one major research university in the United States where the president has no review power of any kind in tenure decisions.

For a hierarchical system to have legitimacy requires regular consultations and explicit forms of monitoring and accountability. Consultation should include all major groups that have a stake in a particular decision, and accountability also applies to all members of the community. We all know that, as applied to professors, accountability is a difficult and delicate concept. Some relation between performance and reward should be mandated.

I do have one specific suggestion that might enhance the legitimacy of ordered ranks, appointments rather than elections, and verticality in general. Throughout the university, everyone should be able to appeal any decision to a level one step above an immediate supervisor. A professor should be able to seek redress above the level of the department chairperson; a student should be allowed to contest a professor's decision at the level of a department chairperson; similar rights should be available to all employees. To be fully effective, these mechanisms of review and appeal have to be clear, simple to use, and highly publicized.

The Best Assurance of Maintaining Institutional Quality is Shared or Cooperative Governance

Academics will know what this implies: some—a share—of policy decisions should be delegated to the faculty. Primarily, this would consist of educational policy—particularly curriculum—and the selection and promotion of academic staff, most especially the award of tenure. Delegation does not imply absolute control. It is desirable for supervisory bodies to review faculty decisions, but their emphasis should be procedural. If procedures are carefully constructed, matters of substance will emerge on their own. For example, if a recommendation for promotion is questionable, the evidence required by good procedures should make that clear. Those who review decisions delegated to faculty bodies exercise mostly negative powers. They can send back for reconsideration or they can reject. Their authority to initiate in a shared system is much weaker, and that is also a good thing because it recognizes that initiation—e.g. the choice of a new professor—should reflect the collective wisdom of selected faculty members in a particular field and not the whim of an individual administrator.

For shared governance to accomplish its purposes, certain attributes are very valuable. At least three seem to me to be necessary.

Firstly, administrations should ensure that a detailed database about individual faculty members has been created. It would show, *inter alia*, current and past teaching assignments with class enrollments, number of Ph.D. students, number of undergraduates under supervision, salary history, leaves, major committee assignments, consultancies, grants, etc. This type of information should be instantly and easily available. Commonly, it is not available in readily usable form and current technology eliminates any excuse for its absence. It may seem odd to insist on this seemingly trivial point, but inadequate information has a destructive influence and creates unfairness. That can harm collegiality, a necessary part of smoothly functioning shared governance.

Secondly, I would advocate that each university formally establish the principal parameters of institutional citizenship: in essence, a social contract. This matters because mutually agreed upon rights and responsibilities too often tend to be left in a state of vagueness, creating internal dissension and, not too rarely, the neglect of students. My preference is for a proposed social contract to be debated, perhaps amended, and then officially adopted by a faculty. An unambiguous understanding of what we can expect from each other and what we owe to the collectivity will help to transform individual entrepreneurs into a group that can responsibly exercise the rights of shared governance. These discussions will be uncomfortable, but that might—in the end—be valuable. A sample agenda item might be: why do salaries and teaching loads differ so greatly by discipline? Is that a defensible situation or should something be done about it? Needless to say, I do not know of any faculty that has looked upon these discussions with eagerness.

Thirdly, bodies responsible for governance should regularly test and verify standards of quality. The use of external peers, visiting committees, and accreditation bodies can all be useful in providing comfort to those who have delegated their authority.

University Governance Should Improve the Capacity for Teaching, Learning, and Research

It is odd that this most obvious of principles is frequently ignored in practice. In designing or modifying systems of university governance, do we start with the very tasks for which we exist, and make everything else support those responsibilities? Not as much as we should.

Maximum output per unit of input is one way in which economists define efficiency. To achieve that goal requires the careful use of scarce factors: in our case, faculty and student time has to be used as productively as possible. For professors, it means avoiding and not being asked to do administrative tasks that can be performed equally well by others; for students, the structure of governance has to reflect the premise that studying is their principal responsibility, and that other activities, while perhaps valuable life experiences, are secondary. I add for my American colleagues: and that includes athletics!

I insist on this principle because the time involved in shared or self-governance is only rarely considered in detail. No one should attempt to replace faculty members in discussions of curriculum, promotions, or examinations. Yet all universities feature innumerable committees that spend hours in fruitless and inconsequential debates about subjects that merit nothing better. The list of such committees and meetings would vary from place to place and country to country, but I am sure that experienced academics will have little difficulty in producing suitable examples.

I find student behavior to be more rational. They are extremely anxious to gain seats on almost any committee. It is, for them, a great symbol. If representation is granted, students quickly discover the profound boredom associated with many of these assemblies, and their poor attendance tends to demonstrate newly gained wisdom. My evaluation of the student role may seem too cynical. I can certainly cite exceptions where student representation has been very valuable, but these cases are confined to subjects where their voices bring new knowledge and where the students themselves are not under the pressure of strong conflicts of interest. Appropriate examples would be the evaluation of teaching—in itself a most inexact science—and issues pertaining to student life, such as housing, recreational facilities, advising, library usage, etc.

The relationship between efficient governance and the purposes of the university is not confined to economizing faculty and student time. Governors of universities and those to whom they are responsible—public or private—also have major assignments. Institutions of higher education—and in this they are surely not alone—require sufficient financial stability to permit orderly development. Financial uncertainty and sharp budgetary fluctuations all hinder the fundamental mission of learning and knowledge creation. Rational planning becomes impossible.

Budgetary practices and financial management are equally important. Rules that permit institutions to carry over budgetary surpluses from one year to the next or to transfer funds from one budgetary category to another counter the "use it or lose it" attitude that encourages inefficiency. By lengthening the period of time over which financial stability is reasonably assured, multi-year budgets permit higher education institutions to stretch planning horizons, thereby creating more desirable options.

Establishing the proper time horizon for an institution is one of the most important and difficult responsibilities of the governance apparatus. The longest possible period is not necessarily the best. In my experience, primarily limited to membership on Harvard's executive board (The Harvard Corporation), I sometimes felt that our time horizon tended to be too long—that we were excessively concerned about the future and therefore insufficiently concerned about the present. (It was not a view shared by my fellow corporation members.) We always worried about our obligations to future generations. I wanted current expenditures to be viewed more as investments and less as consumption, and believed that the highest quality achieved in the present was likely in the future to attract all necessary resources. The way the question presented itself at Harvard may be particular to private philanthropic organizations in the United States, but the general issue applies to all institutions of higher learning.

Faculty compensation also needs to be mentioned in connection with accomplishing institutional goals. Inadequate salaries lead to lack of commitment and excessive outside activities. Even adequate salaries may not prevent "moonlighting." The point is that the most efficient faculties are reasonably compensated, work full-time, and are subject to control of their outside activities.

Financial stability, progressive budgetary practices, and decent faculty compensation are the obligations of the "governors." It is part of their contribution to increasing institutional capacity for teaching, learning, and research.

CONCLUSION

It is beyond my capacities to offer a complete "theory" of governance. I have tried to outline a few general propositions that apply to both theory and practice in universities. By way of conclusion, I would like to comment on some currently popular premises concerning university governance that relate to my brief essay.

The first premise is that university evolution implies changes in the structure of governance. That is obviously true and it is happening all the time. Our critics perhaps believe that we are not changing enough or that we are changing too slowly. Sometimes that is true, but more generally we are changing all the time—incrementally—and specific changes are sometimes less than obvious. An example from my own university will make the point. Until the early 1970's, Harvard's central administration consisted of a president, a vice-president, and a few elderly ladies who provided genteel support. During the next presidency which ended in the early 1990's, the central administration became much larger and highly diversified. Vice-presidencies quintupled, a sizable internal "law firm" was created, lobbyists came on board, and administrative services were thoroughly professionalized. These changes reflected external realities: the growing importance of the Federal Government, changing financial circumstances, a more confrontational local environment, etc. Finally, our current president, who took office in 1991 has dedicated himself to pulling the university together intellectually by creating a series of institution-wide initiatives. One such, just to give an example, encompasses the study of "Mind, Brain, and Behavior," and involves at least four faculties. All these changes require new forms of governance, and are testimony of continual evolution.

Another popular premise (or question) addresses departmental structures. It is not unfamiliar territory: should the department still be the primary unit of organization? Have interdisciplinary approaches made departments obsolete? Is one meant to draw the conclusion that departments are bastions of intellectual reaction? That is not my view. I want to stress the proposition that departments are our main instruments of quality control, and also that disciplines and specialization are—certainly in the last century—the main engines of scholarly progress. Of course we must encourage interdisciplinary work, but we should remember what the term connotes: not the absence of disciplines but the presence of more than one discipline. How can those charged with making choices judge the promise of an interdisciplinary endeavor? An evaluation should include the disciplinary qualifications of participants, and that will inevitably lead us back to departmental specialists.

Furthermore—as is the case with universities generally—departments are not exempt from evolution. To cite another Harvard example, when I became dean of arts and sciences in 1973, we had one biology department. Early in my tenure, it split into two parts: organismic and evolutionary biology, and cellular and developmental biology. Later, cellular and developmental combined with bio-chemistry to form a new unit. These changes reflected intellectual developments. During my time, also, new departments came into being: Afro-American Studies was created, and Social Relations gave birth to three departments—Psychology, Anthropology, and Sociology. I mention this only to stress that departments are not necessarily academic mausoleums. *Ad hoc* groupings reflecting current interests and enthusiasms are valuable, but they are unlikely to perform similar levels of quality control.

Finally, a word about today's trendiest subject: distance learning. How will the governance structure adjust to this phenomenon? Distance learning is not entirely new: open universities and extension studies have existed for a long time. Neither have been central concerns of traditional research universities and, in view of technological progress, that may no longer be true. To my mind, this only underscores the importance of shared governance. Distance learning carries an institutional *imprimatur* for which the faculty must assume responsibility. To leave it in the hands of media professionals and advertising agencies would be a travesty.

Recently, I heard a businessman say that the Internet is changing every business that we know, and that also has to apply to higher education. But we must attempt to draw the right conclusions: core academic values have to be protected, especially in research universities; in fact, they will need greater protection and more vigilance on our part. We should use the Web and information technology to improve our services to students and society—that is what business is doing in its own sphere—and not transform ourselves into hollowed-out institutions of virtual scholarship.

POSTSCRIPT

That my review of governance supports traditional philosophies and structures should not imply uncritical advocacy of the *status quo*. Change is needed, but I am conscious that the specifics will vary institutionally and nationally.

On the American scene, there are at least two glaring weak spots in governance: the departmental chairmanship and a decline in civic virtue. The former involves "middle management" and the problem evokes insufficient general interest. Essentially, in our research universities, departmental leadership in the arts and sciences has all the characteristics of "musical chairs:" short terms, weak authority, no possibility of establishing leadership. There is little respect for the job or for the individual unfortunate enough briefly to hold the position. Too often, the additional administrative burdens are uncompensated and unappreciated. But, as already indicated, this situation may be too affected by local detail to permit the discussion of general solutions.

A problem of much wider applicability and greater significance for research universities is the decline in standards of civic virtue or citizenship among the professorate. By that, I mean the growing and sometimes exclusive focus on one's profession, field, or discipline, and personal advancement, as opposed to institutional obligations—both pedagogical and administrative. I am unable to date the beginning of this trend and to cite quantitative evidence, but disciplinary focus has certainly been growing in the postwar period. A few examples can set the scene. In the United States, all will agree that teaching loads have been subject to enormous decline since the postwar boom, especially in the natural and social sciences. Has this been the result of formal administrative authorization after careful consideration or was it simply—from the perspective of deans—a *fait accompli*, justified by vague competitive pressures? Do professors, in fact, determine their own teaching loads? Sometimes the answer is yes to both questions. Professorial absences from campus have also increased at the expense of "pastoral" obligations, and rules relating to consulting and other outside activities usually are loosely enforced. (The famous rule about "one day a week" that can be devoted to outside activities is, in my estimation, unmonitorable and therefore unenforceable, accounting—no doubt—for its popularity.) As a graduate student at Harvard in the late 1940's, I now recall that only one professor in the economics department had significant outside interests that took him away from the campus on a regular (weekly) basis. Today, there are very few professors of economics without major outside obligations. It would not be difficult to give other examples.

It is the role of governance to re-establish the values of citizenship, undermined by expansion, perpetual shortages of top-notch scholars, and the increased value to society of what many professors know. That will not be easy, but I can see at least three possibilities.

An agreed upon social contract that would detail and incorporate the meaning of good citizenship could be helpful. As noted earlier, it will be very hard to get faculties voluntarily to engage in this process.

I favor post-tenure review as one way of preserving the values of civic virtue. Post-tenure review—defined as formal periodic peer evaluation—does not threaten tenure, and can tie reward to performance using criteria that include both the institution and the demands of the profession.

The lifting of the retirement cap in the United States makes this task all the more urgent. Many observers of universities believe that retirements will continue to occur at more or less "normal" times, and therefore think that there is not much for us to worry about. So far they have been right, but I still disagree. Even relatively brief postponements create obstacles for the young seeking to join our profession: elements of a zero-sum game are present, especially with financial constraints. A reduced number of younger colleagues also entails obvious intellectual penalties. Furthermore, the absence of a specified retirement age combined with tenure raises very serious issues. Under the best of circumstances, our formal obligations will always be a small proportion of our real tasks: if we meet all our classes, is there much else that our "supervisors" can insist on? These may not be grave problems when retirement is economically attractive, as it has been for well over a decade. Now, consider a prolonged recession or a depression. Those whose retirement plans are linked directly or indirectly to the stock market will, I have no doubt, extend their years of active service when they feel poorer. All of the above reinforces the case for serious and fair post-tenure review.

Finally, I urge instruction in professional conduct for all who join faculty ranks, perhaps as part of Ph.D. training. The academic profession appears to be unique in not insisting on this type of instruction. Lawyers and physicians have it; even some trades have it; we do not. To be sure, we learn disciplinary conduct as part of graduate studies—essentially this is training for research. But discipline is not identical to the academic profession: the missing parts are our roles as teachers, mentors, co-workers, supervisors, institutional citizens, etc. These can be taught, analyzed, and discussed. All newcomers can be sensitized to the main issues, ranging from what happens in classrooms—your own and others—to curriculum in your department and in others, sexual harassment, honest evaluations, and many others.

Everything in this section relates to a current watchword in higher education: accountability. I finish as I began, with Caesar. Let us make ourselves more accountable in ways that suit our customs and traditions. Let us do so in good time, thereby keeping Caesar at bay.

REFERENCES [1]

Rosovsky, H.,
— *The University: An Owner's Manual* (1990). W.W. Norton, New York.
— *Dean's Report* (1990-91). Faculty of Arts and Sciences, Harvard University.
— The Task Force on Higher Education and Societ, (2000). [2] *Higher Education in Developing Countries: Peril and Promise*, The World Bank, Washington, D.C.

---

1 For the purposes of this essay, I have borrowed freely from three earlier publications.
2 I co-chaired this international commission with Mamphela Ramphele, the former Vice Chancellor of the University of Cape Town and currently a managing director of the World Bank.

CHAPTER 8

Setting Strategic Direction in Academic Institutions: The Planning Dilemma

Peter Lorange[1]

INTRODUCTION

Academic direction setting has never been clear-cut. It is complex, and often rife with dilemma and even controversy. So it should come as no surprise that, all too often, academic institutions view management ideas and practices with skepticism, if not outright disapproval. "Unfortunately, management in education is still a concept that stimulates a negative reaction from many academics. As a result, organizations in higher education tend to neglect management concepts and practices" (Cyert, R. M., in Keller, G., 1983). Planning and budgeting processes would probably be among those generally regarded with a considerable skepticism, despite widespread use.

This chapter will demonstrate how strategic planning and budgeting can alleviate some of the problems of effective adaptation to changed environmental conditions facing academic institutions. The chapter will also stress some of the shortcomings associated with the planning and budgeting process. We shall treat formal planning and budgeting as strategic process elements within the broader leadership "toolkit" of the academic institution.

---

[1] Gordon Adler, Heather Cairns and Knut Haanes contributed important ideas, which have been reflected in this chapter.

In light of these inherent difficulties, can academic institutions set strategic direction? In the last two decades, several path-breaking works have tackled this question, and their answers provide a useful starting point for further discussion.

A RETROSPECTIVE VIEW

In their 1973 book, "Leadership and Ambiguity," Michael Cohen and James March chose eight metaphors of leadership for the corporate university president. They concluded that the organizational anarchy metaphor is most appropriate. In their words, "each individual in the university is seen as making autonomous decisions. Teachers decide if, when, and what to teach. Students decide if, when, and what to learn. Neither coordination (except the spontaneous mutual adaptation of decision) nor control is practiced. Resources are allocated by whatever process emerges but without explicit accommodation and without explicit reference to some super-ordinate goal. The "decisions" of the system are a consequence produced by the system but intended by no one and decisively controlled by no one (Cohen, M. D. & March, J. G., 1973). This view of the university as little more than "organized anarchy" is more or less similar to the famous "garbage can model" (March, J. G. & Olsen, J. P., 1976). The approach, however, offers little guidance in managing an academic institution in such a way that those entrusted with leadership can actually set the strategic direction – it gives us little support for a planning approach!

Dahrendorf (1995) echoes the notion that academic institutions cannot be managed. "A university neither wants nor needs to be run... basically, it runs itself, by way of its own mysterious "internal channels". Interference with the usual channels should be reserved for extreme situations" (Dahrendorf, R., 1995).

As a counterpoint to these two views, George Keller ("Academic Strategy," 1983) develops a strategic planning model based on six postulates of academic strategy. "Since the fundamental aim of strategic planning is a Darwinian one of linking the forward direction of your organization with the movement of historical forces in the environment, the two critical areas for analysis are one's own organization and the environment. You need to look inside and outside. And in each of these searches there are three elements..." (Keller, G., 1983). Looking inside, Keller sees three internal dimensions of concern to the leader of an academic institution: (1) traditions, values, and aspirations; (2) strengths and weaknesses: academic and financial; and (3) leadership: abilities and priorities. Keller's so-called "external dimensions" include: (1) environmental trends: threats and opportunities; (2) market preferences, perceptions, and directions; and (3) the competitive situation: threats and opportunities.

Keller seems to imply that the setting of strategic direction is a matter of *balancing* several viewpoints, forces, and contextual dimensions. He claims that although the leaders of academic institutions can set strategic direction, the position of the institution in the flow of "historical forces" plays a key role, and may, in fact, severely limit strategic direction setting. He thus seems to offer strong support for a planning approach, but recognizes that a major potential problem might be its heritage – i.e., that past circumstances could seriously constrain planning.

Taking a different emphasis, Blau underscores the role of bureaucracy and structure. He states that: "Academic institutions have the difficult responsibility of providing an administrative framework for creative scholarship, which makes them particularly susceptible to the ill effects of bureaucratic rigidity." (Blau, P. M., 1994) He continues: "Bureaucracy does come into conflict with scholarship. Several bureaucratic features of academic institutions have deleterious consequences for educational performance, but none of these, and no others that could be discovered, have negative effects on research performance, perhaps because research can be separated from an institution's administrative machinery while education is intricately enmeshed in it. This is a bad omen for the future of higher education." (Blau, P. M., 1994) Blau thus recognizes that setting the direction of research may be somewhat "easier" than other kinds of value-creation, most notably teaching. So, while Blau would be skeptical to planning and budgeting in general, he would be particularly concerned with the potential shortcomings of all managerial approaches when it comes to supporting a proactive view of the academic teaching dimensions.

In his recent study of what creates successful dynamic, "entrepreneurial universities", Clark pinpoints five organizational "pathways of transformation" (Clark, B. R., 1998). His "five pathways" model is a good starting template for characterizing an effective strategy for a university.

Clark starts with what he calls the "strengthened steering core," which embraces central managerial groups *and* academic departments. He includes the "expanded developmental periphery," which would encompass outside organizations and groups. Clark adds the "diversified funding base," and also designates a "stimulated academic heartland." This corresponds to the academic values and belief systems. And lastly, he refers to an "integrated entrepreneurial culture," i.e., the people and the processes they follow to create value. Planning and budgeting certainly have a role in Clark's scheme, perhaps the most essential as part of the "integral entrepreneurial culture" dimension. But, Clark importantly implies that planning and budgeting must be entrepreneurial, i.e., creative, positive, alive, *and* that they are part of a broader set of administrative approaches.

Taken together, these authors provide three fundamental messages that must be kept in mind when it comes to grappling with academic value-creation and direction setting. First, since it is the strength of the *individual* academic players, with their own agendas, that drives any direction setting, setting strategic direction happens in a highly individualized, person-by-person context. Second, ways exist to rally these individual forces to *consensus* via *coalition* building for a particular strategic direction for the academic institution as a whole, although they are *de facto* highly dependent on the evolutionary context, values, and key environmental factors. With proper sensitivity to these *power* factors, academic direction setting *might* be a reality, within certain limits. And finally, procedures, rules, and structures drive academic organizations—in other words, they are inherently bureaucratic. But the university's leadership *can* have an impact on this! Beyond research, this bureaucracy especially limits choice in all other aspects of academic value creation, especially teaching. Research may well get done, even in a relatively undirected academic setting, but the rest of the value-creation equation may suffer. In summary then, a pertinent literature review provides strong limitations regarding how planning and budgeting might be practiced in academic institutions.

FOUR COMPLEMENTARY APPROACHES TO SETTING STRATEGIC DIRECTION

But, again, what about the academic leader? What might be done differently to make planning and budgeting more useful? While the aforementioned authors describe limitations or constraints (with the possible exception of Keller and Clark), they fail to value the academic leader explicitly. A president's authority is typically much more limited and tenuous than that of a corporate executive. The dean is appointed by the university board. It is not a tenured position; the person serves at the pleasure of the board. But the president interfaces with his/her faculty, many of whom have tenure. They do not need to please the president and there is ultimately relatively little he or she can do to force faculty members to do things they do not want to do. Thus, the president's job has been likened to that of Speaker of the House – the effectiveness depends on the ability to build coalitions and to persuade faculty members, with their own independent bases of authority and power, to come together in a common effort. Respecting the assumptions above, I will argue that academic institutions still *can* and *should* be managed and that academic leaders *can* play a pivotal role in setting and implementing a deliberate direction for the university. The president and some combination of faculty and staff can set a strategic direction. I will proceed on the assumption that setting and implementing the strategic direction requires both a clear focus and sense of priorities—after all, "strategy means choice"! Also essential is a well-developed sense of building coalitions, creating a power base through managing stakeholders—individuals and groups, most notably faculty. Thus, I will claim that the *way* academic leaders focus their activities inside the academic institution is crucial.

The key success criterion for a university is to *create value!* The definition of this, which is essentially the mission of the university, means emphasis on:

- *research* – creating new knowledge – and the role of the university in the economy and society,
- *teaching* – knowledge dissemination for individuals to learn, and
- *citizenship* – service to the community.

The most effective way to set strategy is to heighten focus on four ways universities can strive to create value. I will call these four approaches (strategies would be another name) "adaptation" and "pro-activism," as well as "entrepreneurialism" and "rational leadership." I shall assume that any planning or budgeting chosen must incorporate these views to be effective as a strategy direction-setting vehicle. For academic leaders to set strategic direction effectively they must worry about creating value, through research, teaching, and citizenship, in each of these four ways; doing well in only one, or two—such as research only—is inadequate. Further, the leaders of academic institutions need to see strategic direction setting as a matter of dynamically balancing the four approaches. And this will mean, I maintain, that the ideal direction for any academic institution (if we can speak of an "ideal") will consist of getting the right tradeoffs among proactive vision *and* adapting to the clients' needs, through bottom-up, faculty entrepreneurialism and top-down leadership. I shall argue that these approaches must be brought into some sort of balance and that the president will have to manage this balance by making strategic choices together with the key stakeholders. The strategic direction of the university at any point in time reflects only a temporary balance of forces or of power. The university's strategy will change over time as the balance of internal forces changes.

THE ADAPTIVE UNIVERSITY…

The *adaptive* university sets its direction and adjusts to the changing needs of its students or its clients e.g., companies, alumni, and business executives interested in continuing education. It will be *driven by the market*; this is a major challenge. If a university cannot adapt to the needs of the students or clients, it will be unable to generate the resources it needs for long-term sustainability. Still, as important as the adaptation challenge may be, it is too one-sided; it only adjusts to the changing needs of the student or client *after* the fact. In effect, although the university may have a strategic direction, the process of setting strategy may be rather passive, spearheaded by the students or client firms themselves. As such, even though listening to learning partners is a critical aspect of direction setting, merely being adaptive is inadequate. Still, caution should be exercised before downplaying the adaptive dimension. One may suggest, for example, that it could be dangerous to change the core curriculum or research agenda too quickly in response to demand shifts in the job market, which may turn out to be temporary, or to make changes that simply respond to the latest corporate fad.

... AND THE PROACTIVE UNIVERSITY

A *proactive* university seeks the direction it needs to take, senses where to go, and gets there first. In concrete terms, this means making sure that one's directional moves ultimately meet the needs of students and clients, not merely by adapting to their needs *post facto*, but by actually leading change, leapfrogging ahead. It means *driving the market!* (Kumar, N. & Scheer, L.K. & Kotler, P., 2000)

The key shall be to balance the adaptive and the proactive strategies. Both dimensions—to be led as well as to lead—have merit, but in a complementary manner. Too much relative focus on proactiveness can lead the university to "jump the gun", with an insufficient revenue base. Too much relative focus on adaptiveness, on the other hand, can lead to milking the market dry, so as to live on borrowed time. The two are equally valid; they are two sides of the same coin. Crucial as this balance of adaptation and pro-action is, I believe that it still misses an important additional point to secure optimal value creation, namely the bottom-up/top-down interplay between the faculty and the president.

ALSO, THE ENTREPRENEURIAL UNIVERSITY...

The *entrepreneurial* university also represents an essential, but still partial, view of what we see as optimal in setting strategic direction. No one would argue that the individual initiatives of faculty members *cum* entrepreneurs are unimportant. In the effective strategic management of a university, this should not be ignored. The effective university unleashes its faculty members' energies, their willingness to take on initiatives and spearhead "pioneer" and "rapid expansion" teaching and research activities. This builds on the individualistic drive of each faculty member, so deep-rooted in academic life. The key here is indeed to create proactiveness, through new research-based discoveries and new pedagogical teaching innovations.

On the other hand, a team approach to creating value in the university is also necessary. Students or clients benefit most from the coordinated activities of a true faculty team to ensure effective adaptiveness. The same holds true for research efforts: eclectic teams of faculty members, working together on a cross-disciplinary basis, are the best hope for value management, or any other academic insights. Finally, and perhaps most fundamentally, the human capital resource base must have a *balance* within the university, with the faculty members comprising a portfolio of human talents. This faculty team can only have its full strength when its members are compatible. This ultimately helps to ensure creativity and proactive thinking, as well as serving the learning partners better by adaptation.

Despite their importance, the *entrepreneurial* elements of a university do not represent an exhaustive label for the value-creating activities of the university, either. The entrepreneurial faculty member, to be effective alone and/or as a team member, must alone possess a sense of maturity and a breadth to find his or her place within the broader portfolio strategy context of the university. Perhaps we need to invent the label "team-based entrepreneurialism" for blending these bottom-up faculty-driven initiatives into a cohesive overall strategy for the school.

...AND THE RATIONALLY MANAGED UNIVERSITY

I shall argue that a university's dean or president must, to a certain extent, manage from the top, project a well-defined role. This includes playing a catalytic role to improve the conditions of, and affect how people work in a university, so that a clearer, more deliberate direction can be the result. To be a source of encouragement, to add support, and to provide positive feedback will thus be a part of the president's strategic agenda—a key implementation task!

Perhaps even more importantly will be the addition of a portfolio focus, a vision for "how things fit together", for what the school should do and not do. A particular strategic initiative may indeed be interesting, but still not fit into *this* university's vision of itself. It is the president's job to facilitate the process of being selective. The task is to manage fit through top-down vision, not to be merely a glorified adding machine of bottom-up initiatives.

A university thus managed can be thought of as *rationally managed*. Still, the mere provision of energy and focus from the top does not give a full picture of the value creation for which I have argued. Input from the top can only be part of a more full-blown value creation process. As noted, real strategic direction thus emerges from the balance of the bottom-up and top-down forces. This is a matter of the balance of power that is likely to determine the ultimate balance of focus, or strategic direction of the university. It must be kept in mind that tenured faculty will often have their own resources, and that some faculty are more powerful than others. Some alumni, companies, and potential donors are more powerful than others. The university's board may make its own claims on the university's resources. University presidents often find themselves clashing with university boards and administrators over control of their financial resources. Also, some of the schools within the university—say, the business schools—will often be the most profitable operations on campus, and revenue generated by them are typically hard to divert to fund activities at less prosperous schools and departments. Important internal dynamics thus have an impact on this top-down/bottom-up balance. To have a realistic chance, the president must bring his or her own resources, coalitions, and connections to the table, to create a certain power balance.

For the sake of clarity, it might be useful to summarize the various forces into two dimensions, as shown in *Exhibit I*.

Exhibit I Forces with an Impact on the Strategic Direction of the University

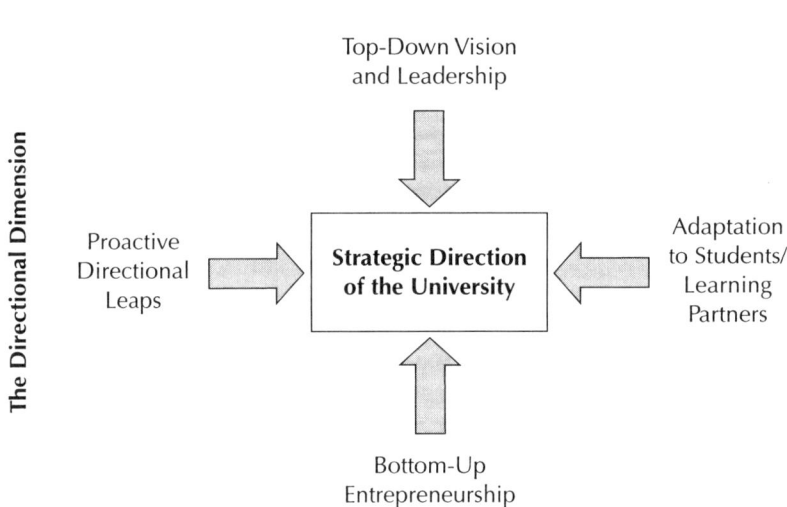

The directional dimension sets out the strategy of the university's research and teaching activities. It is a function of the need to respond to the various customers, i.e., to adapt. It is also a function of the proactive vision of the faculty members and their interest in pioneering and rapidly expanding in new directions, i.e., more of a strategic leapfrogging dimension. The paradox is that a better strategic direction will most likely emerge out of the tradeoffs or sources of positive tension between the two types of directional input illustrated; one might say, market leading *and* market led.

On the other axis of the model are two complementary actor dimensions. On the one hand are the important entrepreneurial inputs by the faculty members, working both alone and in teams, creating what might be called a "bottom-up input." These influence the strategic direction of the university, both by shaping the proactive, so-called "leaps" and by shaping the university's adaptation to the needs of its learning partners. A top-down vision and leadership dimension complements, driven by what the choices the president feels the university *should* make in setting its strategic direction to develop an overall portfolio. The top-down force counterbalances the bottom-up entrepreneurship dimension, so that the emerging direction results from a balances of these forces. Or, as Cyert states: "To survive the difficulties ahead, colleges and universities must have more foresight in management. But, at the same time, universities must maintain their decentralized form and capitalize on the entrepreneurship and idea-generating abilities of the faculty. Thus, there needs to be more active and decisive campus leadership—but it must seek and include faculty contributions." (Cyert, R. M., in Keller, G., 1983)

All in all, the strategic direction of a university can best be depicted as a combination of forces—see Exhibit I—reflecting a temporary balance of power at any point in time. Both the bottom-up, entrepreneurial input, as well as the top-down leadership input, are likely to change over time. So are the adaptive needs of the learning partners, as well as the opportunities for proactive, directional leaps. The relationship between different coalitions of forces changes. Clearly then, the actual strategy of a university at any point in time is the result of the power shifts and interactive forces among key stakeholders—individuals and groups—along the four dimensions in the exhibit. And keeping the dynamic balance among them is extremely important.

MAKING STRATEGIC CHOICES: KEEPING THE BALANCE TO CREATE VALUE

Let us focus some more on the strategic task of the president. How can he or she further define the dimensions that should guide the development of a portfolio strategy, beyond a healthy proactive/adaptive balance?

Setting strategic direction, managing the focuses that have an impact on the value-creating portfolio of activities of the dynamic university, "keeping the balance," is necessarily difficult. The balance does not come by itself, of course. Explicit strategic choices are not only necessary; they form the basis for creating the balance. These choices entail tradeoffs and tradeoffs mean setbacks and frustration, due above all to the multitude of competing needs and concerns that stakeholders in an academic institution typically debate. Still, I believe that a significant increase in the value creation capabilities of the modern university is possible. I recommend that the portfolio strategy of the dynamic university be "operationalized" by following *three* fundamental strategic options for creating value. They must remain at the center of any portfolio tradeoff debate. Essentially, these three options deal with how to create value through activities that yield decreasing and/or increasing economies of scales and/or specialization:

1. *Mass production*, i.e. acknowledging economies of scale. The more students you have, the fuller your classrooms, and the more efficiently you can run your teaching. The larger your research budget, the more efficiently you can carry out your research. Many academic institutions follow this approach to value creation. The more customers you get, the *lower* is the value for the last customer, however, and the *lower* is the price you want to charge for a service given to your last student/customer. However, there is little "upside" to this strategy, one would say!

2. *Mediation through a network*. This approach is based on bringing students *cum* customers together, who add value to all. Thompson labels this approach the "mediating industry" (Thompson, J. D., 1967). In essence, you create value by putting people together—creating clubs! The more customers you get in your network, the *higher* the value for the last customer who joins, and the higher you can set the price of your services! (Gibbons, M. & Limoges, C. & Nowotny, H. & Schwartzman, S. & Scott, P. & Trow, M., 1994) The larger network always beats the smaller networks—the members are basically partners in a club, not individual partners. Here, you do *not* want to create value by isolating each member, say, through having key accounts for each. Rather, you want to have all members participate in each key activity; this way, you create value via key activities for all members! Interestingly, the *more* you do, the better it goes; you can indeed benefit from some "upsides" here!

3. *Unique problem solving as a mode of value creation*. This approach is based on solving unique problems that the customer cannot solve by him- or herself. Much sponsored research follows this mode. Asymmetric information is at work here—the expert, with his or her reputation, versus the customer. Much so-called "problem solving" amounts to the expert helping the client to reach the best understanding of the problem possible, and hence, the most accurate diagnosis. The customer often solves the problem him- or herself. (Sarvary, M., 1999).

In choosing the relative emphasis among the three options for shaping the university's portfolio strategy, there are of course several constraints at work.

One will be the power balance equation—the stakeholder coalition puzzle—already discussed. The president may have no other option, for instance, than to continue a focused emphasis on mass production. Another key factor will be the university's existing capabilities. Are not the choices themselves affected, even significantly, by the university's existing capability to create and exploit economics of scale and/or specialization, as well as its desire to be both adaptive and proactive in responding to customer demand? There is a clear feedback loop between a university's existing organizational capabilities and the strategic portfolio choices the president can make among potential areas of emphasis.

For instance, the president may want to create a network with a designated group of corporations and learning partners. The problem might be, however, that the faculty may *not* be in a position to "deliver" the cross-disciplinary, managerially focused input that this would require; discipline-based fragmentation regularly limits the capabilities of a typical network, and the president must thus be aware of this! For instance, a faculty with a strong focus on conventional undergraduate and graduate-level teaching, backed up by a strong axiomatic research tradition, may simply not have the interest, nor the capabilities, to get engaged in unique, cross-functional problem-solving, based on a lot of interaction also with real life business executives. Again, the president must realize that options may be limited, at least in the short run, in adding emphasis on unique problem-solving as part of the university's portfolio strategy.

A third key factor is the maturity of the market-place itself. This may also highlight the balance of the critical decision between the problems the university should solve and the problems others (clients) should solve, either on their own or with one another. It should be noted that, in this world of expert problem solvers, customers may be referred to each other. The key is to choose the university's area(s) of problem solving. This choice creates an effective flow of information for understanding problems, and by so doing, creates a team of faculty members who work on them in an on-going proactive loop! Stabell and Fjellstad describe this cycle of strengthening the university's own capabilities by choosing in which arenas to engage (Stabell, C. B. & Fjellstad, Ø. D., 1998).

THE PLANNING AND BUDGETING PROCESS

Exhibit II gives an overview of a conventional planning and budgeting process, as first conceptualized by Vancil and Lorange (Vancil, R. F. & Lorange, P., 1975) (Lorange, P., 1980). This step-by-step blueprint for prescribing *who* does *what* and *when* can be the basis for the development of realistic strategies for the university, bringing to bear on the process the various points of view raised so far in this chapter. It should not be denied, on the other hand, that the process can also be the basis for "sheer bureaucratic nonsense". It takes a considerable amount of insight and determination to make the process work and to avoid the major dysfunctions. Let us point out these "upsides and pitfalls":

Exhibit II The Planning and Budgeting Process

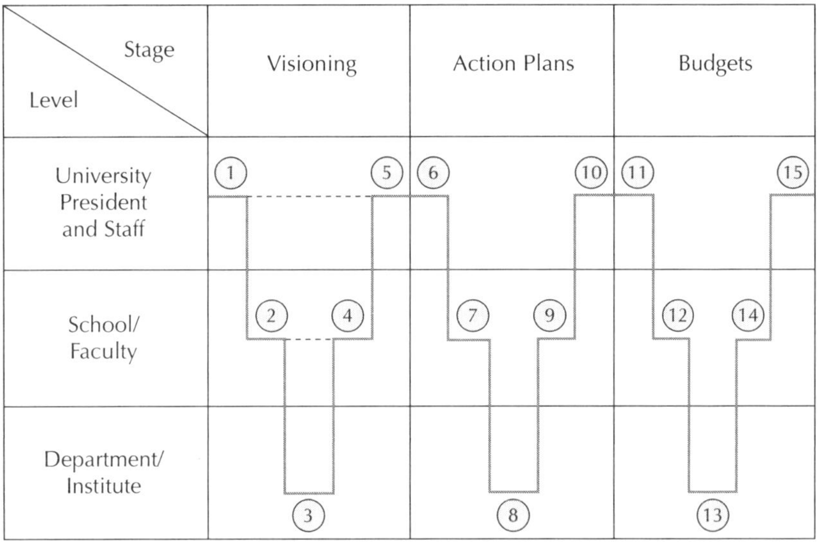

Level \ Stage	Visioning	Action Plans	Budgets
University President and Staff	①　　　　⑤	⑥　　　　⑩	⑪　　　　⑮
School/Faculty	②　　④	⑦　　⑨	⑫　　⑭
Department/Institute	③	⑧	⑬

THE VISION PHASE

Let us first consider the setting of clear premises behind the university's evolving vision. The typical reality *is* that the top leadership of the university issues its view on the future, and on how the university should adapt to it, more or less as an extrapolation of the past. This assumes that the future will bring more of the same and that the emerging challenges facing the university will continue to be of a similar nature. It *should* be a matter of openly attempting to "see" new opportunities—positive as well as threats—*before* they become obvious to everyone else. It thus *should* be a matter of more open-endedly restating the premises that might drive a revised vision, in the age of discontinuity and break points! (Step 1)

Let us now consider how the various schools or faculties might restate their vision premises, in the light of what has been provided for them by the university presidency. The typical reality is that school or faculty visions will often also evolve along proven tracks – assuming essentially more of the same.

Faculty members may *want* the fundamental roles of the school or the faculty to remain essentially unchanged—it would be unthinkable to consider radically different visionary paths! The school or faculty should be more openly ready to reconsider its competencies and its portfolio mix—unburdened by present organizational (i.e., departmental) realities—focusing on the competencies needed within new emerging realities. (Step 2)

How is the academic vision restated at the departmental (or research institute) level? This should look for new opportunities—open-endedly—and assess their consequences when it comes to the department's competence base—"seeing" radically new opportunities. In practice, the departmental vision discussion often tends to "justify" the future relevance of the present competence base—again extrapolating, building plausible cases for the status quo. (Step 3)

How should a school's or faculty's vision now be aggregated and how is this aggregated vision in practice? Analogous to what was argued above, the vision should portray a fresh view of how the direction of the school/faculty might evolve, taking fully into account new environmental circumstances, new opportunities, new threats, new breakpoints, etc. In practice, however, one again typically sees these aggregate vision statements become extensions of the past, not least due to the fact that each school/faculty/department will want to protect itself by building on what it already stands for. (Step 4)

The visioning at the university level is, of course, especially crucial. It should be open-minded and re-examine the overall portfolio of the university in a free-flowing sense, without being bound to the traditional organizational structure and school portfolio. This open-ended visioning should be based on a true assessment of the environmental circumstances, the desire to utilize new opportunities, the internalization of breakpoints (Strebel, P., 1992).

Again, in reality, an extrapolation tends to be the case. The visioning process for the university will typically reflect more of the same. This is often justified by the fact that it will be nearly impossible to change the university structure. Processes such as tenure and self-governance at a highly decentralized level tend to preserve the *status quo*. (Step 5)

As can be seen from Exhibit II, I have inserted dotted lines between Steps 2 and 4, as well as between Steps 1 and 5. Departments and schools should perhaps not be too heavily involved in visioning, in a formal sense, at this stage. Rather, the *formal* visioning may take place primarily at the university level. This might allow for a more open-ended reassessment of the portfolio, thus avoiding to preserve the *status quo*. A variation of this would be that, at the university level, each major school and/or department would be reassessed regularly, a procedure which might also lead to addressing meaningful adaptive changes. This is the case at Harvard, where the president reassesses in depth one of the schools every year.

THE ACTION PLAN PHASE

Now that a clear proactive vision has been established, the next step is to delineate appropriate implementation. The action plan phase attempts to develop programs to drive the implementation of vision and the overall strategy. It might commence with the university president and staff calling for action plan input from each school/faculty. This should take the form of a request for an open-ended set of action plans to support the proactive vision, which also should have been clearly communicated. In practice, presidents instead request essentially an update of the former year's plan. (Step 6)

School action plan premises also need to be set. Here, one should ideally look for premises that are "zero-based", calling for a fresh statement of action to be taken to pursue new strategies. In practice, extrapolative premises often tend to be developed. (Step 7) Departmental/institute premises and plans should be fleshed out. Similar types of issues apply here. (Step 8)

Reconciliation of action plans at the school level should be done in such a way that it creates an opportunistic, rolling action plan framework. Thus, while various action plans are laid out, it should also be recognized that new opportunities could come up during the year, calling for modified action plans. Further, some actions that had initially been envisioned could later become relatively less appropriate. This flexibility of execution is vital. In practice, action plans tend to be laid out in a rigid way, leaving no option for pragmatic, opportunistic manoeuvering during the year, thus not allowing for "making good even better". (Step 9)

The action plans for the university as a whole should be stated as an overall portfolio of action plans; this should reflect the portfolio strategy. In practice, they often end up becoming independent actions, without a contextual role. They may be manifestations of the status quo, "freezing" resources into patterns that are, in essence, an extension of the past. These action plans thus leave little leeway for opportunistic manoeuvering at the top. (Step 10)

THE BUDGET PHASE

This stage attempts to develop a clear budget for the next year – allowing for a distinction between what might be seen as a *strategic* budget versus an *operating* budget (Abell, D., 1993). The so-called strategic budget would fund those aspects of the action plans that are intended to be implemented during the coming budgetary period. This would allow for implementation of the strategic initiatives envisioned. The operating budget, on the other hand, would fund the on-going operations, i.e., "business as usual". At this stage, the university president and staff would send out the budget guidelines, indicating that they would recommend a separation between the strategic budget and the operating budget. These budget guidelines should be "zero-based" regarding the strategic budget part, calling for them to be built up from an open-ended start, taking nothing from the past for granted. In practice, however, both the strategic budget and the operating budget often tend to be built up with a strong focus on the past, in terms of calling for the budget to be developed as "last year's level plus X percent". (Step 11) Likewise, the school/faculty must agree on budgetary guidelines. (Step 12)

Now the departments/institutes should be in a position to develop their budgets. (Step 13) The schools and faculties would then consolidate these budgets. The key here is to move towards a clear distinction between strategic and operating budgetary components. Further, for the strategic component, "zero-based" focus, as well as flexibility, is needed. The developed budgets should be seen as "rolling plans", which are suitable for pragmatic change as new opportunities come up. Thus, agreed-upon budget allocations which later turn out to be less urgent should then, in principle, be "given back", not automatically spent by a departmental unit. Similarly, if a department needs more resources for strategic purposes, they should expect that they can be requested – and normally obtained! The operating budget, on the other hand, should be more firmly fixed for the agreed-upon time period. It should, of course, be closely scrutinized. In particular, head counts and budget allocations to "brick and stone" allocations should be closely re-examined. The operating budget must be tight. (Step 14) Overall budget consolidation at the university level must follow the same issues just outlined. (Step 15)

GENERAL COMMENTS AND CONCLUSION

It is clear that the planning and budgeting process can make a difference to the academic institution. On the one hand, such a process can help the academic institution to adapt more effectively to new opportunities, grasp new initiatives that help the institution to reposition itself for the future, facilitating the development of more appropriate value creation in the light of new, emerging realities, etc. At best, planning and budgeting may thus significantly contribute to the university's value creation!

On the other hand, the planning and budgeting process can also help cement the patterns of the past. Such processes can become very bureaucratic and foster rigid, formal procedures, leading to endless, incremental extrapolation from the past. In practice, such planning and budgeting processes may make it exceedingly difficult for the leadership of the modern university to create superior academic value – break out of the straightjacketing that planning and budgeting processes may, at worst, represent!

I have argued that strategic direction setting *can* take place in academic institutions (Dill, D. D. & Sporn, B., 1995). Strategic direction setting, I have maintained, must be the clear outcome of several tradeoffs between bottom-up entrepreneurial *and* top-down leadership tradeoffs, proactive vision *and* adaptation to the client's focus. I have further asserted that the specific choice of strategic issues must be brought into play, since these tradeoffs have an impact on them: choices having to do with decreasing economies of scale, increasing economies of scale, and specialization. The planning and budgeting process can be a definite positive force here. The output of the strategy can be described in terms of the people the university emphasizes, the processes these people follow in pursuing their strategies, the projects they choose to work on, and the strategic partner's choices. The critical question that I have addressed is: how do the university's leaders amass enough clout—you may say power—enough influence, resources, and authority to *lead?!* They *can* define a strategy for the university, and then make that particular strategy stick!

REFERENCES [2]

Abell, D. (1993). *Managing with Dual Strategies – Mastering the Persent; Preempting the Future*, Free Press, New York.
Blau, P. M. (1994). *The Organization of Academic Work*, Wiley-Interscience, New York, p. 279.
Blau, P. M. (1994). *The Organization of Academic Work*, Wiley-Interscience, New York, p. 280.
Clark, B. R. (1998). *Creating Entrepreneurial Universities: Organizational Pathways of Transformation*, Pergamon, Oxford.
Cohen, M. D. & March, J. G. (1973). *Leadership and Ambiguity*, The Carnegie Commission on Higher Education, McGraw-Hill, New York, p. 33.
Cyert, R. M., in Keller, G. (1983). *Academic Strategy*, Johns Hopkins University Press, Baltimore, p. vi.
Cyert, R. M., in Keller, G. (1983). *Academic Strategy*, Johns Hopkins University Press, Baltimore, p. vii.
Dahrendorf, R. (1995). *A History of London School of Economics and Political Science 1895-1995*, Oxford University Press, Oxford.
Dill, D. D. & Sporn, B. (1995). University 2001: What will the University of the Twenty-First Century Look Like?, in Dill, David D. and Sporn, Barbara (editors), *Emerging Patterns of Social Demand and University Reforms: Through a Glass Darkly*, Pergamon, Oxford.
Gibbons, M. & Limoges, C. & Nowotny, H. & Schwartzman, S. & Scott, P. & Trow, M. (1994). *The New Production of Knowledge*, Sage, London.

---

[2] A more extensive elaboration of several of the arguments proposed here—but applied to the business school—can be found in the article by P. Lorange, 2000.

Keller, G. (1983). *Academic Strategy*, Johns Hopkins University Press, Baltimore, p. 152.

Kumar, N. & Scheer, L.K. & Kotler, P. (2000). "Market Driving and Market Driven", *European Management Journal*, Vol. 18-2, pp. 129-142.

Lorange, P. (1980). *Corporate Planning: An Executive Viewpoint*, Prentice-Hall, Englewood Cliffs, NJ.

Lorange, P. (2000). "Setting Strategic Direction in Academic Institutions: The Case of the Business School", in *Higher Education Policy*, International Association of Universities, Elsevier Science Ltd.

March, J. G. & Olsen, J. P. (1976). *Ambiguity and Choice in Organizations*, Universitetsforlaset, Bergen, Norway.

Sarvary, M. (1999). "Knowledge Management and Competition in the Consulting Industry", *California Management Review*, Vol. 41, n° 2, pp. 95-107.

Stabell, C. B. & Fjellstad, Ø. D. (1998). Configuring Value for Competitive Advantage: On Chains, Shops, and Networks, *Strategic Management Journal*, Vol. 19, pp. 413-437.

Strebel, P. (1992). *Breakpoints: How Managers Exploit Radical Business Change*, Harvard Business School Press, Boston, Massachusetts.

Thompson, J. D. (1967). *Organization in Action*, McGraw-Hill, New York.

Vancil, R. F. & Lorange, P. (1975). "Strategic Planning in Diversified Companies", in *Harvard Business Review*.

PART 4

Improved Governance

CHAPTER 9

Universities as Organizations and their Governance

Peter Scott

INTRODUCTION

'Governance' is a comparatively novel derivation from the root word 'govern' – or, more precisely, it has acquired a new currency and meaning. 'Governors', 'governed' and 'governments' have been familiar terms for centuries. Although 'governance' was not an unfamiliar word in the past, it was often used in an archaic or rhetorical sense; it was not a modern term. But, in the past two decades, a new and more contemporary meaning has been attached to 'governance' to denote a much broader account of the governing process going beyond the actions of 'governors' and 'governments'. 'Governance' embraces a wider set of actors; it ranges beyond the territory of state institutions into the private and voluntary sectors; and, consequently, it is a more ambiguous and volatile process.

Often, 'governance' is used in association with other words that have acquired new currencies and meanings—first, a bundle of words such as 'mission', 'vision' and 'strategy', which emphasizes the dynamic aspects of 'governance' (Bargh, C. & Scott, P. & Smith, D., 1996); and a second bundle such as 'stake-holders', 'ownership' and 'accountability', which emphasizes its representative and fiduciary aspects (Shore, C. & Wright, S., 2000). These semantic shifts and affinities may signify fundamental changes in the constitution of public (and private) authority at the beginning of the twenty-first century. One of these changes is the re-engineering of the state, which has tended to erode wider notions of the 'public interest' and to transform it into the facilitator of individual, and group, ambitions. As a result, classic forms of the welfare state have been superseded by neo-liberal and entrepreneurial forms, which have required a shift from straightforward notions of democratic 'government' to more sinuous notions of stakeholder 'governance'. Another change is the decline, but also the intensification of professional society, and the rise of so-called 'risk society' (Beck, U., 1992). The increasing domination of technical processes (in late-modern society) has been accompanied by a declining respect for, and trust in, experts (in a society that is already post-modern in key respects). These confusing trends have required a re-conceptualization of authority and accountability—which, in turn, has placed greater emphasis on more diffuse notions of 'governance'.

Universities have been deeply implicated in these changes—as (in most cases) state or, at any rate, public institutions, they been adversely affected by the disenchantment with the social democratic state; as mass institutions, they have been intimately involved in the democratization of education and society (and the extension of that project from a 20th century emphasis on the more equitable distribution of life-chances to a 21st century obsession with the construction—and deconstruction—of life-styles); and as expert institutions, they have been shaped by the redefinition of 'expertise', at once more technical and more contested (Gibbons, M. & Limoges, C. & Nowotny, H. & Schwartzman, S. & Scott, P. & Trow, M., 1994) (Scott, P., 1995) (Nowotny, H. & Scott, P. & Gibbons, M., 2001). As a result, the 'governance' of universities has acquired a new relevance and urgency. This wider idea has begun not only to embrace but also to replace traditional notions of academic self-government or, since the 1960s, the democratization of university government.

For the purposes of this chapter, 'governance' is interpreted in wide rather than narrow terms. It is taken to denote the entire leadership function of the university and, therefore, includes not only the formal governing body (university council, board of control, board of governors depending on national and institutional contexts) but also all the other central organs of university government. These include the President, Rector or Vice-Chancellor and his/her senior management team, the Senate or Academic Board and the central administration. Not only is it necessary to adopt a wide rather than a narrow definition of 'governance' for reasons that have already been given; there are also a number of advantages.

- First, it more accurately reflects the real distribution of power and influence in universities. Governing bodies in a narrow sense often validate—and, therefore, legitimate—decisions taken elsewhere. This may be especially true with regard to the university's core academic functions; governing bodies may exercise greatest authority in other, arguably secondary or service, areas such as buildings and bud-

gets. Bagehot's celebrated dichotomy between the 'efficient' power of the government and the 'dignified' power of the monarch in Victorian Britain comes to mind;
- Second, it recognizes that 'governance' in universities is a highly distributed function. In practice it extends far beyond the formal (and legal) authority of governing bodies, beyond 'efficient' power of the senior management and administration, beyond even academic authority of the Senate or Academic Board. In universities, to a greater extent perhaps than in any other type of institution, real authority is exercised as the grass roots—by individual faculty and (in a more limited fashion) administrative staff members. Faculties, Schools and Departments are intermediate arenas in which the formal authority of the governing body, senior management, administration and academic governance must be reconciled with the informal influence of academic guilds;
- Third, it reduces the particularities of different types of higher education institution, which perhaps are at their greatest in terms of formal governance, and emphasises instead the similarities in how power and influence are exercised in different systems and institutions. Instead of concentrating on technical and legal differences, attention can be placed instead on a much broader typology of governance cultures. This typology will be explored later in this paper, but the distinctions it produces are fluid and permeable. Although diversity (arguably) is increasing in higher education, these new forms of differentiation are not aligned with traditional differences in governance. Indeed, some of the most important forms of differentiation are intra- rather than inter-institutional, which may produce greater convergence in terms of governance.

Of course, a wide definition of 'governance' does present certain difficulties. The most significant perhaps is that it tends to fudge the distinction between institutional and systemic governance. It can be argued that, having widened the circle to include senior managers and academic government, the circle should be widening still further to include supra-national and national agencies. This argument must be taken seriously, for two reasons. First, there are real difficulties of definition. For example, in Britain, the higher education funding councils look rather like statewide coordinating bodies in the United States; yet, the former pertain to national governance and the latter, arguably, to institutional governance. Second, governance is a holistic process, best understand by exploring the articulations between national, system or sector-wide, institutional and sub-institutional levels. To focus on the institutional level, as in this paper, offers an incomplete and even misleading picture.

In the rest of this chapter, four main topics will be explored:

- the reasons behind the increasing emphasis on governance
- models of universities as organizations
- different patterns of university governance – by national systems and types of institution
- reforms of university governance.

THE GROWING IMPORTANCE OF GOVERNANCE

There are many reasons for the increased attention now paid to university governance, some generic to all (or most) higher education institutions and systems; others which are particular to different classes of institution and national systems and/or are contingent on 'local' political circumstances.

The generic reasons include:

The Increasing Size of Universities and the Growing Complexity of their Missions

As a result of sustained expansion of student numbers over the past four decades universities have become much larger. Even in Britain, where because of the historical value placed on academic and pastoral intimacy institutions have traditional been smaller, the average size of a university is now 16,000 students. The increasing size of universities has stimulated the development of complex infrastructures, in terms of management information systems, student support services, new communications and learning technologies, maintenance of buildings and plant, and so on. At the same time, universities have taken on multiple missions often involving novel tasks. Better-articulated academic systems have had to be established to cater for new kinds of students on new kinds of academic programs. As a result of these quantitative and qualitative changes the manageability of universities has become a more important issue, which, in turn, has led to a greater emphasis being placed on governance. Reform has become ubiquitous (Kogan, M. & Hanney, S., 2000).

Flexibility and Responsiveness

The increasing importance of higher education in terms of the ambitions of many governments to increase participation and combat social exclusion and their aspirations to harness knowledge production to wealth creation in a highly competitive global environment has led to growing demands and pressure from 'external' stakeholders. As a result, concerns have been expressed about the capacity of universities, as currently managed and governed, to respond with sufficient vigor and speed to these new political agendas. In many cases, changes in governance, particularly strengthening the lay element, have been seen as one way to make higher education more adaptable.

The Erosion of Trust

Universities, like many other professional organizations which in the past enjoyed considerable autonomy, have suffered from the general decline in trust accorded to such organizations. The growing popularity of performance indicators, good practice guidelines and other evaluation mechanisms has contributed to the emergence of a so-called audit culture. This culture affects other professions such as the law and medicine as much as, or more than, higher education. Nor can universities any longer rely on old habits of deference. Student expansion has eroded the 'mystery' that once cloaked elite higher education. The cumulative effect of these changes is that, through their formal governance, institutions must reflect the increasing emphasis on accountability (to non-academic constituencies, whether political and 'market') and also that, through their governance in a wider sense, they must be able to develop the capacity to cope with the ever more insistent and ever more detailed demands for audit, assessment and evaluation.

The Re-Configuration of Budgets

Between 1945 and 1980, higher education became increasingly dependent on public expenditure for its core income. This was a global trend that affected all institutions and all systems regardless of their mix of public and private income. The fortunes of the university rose with the flourishing of the post-war welfare state. The growth of public support for higher education reflected both quantitative and qualitative shifts – student expansion (which would have been impossible without large-scale public investment) and the increasing subordination of more traditional academic purposes to new political agendas. More recently, two phenomena can be observed as the burden of public expenditure on higher education has increased. First, increasing – and, in some eyes, oppressive – emphasis has been placed on achieving efficiency gains, i.e. reductions in income-per-student, and guaranteeing value-for-money. Many governments have developed selective funding mechanisms and special initiatives to secure these objectives. As a result, the structures of university governance and management have had to be strengthened to secure their more efficient operation and to be able to demonstrate that efficiency to external scrutineers. Second, the undermining of the welfare state has demonstrated that there are limits to the expansion of public expenditure. As a result, universities have had to diversify their income sources. The need to generate more non-state income has underlined the need for reforms in governance to make universities more attractive to possible private founders.

The Re-Positioning of the University

Although the degree of autonomy that traditional universities had enjoyed can easily be exaggerated, the academic system was conceived of a discrete sub-system of society, which in important respects could be distinguished (and, therefore, was insulated) from other sub-systems, notably the market and politics. In this general sense, the university was regarded as an autonomous space, regardless of detailed constitutional, legal and administrative arrangements. This general condition no longer holds (except, possibly, in the case of a few elite institutions). The academic sub-system is no longer so clearly demarcated from other sub-systems. The university, although perhaps pre-eminent, is only one among a range of 'knowledge' institutions (with which it is often linked in partnerships and through networks). Science, scholarship and higher education are now highly distributed; traditional linear accounts of knowledge production have been challenged. The old (and perhaps inward) academic culture is being complemented—even eroded—by exposure to a new lifelong-learning environment. As a result the conception of the university as an autonomous space, and of science as an autonomous system, on which detailed arrangements for institutional autonomy ultimately depended, has been weakened. This shift has placed greater emphasis on governance – in the sense that it is the key brokerage mechanism between the university and its stake-holders, partners and rivals.

The Diversification of Higher Education Systems

A similar effect has been produced by the diversification of higher education systems far beyond a core of traditional (and often elite) universities. This diversification has taken different forms. In most of the United States, a strategy of stratification has been pursued in which different 'levels' of institution have been allocated different functions; in much of Europe 'binary' systems have been retained in which a (reasonably) clear demarcation has been maintained between universities and other institutions with a more precisely defined vocational mission (*Fachhochschulen*, *HBO* schools etc.); in a few countries, including Britain, unified systems have been created in which the category of 'university' has been expanded to include newer kinds of higher education institutions. But the general effects have been the same. First, higher education systems now include many institutions that have a strong tradition of engagement with, rather than autonomy from, the rest of society. Second, they have introduced new cultures of governance, which reflect that closer engagement (whether in populist/democratic or quasi-corporate terms).

The locally contingent reasons for the increasing emphasis on governance, inevitably and inherently, are more difficult to describe. But they include:

Delegation of Administrative Responsibilities

In several European countries during the past decade universities have been given greater responsibility for budget, personnel and property issues, which previously were entirely within the competence of the State. This delegation of administration has made it necessary to develop management systems, which, in turn, place greater emphasis on governance. This has been intensified by the encouragement universities have also received to use the greater freedom of organizational manoeuvre they now enjoy to pursue more entrepreneurial policies (which reflects the re-positioning of universities already discussed).

The Cult of Managerialism

The erosion of welfare-state social-democratic values has led to a growing emphasis on 'corporate culture'. Universities have been re-conceptualized as 'businesses', which, therefore, must be run on corporate lines. As a result, a new managerialist discourse has developed in which both traditional academic and public service values have little place (Pollitt, C., 1990) (Willmott, H., 1995). This shift, although superficial in the context of the deep value-structures of the university, has had a significant impact on the culture of governance. This trend perhaps is most marked in Britain, as an after-shock of Thatcherism.

Such influences, and others, have contributed to the growing importance attached to governance in higher education in a broad sense. But their impact on the separate strands of governance has been different. Although it is always dangerous to attempt to generalize across institutions, systems and nations, their general effects appear to have been to leave external, or lay, influence on university governance relatively unchanged (which is puzzling in the light of the re-positioning the university and diversification of higher education systems); to reduce the influence of the academic guild (although the power of professors as individual entrepreneurs has substantially increased); and to increase the influence of senior management and the administration. If this is correct, it suggests that the most powerful of these trends are the organizational complexity of higher education institutions, the re-configuration of budgets, and the growth of audit and evaluation systems. The other, apparently more fundamental, trends appear to be less significant. But this may be a question of time-scale. The current pattern of university governance, in which senior managers have certainly become more powerful, may reflect immediate pressures from the State, still higher education's predominant funder, for greater efficiency (the decline of the welfare state) and a more direct contribution to economic competitiveness (the knowledge society). In other words, the university has been re-engineered as the result of external imperatives. Future patterns of governance may reflect more radical and fundamental pressures produced by the re-visioning of the university, both in terms of wider social perceptions and institutional self-realization. In these circumstances both lay and academic elements in governance may be more powerfully re-asserted.

MODELS OF THE UNIVERSITY

The governance of universities cannot be divorced from their purposes, which are reflected in their institutional values and organizational structures. This paper is not intended to discuss the core purposes of higher education. However, it is important to recognize that in the highly volatile and unstructured environment that characterizes the new millennium (in the construction of private, social, economic and intellectual life), the university has a dual role. The first, which receives most emphasis, is to act as a (possibly the) leading institution within the emerging knowledge society—as a producer, and disseminator, of knowledge and of knowledgeable people. It is largely in this context that universities are valued by governments, employers and, of course, many of their student-customers. This is also the image that university leaders typically present—of the university as a dynamic and innovative institution. The second role, however, may be equally important: the university also has a responsibility to conserve, to protect, to discriminate and to criticize (in the best sense)—in short, to be an agent of stabilization in a highly unstable society. Much less attention is paid to this second role. Too often it is judged to be a conservative, even reactionary, project that harks back to some mythic 'golden time' of university freedom – but it too has been given urgency and relevance by the transgressive and pervasive characteristics of (post?) modern life.

It is in the context of this double mission of the university, to innovate and to stabilize, that the various organizational models (and ultimately, therefore, their patterns of governance) should be judged. Viewed from one perspective, the university is a corporate bureaucracy; from others, an academic guild—a 'donnish dominion' in the alliterative phrase of the British sociologist, A. H. Halsey (Halsey, A. H., 1992); from others again, a political organization. Several theoretical models have also been suggested:

The University as 'Organized Anarchy'

This model of the university is derived from a particular view of the nature of academic work (Cohen, M. & March, J., 1974). Because academic staff have a high degree of discretion over the tasks they perform, organizational goals are often unclear (or irrelevant?) and the 'fit' between people and structures is fairly loose. This tension between individual aspirations and corporate goals is reduced by a high degree of participation in decision-making. In effect, goals are subordinated to aspirations or are simply defined in terms of the aggregation of individual aspirations. This is not as conservative as it sounds, because such aspirations are shaped by institutional environments and cultures and because they are often highly innovative. Nor has this model necessarily been superseded by newer and more dynamic models. It is still a fair description of how elite universities are managed and governed, and even in apparently more managed institutions key academic decisions remain highly devolved and often impervious to managerial intervention. In Britain, for example, the apparatus of examination boards and external examiners sustains a high degree of delegation. In this model of the university, there are significant implications for governance; the most important perhaps is the legitimization of a division of labor between lay influence and academic discretion, which has been institutionalized in the bi-cameral government of university council/governing body and academic board/Senate.

The University as a Cybernetic System

According to a second organizational model, the university is best regarded as a cybernetic system (Morgan, G., 1986) (Birnbaum, R., 1986). It is a flexible, adaptable and resilient institution with a formidable capacity for self-organization in the face of changes in its external environment. In this model, the emphasis is placed on the creative interaction between different elements, and levels, within the university rather than on the tension between individual and corporate goals. The processes, structures and systems by which the university is managed and governed assume great importance – because they embody its capacity for self-organization. They also enable the institution as a whole to 'learn' from its external environment. A variant of this model is relevant to the early discussion of declining trust and the rise of an accountability culture. An alternative way to view these changes is as an internalization of audit, the development of habits of self-evaluation and self-correction, which are essential for successful self-organization. The combination of peer-review with more formal systems of research assessment and quality assurance may be an example of how higher education (as a system but also as institutions) responds to external demands and 'learns' from their experience. Certainly these systems, initially regarded as intrusive, are quickly internalized. If this organizational model of the university is accepted, the implications for its governance are that the aim should be a balanced constitution – an integrated effort by lay members, academic staff and senior managers, rather than a division of function (and territory) as implied by the first model.

The Entrepreneurial University

In this third organizational model, the university is seen as a 'trading' institution which engages in a wide variety of exchanges – with the State and other funding agencies, with its students, with employers of graduates and users of research and, wider still, with society, culture and the economy. In terms of its management and governance, therefore, the university must move beyond self-organization. Instead it must focus on links with the external environment—identifying new partners and markets, developing trading relationships and competing in the academic market place. This external orientation may lead to tension not only with the academic guild but also with the administrative bureaucracy, partly because there may be value-conflicts but partly because speedy decision-making assumes greater importance. The focus shifts to re-engineering the university. According to this model, the role of governance is to change the internal culture to make the university more competitive in the market place. This implies that the lay members and senior managers, the first group because they represent external constituencies (and so potential trading partners and/or rivals) and the second group because they have change-management skills, should have the preponderant voice with the academic guild relegated to a subordinate, or even oppositional role.

In practice, real-world universities have elements of all three models—organized anarchy ('donnish dominion'), cybernetic system (self-organization) and entrepreneurial institution (academic market-place). How these elements are combined, and in what proportions, are influenced by the characteristics of the higher education systems of which they are part and their status, or level, within these systems. Elite institutions are thought to be closest to the first model – but several have successfully demonstrated their capacity for entrepreneurship, as Burton Clark has argued (Clark, B., 1998). Similarly, newer kinds of universities, characterized by apparently more managerial cultures, are thought to be closest to the entrepreneurial model – but, again, this may underestimate the looseness of the 'fit' between the priorities of academic staff and corporate goals (and their capacity to pursue these priorities within the extensive territory of delegated powers). It is perhaps more accurate to see these models as relevant not to whole institutions but to separate units within them. Disciplinary and professional cultures are also highly influential because often they have the first, and most powerful, call on the loyalty of academic staff. Inner-directed 'donnish' values often co-exist in close proximity to outer-directed entrepreneurial behavior. This highly differentiated pattern presents particular difficulties in the context of governance. Governance pertains to whole institutions, and the scope for differentiating it to match institutional diversity is limited. The three organizational models of 'donnish dominion', self-organization and academic market place, therefore, may still be useful in shaping discussions of the role of governance in higher education.

PATTERNS OF GOVERNANCE IN HIGHER EDUCATION

The historical evolution of university governance has produced five main types. These are (i) academic self-government (Oxford and Cambridge with their absence of effective, or any, lay participation in their government are good examples); (ii) lay trusteeship, which is typical of private universities and colleges in the United States; (iii) coalitions of lay and academic members, or 'balanced constitutions' in which spheres of influence are clearly demarcated; (iv) political patronage—of which the regents of state-wide systems or state-appointed members of boards of control may be examples; (v) state bureaucracy, in which universities are embraced within the administrative apparatus of the state (continental Europe provides the best examples of this type).

Academic Self-Government

This is still regarded by many people in universities, sentimentally perhaps, as the ideal type. But since the waning of the Middle Ages, few universities have conformed to it. Even Oxford and Cambridge, although still organized as academic guilds, do not conform to this type in all respects. On three occasions in the nineteenth century, Parliament intervened to re-order their governance, and in the twentieth century they have become subject to virtually the same degree of regulation as other British universities. However, it would be misleading to regard academic self-government as an anachronism. Although it is no longer current at institutional level, it is still pervasive at sub-institutional level. In many universities, faculties and departments are organized according to its principles. There is little lay involvement, except in an advisory capacity or in professional arenas where issues of recognition and accreditation arise. The influence of senior managers may also be limited, partly because they share the commitment to academic self-government and partly because they lack the appropriate expertise. To the extent that the real governance of universities takes place at these intermediate levels, academic self-government is far from moribund. It is a formidable influence, even in institutions that ostensibly conform to other types of governance.

Lay Trusteeship

Many private American colleges and universities are the product of the 'civil society' that De Tocqueville so much admired in the first half of the nineteenth century. They are embraced within a larger tradition of philanthropy, both religious and secular. As a result, their formal governance remains in the hands of lay trustees, who see it as their responsibility to maintain the ethos and tradition of the institutions they govern. This sense of responsibility is heightened by the fact that many are also alumni/ae. Although generalizations are dangerous, lay trusteeship in many cases is interpreted as fiduciary duty rather than as a strategic responsibility. In this respect it may share some of the conservative traits of academic self-government, but without the internal dynamic of a progressive research culture. Their job is to conserve, not to innovate. Conservation, of course, can be expensive; trustees are sometimes expected to be major donors or to act as social and cultural intermediaries through which donations can be obtained. But, in other respects, institutional development is regarded as the responsibility of the president and administration. The successful president who enjoys the confidence of his/her trustees is in a powerful position.

Lay-Academic Coalitions

Some universities are governed by coalitions of lay and academic members. Typically, they have large governing bodies (or councils) on which both groups are well represented. The so-called civic universities established in Britain during the Victorian period are good examples. Initially, lay governors were the dominant group because they represented the civic and business elites that had been prominent in the foundation of such universities. But, as these universities became more dependent on state support, their influence waned. In the third quarter of the present century, academic governors were in the ascendant. Their influence was compounded by the effective delegation of key academic decisions to Senates (or Academic Boards). In effect, a bicameral pattern of governance emerged. More recently, senior managers have become more powerful, but the size and heterogeneity of governing bodies restricts their room for manoeuvre and the maturity of many of these universities obliges managers to operate in harmony with the values of the academic guild (of which they are members—in contrast to the sharper demarcation between faculty and administration in many American institutions).

Political Patronage

The governance of many American state universities and colleges is shaped by political patronage. Members are appointed by the Governor, with or without the involvement of the legislature. However, appointments may be made for lengthy terms to muffle the impact of short-term political change. In the case of statewide systems, governance may be undertaken by coordinating boards (although it may not be correct to include these boards in a discussion of institutional governance); multi-campus institutions are often governed by boards of regents; in the case of individual universities, responsibility rests with a board of control (in all three cases the nomenclature may vary). The degree of politicization is less than might be expected. Many appointees regard themselves as the peers of the politicians who appoint them and not as their delegates; for example, they may have major donors to political campaigns (and see appointment to boards as a pay-back, which raises another set of difficult issues). Also, there are examples of political appointees going 'native' and defending their universities against illegitimate political interference. The influence of the faculty in institutional governance varies according to the prestige of their institutions; in major research universities, it is likely to be considerable. But, partly because these universities operate in a political environment and partly because they are typically large and complex institutions, the driving force is often provided by presidents and their administrations.

State Bureaucracy

In most of Europe, universities are—formally—part of state bureaucracies. But it would be highly misleading to suggest that, as a result, they are subordinated to political agendas. The reverse may possibly be true—that what may be termed 'civil service' universities enjoy greater freedom of manoeuvre than autonomous institutions, whether in the public or private sectors. First, their connection to the State is through its administrative apparatus and not its political processes. Second, senior academics (notably professors) enjoy a high degree of job protection as state officials—even if, in isolated instances, they have also been subject to civil-service rules irksome to the exercise of academic freedom. Third, governance at the institutional level has remained comparatively weak, because key management functions have remained within the competence of the state. University boards and councils have often been highly politicized arenas, because of the high degree of state-mandated representation on such bodies. Almost invariably, rectors have been drawn from the professorate (usually within the same university). However, the ebbing of the welfare-state tide has left 'civil service' universities more vulnerable because, until recently, they lacked the entrepreneurial systems to respond to new challenges. As a result, the links between universities and the state have been loosened and more robust patterns of institutional governance and management are emerging.

These five types of university governance cover public and not-for-profit private institutions. However, in recent years, a number of corporate 'universities' have been formed. These vary greatly in scale and substance. Some, such as the British Aerospace Virtual University, amount to little more than a re-branding of existing corporate training and research and development activities (much of which may already be out-sourced to, or provided in partnership with, existing universities). Others, such as Phoenix University, are real attempts to compete—and compete profitably—with existing institutions. The extent to which the corporate sector will develop is still unclear.

The multinational mass-media corporations have yet to show their hand (Committee of Vice-Chancellors and Principals, 2000).

However, despite these differences and this doubt, the governance of these new institutions has little in common with any of the traditional types of university governance described above. Instead, they conform closely to patterns of corporate governance. In the case of in-company universities, they are 'governed' by appropriate line-managers. Other forms of scrutiny, whether by share-holders or supervisory boards, which could be said to approximate to what is meant by 'governance' in higher education, are vestigial or absent entirely. It is worth noting that corporate governance varies almost as much as university governance. In some countries, power is concentrated in the hands of the chief executive, a role that is often combined with that of the chairman of the board; in others, the two are kept firmly distinct; in others again, two-tier structures of supervisory and management boards are common.

However, it would be wrong to exaggerate the differences between governance cultures, particularly among the five main types outlined above and arguably even between public and not-for-profit private institutions on the one hand and corporate 'universities' on the other. First, although the formal differences appear to be substantial between, for example, academic self-government and lay trusteeship, the actual balance of power in Cambridge (England) and Cambridge (Massachusetts) is probably broadly similar. 'Civic' universities in Britain, land-grant universities in the United States and 'civil service' universities in continental Europe, too, have a great deal in common in their value structures and organizational cultures, despite their very different patterns of governance. Second, all higher education systems and institutions are subject to similar imperatives, whether threats or opportunities. All are expected to play their part in the completion of educational revolutions that have made participation in higher education close to a civic right or democratic entitlement; all are also expected to make a key contribution to the development of a knowledge-based economy; all are expected to conform to a wide range of requirements concerning organizational probity (for example, in employee relations, health and safety, value-for-money audits and many more). For both reasons—the convergence of actual and informal patterns of governance, and the commonality of external expectations of higher education—it would be a mistake to emphasize the technical differences in governance at the expense of the similarities and synergies.

CONCLUSIONS – REFORMING UNIVERSITY GOVERNANCE

Two, apparently contradictory, forces appear to be shaping institutional governance. The first is the need to centralize, to act corporately. The second is the desirability of de-centralization, the urge to empower potential innovators. The tendency to centralize, in turn, has two main components. The first is that institutional identity must now be more strongly reasserted as the competition between universities, both within and between countries, has intensified. Global competition for world-class researchers or international students is a pervasive phenomenon, which is only marginally mitigated by growing collaboration between institutions across national frontiers. But competition within systems is also increasing in many countries, as once-rigid binary systems are softened or abandoned and even firmly stratified structures are eroded. Nor can these tendencies be reduced to 'upward' academic drift as mass institutions aspire to the status (and resources) of elite universities; there are also examples of 'downwards' drift as elite universities engage in new forms of academic outreach. Competition, therefore, is now multi-dimensional. In this new and less stable environment, universities must develop stronger institutional personalities, or identities. External factors have accelerated and exacerbated this tendency, such as the febrile condition of post-modern politics, with its near-instantaneous success or failure, and the ephemerality and volatility, but also the intensity, of life-style consumerism. Universities now have to be their own persuaders. They can no longer rely on a culture of deference or elite connections to make their case.

The second component of the drive towards greater centralization is the rising tide of regulation to ensure that academic quality can be formally assured (and, in the process, appropriate benchmark and comparative information made available to academic 'consumers' whether students or research users), to guarantee value for money (especially when the money is provided by taxpayers), to police compliance with a host of regulations concerning employee rights, health and safety and so on. The so-called audit culture is now firmly established in many countries. Of course, there is a close, even symbiotic, relationship between competition on the one hand and regulation on the other. The two trends are awkward allies, not opposing forces. As a result, two particular aspects of institutional governance have gained new prominence. The first is marketing and customer care. Universities now have much increased 'sales' budgets; the management of 'reputation' has become a key corporate responsibility; and governing bodies too pay growing attention to how their institutions are 'positioned'. Indeed, the development of core strategies is often heavily influenced by, and even derived from such activities, which some argue is the wrong way round. Mission statements, for example, straddle these two worlds of strategy and marketing. The second aspect of institutional governance that has become more prominent is its increasing subordination to new regulatory regimes, which differ significantly from the planning regimes of the past. Governing bodies and senior managers are becoming prisoners of a compliance culture in which reporting requirements are proliferating and evaluation mechanisms become more intrusive. Governance is one of the most important means by which these external messages, and demands, can be communicated to broader academic communities and by which institutions can answer back, either through compliance or critique.

However, the pressures to decentralize are also increasing. It is now increasingly recognized that the managers of basic units (deans of faculties, heads of academic departments and directors of research centers) must be given appropriate incentives both to operate more efficiently to reduce costs and to behave more entrepreneurially in order to stimulate greater innovation. To become more responsive, therefore, institutions must devolve responsibility from central bureaucracies, arguably slow moving, to these allegedly fleet-footed basic units. Budgets are delegated, with surpluses being available for local reinvestment. Corporate rules and requirements provide a framework within which local variation is permitted. As a result, the balance of institutional governance has changed. Not only must members of governing bodies (and senior managers) be 'brand' managers and compliance-enforcers, they must also become facilitators of innovation. They must develop new capacities to assess and to manage risk, without inhibiting enterprise. Governance, in one sense, becomes a 'service' function—in addition to its more traditional responsibilities. This view of governance is at odds with an alternative conception, so-called corporate governance, which is increasingly popular, for example, in the National Health Service in Britain. According to this conception, governance is a dominant, even totalizing, enterprise, which makes use of performance indicators, guidance and protocols of good practice, benchmarking and the rest to reduce the autonomous spaces occupied by professions such as medicine or the law (or higher education?).

It is not easy to move beyond this broad description of the re-balancing of institutional governance to detailed recommendations for reforming existing patterns and structures. But perhaps an important change is a shift from emphasizing governance's contribution to the management of change to its responsibility for changing institutional cultures. Although control systems will continue to be important (not least to satisfy compliance demands and to maximize the resources available to support innovation), governance may also recover a more symbolic role—not, of course, in a static and traditional sense, but in more dynamic and innovative terms. To be able to discharge this new kind of cultural role, institutional governance must be open and transparent. If it is to help establish 'identity', it must take place largely in a public arena.

Whatever the drawbacks of openness and transparency in the context of control management, 'identity' and 'ownership' cannot be achieved behind closed doors. Changing the culture can only happen if a new consensus about values (and, subsequently, about management) is established. This requires debate, dissent and even dissonance.

Changing the culture is not enough. It must be translated into strategy. Institutional governance has a key role to play here – but, to be effective, it must be seen as a pluralistic arena in which the views of lay members of governing bodies, senior academic and administrative management and academic government are all heard. Rather than seeing governance as a layered and hierarchical system, it is better seen as a negotiation, or even a conversation, through which new values and perspectives are generated. The temptation to streamline, to exclude, to reduce—although readily comprehensible in the context of the growing complexity—should be resisted. If the aim is to produce new 'identities', and strategies, owned rather than imposed change, such an approach is likely to be dysfunctional. Finally, of course, institutional governance must still be arranged in a way that its control and management responsibilities can still be effectively discharged. Although this last task appears to be difficult to discharge because 'control' governance is in conflict with 'cultural' governance, this apparent conflict is less if a broad and pluralistic definition of governance is adopted.

There has only been space in this chapter to discuss the wider context in which higher education governance is situated and to sketch the principles and broad characteristics of a new form of governance. Two important gaps have been left. First, a detailed and pragmatic examination of institutional governance has not been attempted. For example, the impact of new information systems on governance has not been explored – but it is likely to be fundamental. Management information no longer has to rationed; instead it can be widely distributed. In that sense it tends to distribute decision-making power and to make governance an even more diffuse (and difficult) process. On the other hand, management information systems encourage the standardization of processes (and relationships), out of which new accounts of institutional purpose and mission may be constructed. Once, it was cynically said that universities were organisations held together by a common grievance over car parking; under contemporary conditions they may be held together by management information systems. Second, this chapter has concentrated exclusively on governance at the institutional level. But, at every turn, the inadequacy and artificiality of the distinction between systemic and institutional (and, maybe, sub-institutional) forms of governance have been exposed. My emphasis on governance as a pluralistic arena with (fairly) open frontiers makes my concentration on the institutional level even less defensible. Governance must be explored through the complex articulations between different levels not by concentrating on arbitrary sub-divisions; indeed, the new meanings attached to the word, and the idea, consist largely in these articulations.

REFERENCES

Bargh, C. & Scott, P. & Smith, D. (1996). *Governing Universities: Changing the Culture?*, Open University Press, Buckingham.

Beck, U. (1992). *Risk Society: Towards a New Modernity*, Sage, London.

Birnbaum, R. (1986). "The cybernetic institution: towards an integration of governance theories", *Higher Education Quarterly*, Vol. 18, pp. 239-253.

Clark, B. (1998). *Creating Entrepreneurial Universities*, Pergamon, Oxford.

Cohen, M. & March, J. (1974). *Leadership and Ambiguity: the American College President*, McGraw-Hill, New York.

Committee of Vice-Chancellors and Principals (2000). *The Business of Borderless Education*, CVCP, London.

Gibbons, M. & Limoges, C. & Nowotny, H. & Schwartzman, S. & Scott, P. & Trow, M. (1994). *The New Production of Knowledge: The Dynamics of Science and Research in Contemporary Societies*, Sage, London.

Halsey, A. H. (1992). *Decline of Donnish Dominion*, Clarendon Press, Oxford.

Kogan, M. & Hanney, S. (2000). *Reforming Higher Education*, Jessica Kingsley, London.

Morgan, G. (1986). *Images of Organization*, Sage, London.

Nowotny, H. & Scott, P. & Gibbons, M. (2001). *Re-Thinking Science: Knowledge and the Public in an Age of Uncertainty*, Polity Press, Oxford.

Pollitt, C. (1990). *Managerialism in the Public Sector*, Blackwell, Oxford.

Scott, P. (1995). *The Meanings of Mass Higher Education*, Open University Press, Buckingham.

Shore, C. & Wright, S. (2000). "Coercive Accountability: the rise of audit culture in higher education", in Strathern, M. (ed.), *Audit Cultures*, Routledge, London.

Willmott, H. (1995). "Managing the Academics: commodification and control in the development of university education in the UK", *Human Relations*, Vol. 48, pp. 993-1027.

CHAPTER 10

Initiatives for Improving Shared Governance

Werner Z. Hirsch

INTRODUCTION

"If men were angels, no government would be necessary. If angels were to govern men, neither external nor internal controls on the government would be necessary. In framing a government... the great difficulty lies in this: you must first enable [it] ...to control itself. A dependence on the people is, no doubt, the primary control on the government; but experience has taught mankind the necessity of auxiliary precautions.
This policy of supplying, by opposite and rival interest, the defect of better motives, might be traced through the whole system of human affairs, private as well as public. We see it particularly displayed in all the subordinate distributions of power, where the constant aim is to divide and arrange the several offices in such a manner as that each may be a check on the other".

James Madison, *The Federalist*

These ideas are relevant today, to some extent, even in the governance of universities, which in America is carried out in rather complex ways by three major stakeholders – governing boards, administration and faculty (the latter usually organized into a Senate). The three are partners in the university's system of shared governance. Ideally, their rights and duties should reflect their specific responsibilities, competence and experience as well as commitment and devotion to the university. Mainly implicit, rather than explicit, contracts within a system of shared governance determine the relations among its stakeholders.

This paper explores some current and future developments that can impact on the governance of universities, especially shared governance of research universities. The uniqueness of universities is explored, together with the question why and how shared governance is responsive to these unique characteristics. Next, weak elements in today's system of shared governance are identified, followed by an exploration of possible remedies.

DEVELOPMENTS CONFRONTING SHARED GOVERNANCE OF THE RESEARCH UNIVERSITY

While we are living in a world that, according to William Carlos Williams, is typified by "the rare occurrence of the expected", we can point to some present and near term circumstances, which bear on the governance of universities.

Society demands that universities educate ever larger numbers of students; provide lifetime learning opportunities as life expectancy lengthens; continue to be leaders in research, especially fundamental research; and provide public service. Even as college age students are increasing in numbers, Americans continue to be committed to providing all those with the potential to benefit from education with access to it, regardless of their financial circumstances. While the demands made on universities have been on the rise, financial support for public institutions is inadequate to their task, for at least two main reasons – society's reluctance to fund a public good whose cost is immediate while its benefits are speculative and delayed, and society's unease about academics because of perceived arrogance and irrelevance of some of their work, as well as universities' managerial backwardness and inefficiency.

Superimposed on these developments are the explosion of knowledge creation, especially at the boundaries of disciplines, and the information-communication cyberspace revolution, both of which promise to accelerate in the future.

New knowledge is created at an amazing pace and often in altogether new academic fields, usually aided by powerful new concepts; much of it requires extremely costly instrumentation. More and more inventions are made and their half-lives are becoming shorter and shorter. Under these circumstances, research universities particularly are facing the challenge of attracting and keeping the very best faculty, raising large amounts of capital for their support, and facilitating their teaming up with members in other disciplines and other universities as well as industry. Departments, schools, and the entire university must become increasingly flexible and adaptive, so that they can excel in the education of their students and in the research quality of their faculty. However, though the creation of new knowledge has many salubrious effects, it can create governance problems. For example, as new scientific knowledge increases life expectancy, including that of tenured faculty, staffing flexibility will decline.

Thus, research universities in particular are shedding their cloistered existence and are dismantling walls, both those that in the past have existed within their confines and those to the outside world. Inside the university, many disciplines are losing some of their distinctive boundaries, which before were seldom transgressed. As a consequence, the old building blocks of universities, i.e., departments with uni-disciplinary courses, are increasingly supplemented, and sometimes even replaced, by new academic units, which allow the easy crossing of disciplinary boundaries. Thus, the structure of the research university is undergoing significant change, while becoming increasingly complex.

At the same time, boundaries of research universities have been forced open to the outside world—many of the best scientists and engineers actively cooperate with high-tech industry. Commitment of time and energy as well as devotion and loyalty to the university have been declining, while dual loyalty is on the increase, and with it come serious conflicts and governance challenges. Universities, thus, must find new ways to assure their academic integrity.

The rapid creation of new knowledge in a society of increasing life expectancy also confronts universities with the challenge of opening their gates to students of all ages and offering them opportunities for lifelong learning.

A second major development with defining implications for shared governance in universities is the information-communication cyberspace revolution. Governance structure and process are profoundly affected by this revolution, which in some respects resembles Gutenberg's invention of the printing press in the 15th century; it widened access to information and, in doing so, loosened central control. The cyberspace revolution goes a lot further in terms of speed, reach and universality in disseminating information; networks are emerging all over the world, replacing hierarchical organizations (many of which in the past benefited from withholding information) by significantly flatter ones. One result is what is at times referred to as Instant Infinite Partnering. At the same time, the half-life of many new inventions, especially in the cyberspace area, is becoming shorter and shorter.

For universities the implications are major. As time and distance are receding in importance, exchanges of information and ideas can be virtually instantaneous to any location in the world, while not requiring the physical presence of any participants at a particular location. In an age of Instant Infinite Partnering, globalization of the knowledge industry will march forward, not only producing and imparting knowledge, but also applying and exploiting it all over the world. With Instant Infinitive Partnering, hierarchical governance and management structures of the university are making room for increasingly horizontal ones. Rather than being withheld, information will become universally available, affecting in a major way research and teaching, as well as the structure of the university. Governing and managing the university will have to adjust itself. In relation to the former, new powerful computational techniques are becoming available. In relation to the latter, universities can become more sophisticated in distance teaching, particularly of undergraduates and professionals, as well as in support of lifelong learning; they can also improve their administrative and housekeeping functions. With relevant information available in a timely manner not only to the three stakeholders, but also to government, students and the public, governance becomes more transparent. While posing increasingly complex challenges to the system of shared governance, opportunities are enhanced for universities to provide quality education and to engage in research of high quality.

UNIQUENESS IN THE GOVERNANCE OF THE MODERN UNIVERSITY

Governance of universities differs from that of other institutions. It is very different, for example, from that of the military, which within its hierarchical structure has lower levels in the establishment taking orders from higher ones; moreover, a carefully crafted governing process exists to enforce orders. Universities with their democratic, egalitarian culture have a more horizontal organizational structure, so essential to fostering individual initiative, creativity and excellence and with it great teaching and research. In line with these objectives, universities have long realized that their greatness depends on the distinction of their faculty, which in turn attracts high quality students, worldwide recognition and funding. Thus, the attraction and retention of world-class faculty are an overarching goal, whose attainment is threatened by faculty "voting with their feet." (Tiebout, C. M., October 1956) Faculty goes elsewhere, and thereby deprives the university of their services and the value of their reputation, when decisions taken by the university are sufficiently detrimental to their interest. Specifically, this comes about when the gain of being associated with another institution promises to be greater than the costs of making the move. Presidents, who in this paper also mean chancellors, rectors, vice chancellors and even deans, make similar trade-off decisions.

The university's three major stakeholders can be looked upon as seeking rents, some of which are tangible while others are intangible. These rents have two major sources—power, which by law and precedent is given in decreasing order to governing boards, administration and faculty; and information, which at present is asymmetrically available to the three stakeholders. Governance systems in general specify, in mainly incomplete contracts, who has the right to make what decisions, by what procedures and under what circumstances.

It is not surprising that in the post-World War II era, a particular form of university governance, i.e., shared governance, has become common. It was given a boost by a 1966 statement of the American Association of University Professors, laying out the roles that trustees, administrations and faculty should play in their shared responsibility and cooperative action (American Association of University Professors, 1966). Ideally, shared governance in universities assigns specific rights and responsibilities to its three stakeholders i.e., provides for a separation of powers, and establishes a structure and process for stakeholders to interact in specific undertakings. To carry out their duties responsibly, implicit contracts provide administration and faculty with monetary as well as intangible incentives. Board members, however, are awarded only intangible ones, mainly in the form of prestige and recognition.

Even the more circumspect separation of powers under shared university governance can have a salubrious effect, which depends particularly on:

- rationale and practice of the assignment of specific rights and responsibilities to each of the three stakeholders, including the right to set the agenda,
- effectiveness of the organizational structure of each stakeholder,
- effectiveness of the governance structure and process that link the three stakeholders and facilitates matters to be brought to timely and mutually satisfactory closure,
- extent to which cogent information is shared with all stakeholders and their capability to make effective use of it,
- flexibility of adapting to changing conditions, and
- degree to which creative, confident and mutually respectful interaction exists between the different stakeholders.

To the extent that these preconditions are met, separation of powers under shared governance, even in a diluted form, can lead to heightened faculty loyalty and commitment to the university as well as to accountability. Efficiency is fostered if the subsidiarity principle is respected, i.e., decisions are made at the lowest possible level that has the required competence.

WEAK ELEMENTS OF UNIVERSITY GOVERNANCE

Although American research universities are the envy of many countries, their governance, both structure and process, is often found wanting. And as the new millennium unfolds, rapidly changing conditions will confront universities and exacerbate their problems. Thus, a critical review of shared governance, in the light of future changes in the environment likely to face universities, is urgent and timely.

Let us begin by reminding ourselves of the role, competence and present status of the three stakeholders who are partners in shared university governance.

Clearly, policy formulation, oversight and top level appointments are the domains of governing boards, which, except for their fiduciary responsibility, can be said to lack formal accountability. Moreover, instead of concentrating on policymaking and oversight, they often tend to micro-manage, and have little contact with faculty who, however, are ultimately responsible for implementing the university's mission.

The president and the administration, who occupy a place in the governance system between board and faculty, provide the board with information needed for oversight and development of policies; translating policies into programmatic initiatives, a function which must be carried out in close cooperation with faculty; and ensuring that agreed upon initiatives are effectively brought to timely fruition. In a sense, the ultimate role of presidents is to facilitate productive work by faculty and to make sure that students are given a quality education.

The effectiveness of presidents is often severely constrained by the fact that so many faculty members have tenure and thus only limited incentives to cooperate with the administration. In public institutions, with state funding having drastically declined, presidents as well as deans have been spending much of their time (in some cases up to half of their time) on raising funds from private sources (Hirsch, W. Z., 1999). It is often said that different skills are needed to stimulate gift giving than to lead an academic institution. Moreover, gifts today become available on a selective basis —mostly for medicine, engineering and the physical and biological sciences, and little for the humanities and the arts. The result can be fearful intellectual imbalance. Raising of private funds and their investing as well as the emergence of a host of university-high-tech industry alliances pose great challenges to presidents and the academic integrity of their institutions.

Finally, all too many presidents have developed an "add-on-culture". While business has pursued a downsizing and slimming-down policy, universities appear to continually add on functions, many only marginally related to their teaching and research mission. (By the way, this add-on culture is not unique to American higher education. When in a discussion with the president of Tokyo University, I asked whether he had recently added new departments and programs, he proudly answered in the affirmative. But when I went on to ask whether any had been phased out, after a long hesitation he said such steps, to the best of his knowledge, had never been taken.) Many universities own a host of large business enterprises, including fleets of busses and cars, huge amounts of real estate, insurance companies, stores, hotels and restaurants. (As a consequence, for example, some of the University of California campuses spend about half of their operating budgets on activities other than teaching and research). Not only is the time of presidents taken away from guiding the academic enterprise, but the large-scale influx of high-level business managers into the administration, holding vice president, vice chancellor or director titles, and the infusion of their business ethos can conflict with the ethos of academia.

Faculty by training and expertise holds a unique position. It is the sole body with teaching and research competence, which are needed for decisions about academic matters. These include hiring and promoting of faculty, as well as determining entrance and graduation requirements of students and their curriculum. Faculty are the ones who carry out the mission of the university—teaching, research and public knowledge. And yet in governance matters, faculty, organized into an academic senate (or similar institutions) with a host of committee and/or councils, are often the stakeholder who fights for maintaining the *status quo*. A consequence is often a conservative senate of great complexity whose structure and process usually are incorporated into a series of formal rules and by-laws.

In the recent past, Senates in many research universities have been suffering from a declining faculty interest in governance matters, a cumbersome internal governance structure and process and, all too often, an unrealistic view of their rights and obligations. Should the waning interest become a trend, the influence of senates in a system of shared governance would tend to erode.

INITIATIVES

Shared governance has served America's Higher Education well in the postwar era. Clearly there have been ups and downs, and today's complaints deserve to be carefully evaluated and remedial steps explored by taking into account changes that can be expected to occur in universities. Increasingly, as was argued earlier, they will have to respond to the information-communication cyberspace revolution, explosion of knowledge, their own internal and external permeability, and society's insistence on greater accountability, transparency and efficiency. When searching for governance initiatives that deserve exploration, our strategy can resemble that of engineers charged with strengthening a bridge across a major river. They must look at the condition of the bridge itself, as well as at the towers on the two sides of the river that support the bridge. The same holds true with regard to shared governance. Therefore, there is need for initiatives that strengthen each of the three stakeholders' capability to play an effective role in shared governance as well as strengthen the interface among stakeholders.

Exploration of remedial initiatives must be sensitive to the university's existing circumstances, including its system of governance; to its prevailing culture, tradition, and ethos; and to the likelihood that if it were alone to introduce a major drastic change in shared governance (for example, abolition of tenure), a wholesale exodus of top faculty might occur. Therefore, change has to be evolutionary rather than revolutionary and the result of close cooperation between the stakeholders.

Governing Boards

Boards have been accused of lacking formalized accountability except in their fiduciary responsibilities; of aloofness that, in the eyes of many faculty members and students, borders on that of the Supreme Court; and in engaging too often in micro-management rather than in policy making (Fishman, B., March 2, 2000).

Initiatives for increased accountability, however, must neither deter able, knowledgeable and committed citizens to join boards nor become a straitjacket that prevents them from acting decisively. While it would be inappropriate to review individual board members, it might be helpful to constitute visiting committees that periodically, for example every 5-8 years, spend one or two days with the board to discuss the making of major recent policy decisions, etc. Such committees could be assembled by the National Academy of Science and be assisted by the Association of Governing Boards. They could include former board members, presidents and one or two faculty members of the same institution. Findings would not necessarily be made public.

In order for boards' time not to be monopolized by mainly ministerial concerns, but rather be devoted to policy issues, boards might set aside annually two meetings which are devoted exclusively to policy matters. While the power to appoint board members is important, and especially for public universities, the board's composition is also significant. Governance is more effective if the president serves a full-fledged board member, thereby contributing to the informed cooperation between board and president. Consequently, the president can feel free to consult informally ahead of board meetings with other board members on path-breaking and controversial matters. Moreover, since the board appoints the president as its chosen and publicly designated agent in whom it has vested confidence, and to whom it has delegated authority to administer the university, the president should be able to expect that carefully developed recommendations will be supported, or if not, then for reasons grounded in the merits of the proposal rather than in its politics or other extraneous considerations.

Likewise, governance is more effective when the senate chair, and perhaps also vice chair, are voting board members. Both of these appointments can facilitate information flow to the senate and also increase the legitimacy and acceptability of board decisions. Turning to interaction between boards and the other stake holders, the AGB Statement on Institution Governance can form the basic guidelines. Accordingly, boards should seek to reach consensus, and toward this end should recognize that institutional consensus is more likely when all parties have agreed on process and criteria (Association of Governing Boards of Universities and Colleges, November 8, 1998). Therefore, it would be helpful for boards to schedule periodic meeting with senate leaders. Presidents should be present in such meetings. However, at no time should individual faculty members or students given access to board members. It could be looked upon as going over the head of the president and can be counterproductive.

Administration

The administration's foremost competence relates to providing the board with information necessary for carrying out its responsibilities, implementing board directives, facilitating productive work by faculty and assuring that students gain a first-rate education. The effectiveness of presidents often is constrained by faculty's tenure, particularly as the proportion of tenured faculty continues to increase with lengthening life expectancy. Moreover, in many universities, especially large public research universities, presidents' academic responsibilities are severely impacted by ever increasing workloads, complexity of problems, and all too often archaic governance processes and management practices.

In response to these circumstances, the first challenge is to find ways to lighten the burden of presidents and other high level administrators. Note that today presidents are forced to spend more and more time and effort on private fund-raising and on managing ever more and ever larger business enterprises. While universities have no alternative but to seek private gifts, they could significantly reduce the scope and functions of in-house business-type enterprises. Year by year, presidents who often lack much training and expertise, have assumed increasing responsibilities (admittedly voluntarily), for a large variety of business-type functions. Reducing the number and scope of business-type services and out-sourcing others has great merit, though the latter step might have to be undertaken in the face of union opposition.

University administrations also can benefit from the introduction of more powerful information systems which can provide enhanced transparency of their decisions and activities. One such system, in use already in a few universities, is Responsibility Center Management that is output-oriented and facilitates the making of informed transparent trade-offs. Admittedly the installation of a sophisticated computerized information system can be a double-edged sword. It can provide the three stakeholders and, to some extent, staff, students, alumni and the population at large with timely and easily accessible cogent information. As a consequence, the power that, as Machiavelli has pointed out, goes with being in possession of information becomes more equally distributed throughout the university. As decisions become more transparent, however, presiding over a university with shared governance can become more difficult.

The unique competence of faculty is its teaching and research and thus mainly relates to micro- rather than macro-academic matters. While faculty cherishes freedom, and rightly so, it is not always willing to be accountable to its university and to students. Commitment by faculty to their university has been on the decline, particularly as the walls between research universities and industry are coming down. Academic senates appear to be held in lower esteem by faculty and are less effective today than they were only a few years ago. One manifestation is that fewer and fewer faculty members are ready to devote time to serve on senate committees, so essential for making shared governance work. Slots on senate committees all too often go begging and so do chairmanships. (For example, one great research university, which contacted all senate members with a request to serve on one of its committee, found only 4 percent interested.)

In order to stimulate a broader interest and esteem, the senate could take a number of steps, which could strengthen its standing as a partner in the shared governance system. For example, the senate could provide more significant, readily available information to faculty. To this end the development and installation by the senate of a sophisticated computerized information system can be helpful. This system should supplement the university's information and provide senate members with information germane to their concerns.

Moreover, the senate could benefit by having attached to it a research capability, even initially merely a rather limited one until its usefulness has proven itself.

In addition, the senate could sponsor more frequent town hall meetings on issues of major concern to faculty. President and members of relevant board committees could be invited. The purpose would be to inform the faculty and engage them in first hand deliberations toward advancing solutions to major issues confronting the university.

Finally, attention should be given to reducing the commonly large number of senate committees with which the senate feels the administration is obliged to interact.[1] Also procedures should be explored that can bring matters to a more timely closure.

---

[1] For example, in the University of California with its nine campuses, where many proposed initiatives are sent by the president to the statewide senate chair. The chair in turn asks each campus to review the proposal, which is done not infrequently by as many as 2-4 committees on each campus. Thus, 15-30 senate committees are often asked to review long documents. Because of the large number of reviewers, each one has very little effect on the outcome and proposals go through a very long gestation period.

Chapter 10: Initiatives for Improving Shared Governance

In order to make interaction between faculty and administration more effective and bring deliberations about academic matters to a judicious and timely conclusion, the following specific initiatives deserve consideration.

One initiative could more carefully define criteria for determining the issues about which faculty have the right to be "informed and advised", or "consulted" or "given delegated decision making authority" (though formally still subject to board approval). As a result, fewer senate committees and meetings would be needed and university decisions could be made more expeditiously.

A second initiative could more carefully define the reasons for joint faculty-administration committees and the role of faculty on such committees, of which there are four major types:

- administration committee with faculty representation,
- administration committee with senate representation,
- senate committee with administration representation, and
- senate committee with administration observers.

A third initiative could, by agreement, reduce the number of major issues to be advanced jointly by the senate and the administration in any given year. Toward this end, administration and senate leaders could meet at the beginning of the academic year, each presenting a list of issues likely to loom large in the coming year. Triage could be jointly undertaken and a manageable number of weighty issues and datelines agreed to as consultative undertakings.

These initiatives can have a salubrious impact on shared governance. They can rein in what Henry Rosvosky refer to as "excess democracy (that) can lead to chaos; more frequently... slows-down or prevents change." (Rosovsky, H., 2001) Moreover, they can not only improve efficiency of the consultative process and timeliness of its results, but also help senates prove to alienated members their ability to effectively work with the administration in bringing weighty academic matters to a satisfactory and timely closure. Seeing tangible results of their service on senate committees, faculty is likely to devote time to committee work even though such a decision might take time away from research and teaching.

CONCLUSION

Governance is the defining link between a university's aspirations and their fulfillment. The present structure and process of shared governance have in the past served America well. Nevertheless, experimentation with specific new initiatives is in order since rapid changes in the world make it imperative. For example, to the extent that research universities in the past had a hierarchical structure, low cost and virtually instantaneous information dissemination will flatten this structure and lead to greater transparency. As the walls between the university and industry come down and globalization of knowledge gains speed, mobility of faculty, particularly in the sciences and professional schools, will increase and new structures will be needed to accommodate these tendencies. But also departments see their walls coming down. They are losing their distinctive boundaries as major contributions to knowledge are made increasingly not merely at the core but at the boundaries and intersections of disciplines. Thus, the venerable structure of universities, with departments as building blocks, must increasingly accommodate new, multi-disciplinary organizations, which very often transgress the boundaries of schools and colleges. As new university structures are evolving, new governance structures and processes are needed.

Toward this end, a number of initiatives are proposed, some to be taken by a single stakeholder and others by collaborative efforts of two or all three of them. President and senate, as well as thoughtful outsiders, are likely to be the prime change agents. They can offer new ideas for tailoring governance to suit the new environment universities can expect to face. Boards can have a defining effect by stimulating president and faculty to contribute to the timely evolution of forward-looking governance structures and procedures.

I would like to close by quoting Harold Williams' admonition – "I would urge that we begin the colloquium thinking 'out of the box' and consider what the ideal university will look like to meet the needs and challenges of the 21st century as best as we can imagine them." [2] It is my hope that this paper will prove to be a modest attempt in this direction. Specifically, I hope that we will think "out of the box" when we explore how to experiment with and ultimately implement new governance initiatives.

REFERENCES

American Association of University Professors (1966). *Statement on Government of Colleges and Universities*, Washington, D.C.

Association of Governing Boards of Universities and Colleges (November 8, 1998). *AGB Statement on Institutional Governance*, Washington, D.C.

Fishman, B. (March 2, 2000). "Regents Out of Touch With Campuses", *Daily Bruin*, pp. 21, 23.

Hirsch, W. Z. (1999). "Financing Universities Through Non-traditional Revenue Sources: Opportunities and Threats", pp. 75-84, in Hirsch, W. Z. & Weber L. E., eds., *Challenges Facing Higher Education at the Millennium*, American Council on Education/The Oryx Press, Phoenix.

Rosovsky, H. (2001). "Some Thoughts About University Governance", in this book.

Tiebout, C. M. (October 1956). "A Pure Theory of Public Expenditures", *Journal of Political Economy*, n° 4, pp. 416-424.

---

2 Letter from Harold M. Williams as of April 9, 1999.

CHAPTER 11

Variety and Impact: Differences that Matter

Some Thoughts on the Variety of University Governance Systems and their Impact on University Policies and Strategies

Hans van Ginkel

INTRODUCTION

"I am very proud of the progress we made, while I was president, even though we followed policies that some people now prefer to fault. I'd hate to think where we'd be if I hadn't followed those policies and I refer to affirmative action policies. And by affirmative action policies I don't mean what some other people mean by it. What I mean is that we make a determined effort to increase the pool of historically underrepresented minorities who are eligible to be admitted out of high school…"

David Pierpont Gardner [1]

In 1995, the Board of Regents of the University of California decided to halt all forms of affirmative action on its university campuses. President Gardner had discussed at length the pros and cons, and the advantages and problems of affirmative action policies in contracting and purchasing and in personnel and admissions with the Regents in 1990. The Regents had agreed in 1990, but no longer did in 1995. The Board of Regents, created to keep the university free in its internal affairs from political and sectarian influences, had itself become a highly politicized institution.

---

[1] Kreisler, H. (October 21, 1998). *Leadership in Education – Conversations with David Pierpont Gardner*, Institute of International Studies, UC Berkeley.

In California, but even more so in the rest of the world, particularly Europe, the decision of the Board of Regents attracted a lot of attention. Indeed, such political interference with established university policies would be un-imaginable in many countries. In countries where public universities do not have a Board of Trustees or Regents—or where persons holding office in government cannot be members—a decision this would at least have resulted in direct involvement of the Minister of Science and Education. This action of the Board of Regents would have most certainly been interpreted as an unacceptable violation of *university autonomy*, a basic value upheld by all, and guaranteed by law, if not the constitution.

This example illustrates clearly two important facts:

- The governance structure has an important impact on the outcome of university debates on policies and strategies;
- The same institutional framework can bring about very different policies and strategies depending on the people operating in it.

Both of these facts have not been given much attention in the rapidly expanding literature on higher education. In particular, legislation regarding the way(s) in which universities govern themselves, and the actual ways in which they do this, has not yet received much analytical attention. Characteristically, the *World Declaration* and the *Framework for Action* of UNESCO's World Conference on Higher Education (Paris, 1998) do not mention these topics at all. Nor does the *Follow-up Strategy* for 2000 and beyond.

Still, there does exist an astounding variety of governances system in academia: with or without intermediate layer(s) between the government and the individual institution, with elected or appointed or elected and appointed heads of the institution (rector, vice-chancellor, president), from outside or inside the institution, only from the body of full professors or also others, linked to university policies only or based on nationwide political parties, with a strong direct line from the chief administrator to the minister or not, with an academic senate or a much broader university council with representation of students and technical/administrative staff in very varying strengths, with much institutional independence in management issues or more strictly regulated by the ministry, etc. In this chapter, we look at some of the choices that can be made, and the impact these might have.

GOVERNMENTS AND UNIVERSITY GOVERNANCE

Governments pay growing attention to proposals to improve university governance. This has most certainly been the case in Western Europe, and since the fall of the Berlin Wall in 1989, increasingly also in the rest of the continent. The rapidly increasing numbers of students and, related to that, the rapid expansion of academic, technical and administrative staff of higher education programmers as well as teaching and research facilities are among the main reasons for this drive towards "improved" university governance systems.

The general trend towards democratization since the *cultural revolution* of the late sixties, as well as the need for more transparency and accountability contributed importantly, too. The size of operations, the need to diversify programs, to diversify also financial sources for expanding budgets, and to increase cooperation with the world of work, all necessitate more effective, more efficient and more flexible governance structures and regulations.

Most of the reports and proposals aimed at improving university governance systems, however, focus largely on legal aspects and broad interpretations and pay scant attention to the realities of university life. In the Netherlands, for instance, successive measures to reduce government expenditure on student grants, combined with a highly consistent financial policy to not adapt university budgets to yearly inflation did more to bring about Guy Neave's mode 2 revolution than any action to change the university governance system. It is therefore good to understand governance in a broader way than just a system of legally defined structures and processes. The people implementing the system and the way in which they interpret the rules from within the system, as well as from outside the system (the "*environment*") are also of paramount importance, as are their various differently motivated and sometimes very individual and specific actions.

In the more complex society of today, it is questionable whether governments can still perform in much detail the wide variety of functions they were used to perform. Hence the trend towards decentralization, delegation, and for instance, privatization of formerly state-owned companies in the public utilities sector (transport, mail, communications, etc.). In Japan, the government is moving now to make the public universities more independent public agencies. Characteristically, the government of the Netherlands decentralized the construction-investment budgets to the individual universities (1995) when it had no capacity left within the ministry to pursue the construction policy and implementation schemes for university buildings in the traditional way.

Responsibilities are more and more decentralized to the universities. The strength and kind of their governance system, as well as the character and personality of the people operating it, become ever more important. This chapter deals with variety in university governance systems and the impact this may have on policies and strategies, with differences in governance systems, therefore, that matter. Much change has taken place in the Netherlands, where the Higher Education Law changed fundamentally three times in the last three decades. The experience of this country, which can almost be regarded as a laboratory for higher education policy, will receive much attention.

The crucial question will be: what functions does the university governance system have to perform? And how is it equipped to do so? Rather than to make a complete typology and analysis of university governance systems in the world, I would like in this chapter to give a more sketchy overview and to focus only on some key aspects of university governance. How is the relation between the university and the government organized? Are internal democracy and leadership development guaranteed? To what extent is the university allowed to develop its own policies with regard to finance, personnel, and physical infrastructure; its own research as well as education and training policies and its own package of services to society?

THE RELATION WITH THE GOVERNMENT

In continental Europe, it is a generally held view that it is a core responsibility of governments to ensure the availability and adequate supply, as well as the quality of and access to higher education. All citizens, regardless of their socio-economic background, should have full opportunities to enter higher education, provided that they have shown their capability to participate with a fair chance on successful completion of the chosen study programmed. Whatever has changed in the financing levels and the governance systems, there is no indication whatsoever that this conviction has changed in recent years.

In the Netherlands, there may be debate on the efficacy and efficiency of the universities, or on questions like how many years students should be supported by government grants, whether there should be a special academics tax or any other way of repayment for higher education received, but there is no indication that the interest of the politicians and the public in issues of supply and quality of and access to higher education has decreased. The debates rather point in the other direction, including preparedness to accept the financial consequences in the national budget. In Germany, direct interest in these issues exists rather on the Länder level in the framework of an overall policy to strengthen cultural identities within an emerging Europe. In Belgium, too, higher education is dealt with largely at the level of Flanders and Wallonia, or the Dutch-speaking and the French-speaking communities, but the interest there is still unabated.

At the same time, however, we have seen regularly that governments try to strengthen the effectiveness and the efficiency of universities and to reduce costs by granting them incrementally more autonomy and by placing them at more distance from the ministry. As a previous Minister of Education of Finland once said: *"We have given the autonomy to do more with less"*. These same governments, nevertheless, are urged time and again to show that by doing so, they are not losing control over the universities, in particular not over the supply and quality of and access to university study programmers.

In the Netherlands, regulations with regard to students and study grants; budget rules to influence financial policies; rules with regard to the supply, orientation and duration of programmers; general regulations with direct consequences for personnel management and policy, among others, were used to force universities to "*make the right choices*". Quality evaluation and control mechanisms such as "*meta-evaluations*", focusing among others on "*macro-efficiency*", were other tools to show the earnest wish of successive governments to keep control while granting more autonomy.

In the relationship with the government, two issues are of prime importance:
- the willingness of the government not to interfere with the academic policies of the university and the management process to implement these;
- whether or not there exists an intermediate body or bodies between the government and the individual university.

What is important, indeed, has been phrased clearly by David Gardner in his conversations with Harry Kreisler on October 21, 1998 in one of the *Conversations with History*, developed by the Institute of International Studies, UC Berkeley:

"What I mean by that is that universities require a high degree of independence, a high degree of autonomy. They really need to have control over who's admitted, what courses are offered, what constitutes grounds for awarding a degree, who's employed on the faculty, who's advanced to tenure, who's promoted, who isn't, who is awarded degrees, the standards in the classroom. Those are decisions that the university needs to be able to make without interference from the outside. They need to be accountable for those decisions. They need to explain those decisions. But the locus of authority to make those decisions rests with the institutions"...

Many governments have followed a policy line to give universities an opportunity to slowly develop more mature governance systems, more likely to cope with the type of problems more entrepreneurial universities would have to face. On the one side, they have tried to maintain a high degree of independence, of autonomy for the universities. On the other, they have tried to improve the transparency of university policies and the accountability of university management as well as to enhance the supply and quality of and the access to university programmers.

TOWARDS MORE INDEPENDENT, DEMOCRATIC INSTITUTIONS

In the Netherlands, for instance, the universities were until 1963 in formal terms a part of the Ministry of Education, Culture and Science and had no separate legal personality of their own. This meant that they were subject to the same budgetary rules and personnel policy as the civil service in general.

The secretary(-general) of the university, like the Kanzler in the German universities and probably the director of administration in Japanese universities, was in daily practice the most powerful person, as this person had the direct links with and information from the ministry. The rector chaired the academic senate and had the academic legitimation and credibility, but changed every year according to seniority. The Board of Trustees consisted of high-ranking citizens not otherwise directly involved in university matters, meeting only once or twice a month on an agenda prepared by the secretary (-general) and the rector. The Ministry not only approved the annual budget and report, but also the detailed staffing table, and prepared the appointment of full professors by the Queen. The construction of buildings was a matter to be dealt with by the government as a whole, in particular by the ministers of education, finance and construction. The buildings were financed at once from the state budget and remained, therefore, state property.

Probably the most important single, legal decision with regard to the university was the decision in 1963 to grant universities autonomy as individual, independent, legal entities. The fact that a complete renewal of the university governance system was not envisaged at that time is illustrated by the observation that for the rest nothing had changed. It took the cultural revolution of the late sixties, before, in 1971, the *Wet Universitaire Bestuurshervorming* (WUB, the Law on University Administrative Reform) was adopted and the governance system changed. It may be clear that the old system, maintained almost a decade after 1963 had proved to be very unsatisfactory in view of the increased responsibilities of universities.

The new system was largely based on the three-layer system in public administration (municipality-province-country, department-faculty-university) as a response to the democratic ideals of the *cultural revolution*. Because of the special character of academic institutions, however, the one man-one vote system was not adopted. On the university level in the university council, the academic staff, the technical/administrative staff and the students each had one third of the seats. In the faculty council, however, the academic staff had one-half of the seats. The Board of Trustees was abolished. To establish a link with society in particular in the university council, some representatives from society could be added. This, however, soon lost most of its function when only such representatives were chosen by the councils who made sure that the balance of power between the different parties and factions in the university council was not changed. Therefore, the only effective link with society was operated through the appointment by the minister of two members from outside the university, the so-called *crown members*, to the university executive board.

Among the five members of the board, the rector was only one—however, in most cases, the most influential one, as he or she had the backing of the board of deans and the faculties. The position of the rector was further strengthened when he or she was duly elected by the board of deans and then recommended for appointment by the university council to the minister for a period of up to four years, comparable with the other members of the university board. The university council elected two members of the university board and the minister appointed the other two. Of course, a lot of confidential discussion between the minister, the council and the board of deans was necessary to get a workable result. The minister also appointed the chair from among the five: in most cases, one of the two political appointees. The democratization of the university governance system was so highly valued, however, that this never raised too much open criticism and all decisions in the Board could be taken by simple majority.

The system introduced in 1971 never functioned very well. In the beginning, it was a problem that much the same people who had operated in the previous system were still in the most influential positions. With a university council dominated by the participation of many who had taken an active part in the *cultural revolution*, this did not work too well. Beyond that, there were in fact three centers of power in this new governance structure, personified in the chair of the university board, the rector, and the chair of the university council. The chair of the board, who soon began to name himself the president, based his position on a strong relation with the minister; the rector on his chairmanship of the board of deans and, therefore, the support by the faculties, and the chair of the university council on his/her support in particular among the students, the technical/administrative staff and at least the progressive part of the academic staff.

Two other problems had to be overcome to make the system work. The first related to the secretary (-general) of the university. Before, this had been a very powerful position, when the rector changed every year and a board of trustees could devote only limited time to the university. Under the new law, the secretary (-general) got five new "bosses" in the university board and had to be prepared at any time to give full information to the members of the university council on any issue they were collectively or individually interested in. It took more than a decade before a new generation of secretaries-general had come into the universities, capable and prepared to play this role.

Many of the previous secretaries-general involved themselves directly in the power game and adopted a position between the university board and the university council. This quite often aggravated the second problem that had to be solved in the practical functioning of the system: the tension between the university board and the university council. This, too, took more than a decade before workable arrangements had developed. For this situation to come about, it was crucial that university boards could serve longer than the university councils. By serving longer, the members of the boards slowly gained more experience to handle difficult matters better.

It is important to know that the university council had the right to approve (or disapprove) the university budget and annual accounts, as well as the strategic plan. It may be clear that in many cases in particular the relationship between the chair of the board and the chair of the council was not very easy, in particular not in times of severe budget cuts by the ministry. This happened two times in the eighties: in 1982-83 under the name *Division of Labor and Concentration*, and in 1987 in the action programmed *Selective Growth and Shrinkage*. Nevertheless, the system gradually worked well after a balance had developed between the system of structures and regulations and the people operating it.

TOWARDS MORE EFFECTIVE, ENTREPRENEURIAL ORGANIZATIONS

The eighties and the nineties saw two further major changes in the higher education law. In 1987, under the name *Law on Higher Education and Scientific Research* (WHW, Wet op het Hoger Onderwijs en Wetenschappelijk Onderzoek) and in 1997 with the adoption of the *Law on the Modernization of University Administration* (MUB, Modernisering Universitair Bestuur). The first law (WHW) tried to rationalize the democratized university governance system of 1971 and to reduce the system-inherent tensions and conflicts. The second (MUB), however, changed the course of developments fundamentally: it reduced internal democracy in the university importantly, but gave at the same time more autonomy to the university by re-introducing a board of trustees and, by doing so, placing the university at greater distance from the ministry and reducing direct interference by the minister (one might add, also, reducing the workload in the ministry with regard to the universities).

In 1987, the new law (WHW) reduced the number of people in the governing bodies: the university board decreased from 5 to 3 members and the council to a maximum of 30 members and even less for smaller universities. The chair of the university board also o a clearer position, but was still in a more difficult position as that person had no in-house constituency. Gradually, the university learned not only to be democratic, transparent and accountable, but also to become more flexible and entrepreneurial. Each university developed its own profile, procedures and support structures. Such support structures were, among others, specific-purpose foundations for applied research and cooperation with industry or for constructing buildings that were not (yet) included in the government's investment schemes.

In the law of 1997 (MUB), the minister delegated the authority to appoint up to three members of the university board to the new board of trustees. These new boards should remain small—generally five members not related to the university in any way— and they should also not hold a position in government or parliament. In this way, a new effort was made to link the university better to society in a non-political, broad sense. The new board of trustees got the right to approve the annual budgets, accounts and annual reports, as well as the strategic plan. The university council remained, but clearly with much reduced authority. Although the minister kept the authority to appoint the trustees, in practice the individual universities were asked each to come up with a proposal and after some discussion, in a few cases, the minister appointed them all. It would have been difficult to act differently, as all the universities together needed at the same time so many highly qualified and dedicated candidates.

An overarching tendency in the sequence of the new laws was that each new law tended to strengthen the position of the chairperson of the university board. Since in the division of labor between the chair of the university council, the rector and the president, the contacts with the minister and lobbying were left largely to the president, this overall development may not be a surprise. There is, however, a threat that the top "management" of the university becomes more hierarchical and more distanced from the university community. The other aspect is that the new boards of trustees are less likely to make political appointments. In Twente University, for instance, the rector was recently appointed to be, at the same time, the president.

Developments to create a kind of intermediate layer between the minister and the universities are quite common now. These can, however, take two very different forms: either as a collective layer between the minister and all the universities, or more individual – between the Minister and one specific university. In Sweden, for instance, the chancellor relates to all the universities; in Finland, only to one. In the Netherlands both forms exist now: the Association of Universities in the Netherlands (VSNU), as well as the boards of trustees. Increasingly, however, the VSNU is focusing on its task as an employers' union, as the universities have become responsible for their own personnel policy, including the negotiations with the trade unions.

All this refers very much to the governance system, the structures and regulations. It may, however, be clear that the ways in which these work out very much depend on developments related to the primary tasks of the university: teaching and research. In the years described, there were dramatic changes in the length and structure of study programmers, in the system of study grants and student fees, in the financing system of the universities and the level of the financing, in the organization and evaluation of research, and the degree in which more competition for research money was introduced, the evaluation of teaching and faculties or universities as a whole, and the transfer of the property rights on real estate to the universities themselves, the transfer of negotiations on personnel policy with the trade-unions to the universities, etc.

Rapid changes in almost any aspect of the university have put the governance system under many diverse and great pressures. The most important gain has certainly been the opportunity given to the university to govern itself increasingly independently in almost every aspect. It has given opportunities to the universities to shape their own future. It has also given the opportunity to see what really matters in university governance.

WHAT MATTERS

From the previous description, it may have become clear that the universities in the Netherlands underwent important change, in particular also in their governance system. Looking back, however, the conclusion must be that universities are characterized by a remarkable adaptability, and profit from the availability of people who have the capacity to make almost any system work. The variety of university governance systems around the world is accordingly surprisingly large. Some differences, however, are of the utmost importance for the policies and strategies as well as for the management of universities.

1. The watershed decision is to grant universities the status of autonomous, semi-independent, individual legal entities. Only if this is the case does it become possible to award them full responsibility for their long-term commitments in finance, housing, equipment and personnel.
2. In connection with this, it is important to create the adequate distance between the ministry and the university, for instance by introducing a board of trustees, with highly qualified, and dedicated representatives of society not holding political positions. Such boards of trustees should, however, keep distance from the internal affairs of the university and should focus instead on issues like sound management, quality and access and they should not be politicized.
3. Universities are increasingly in competition with each other, but this should not let them forget their inherent complementarity and joint responsibility for high-level study programmers, research and service to society. They should not forget their joint responsibility, in particular, for young generations. To regulate competition and to improve their joint performance, it is important to work together in a strong intermediary organization, which can perform important tasks in shared responsibility.
4. Responsibility strengthens the quality of governance as well as the people prepared to play a role in that governance, and vice versa. For the university to operate in a more mature and entrepreneurial way, it is necessary to have a clear picture of the medium-term financial frame-

work in which the university has to operate. It has to be clear how large the contribution of the government will be by approximation over the next years and for what functions. It has also to be clear what sources of additional income the university may tap within its own responsibility, in particular in cooperation with the private sector.

5. This implies the right to shift funding from one year to the next and to create financial provisions for specific purposes on the medium-term, as well as the right to use money freely within the framework of the properly approved budget, without being restricted by governmental financial rules related to the variables in the formula on which the lump-sum contribution to the university is decided. This also includes the right to develop profitable contract activities and to use the income freely without any consequence for the lump sum granted to the university on the basis of its primary activities (research and teaching).

6. A more entrepreneurial behavior of universities is impossible under conditions where the staffing table as well as the major appointments of personnel must be approved by the ministry and the labor conditions are negotiated by the ministry with the trade unions. Universities need a very flexible personnel policy, which promotes and rewards commitment and quality, not just seniority. The strict personnel policy rules of the traditional civil service do not contribute to the best results. Inputs in the financial formula for deciding the lump-sum budget of the university can also be based on *"ideal-type"* personnel formations in different disciplinary areas.

7. It is clear that in the name of such modern, flexible, personnel management, academic freedom may not be threatened. It may also be clear, however, that ill-conceived interpretations of academic freedom should not make the proper organization of the university and its programmers impossible. The balance needed in truly academic personnel management, promoting commitment and quality as well as originality and creativity requires tailor-made regulations for which universities themselves must take responsibility. For more entrepreneurial and responsible university governance systems, more control over labor conditions and personnel management is absolutely essential.

8. In order to induce a more efficient use of buildings and equipment, the university itself must be responsible for investment, maintenance and renewal, and have full ownership of their physical facilities, as is the case in the Netherlands since 1995. The lump sum made available by the government to the university must therefore include an investment and maintenance component. This implies the right of the university to buy and sell buildings, as well as to construct new buildings and to take mortgages, as appropriate within the

approved budget and taking account of the reservations of funds already made available.

9. A major trend in higher education is the trend towards diversification. This includes the development of more non-university (or non-academic), vocationally oriented higher education programmers, such as previously provided by the polytechnics in England, and still nowadays by the German *"Fachhochschulen"* and the *"hogescholen"* in the Netherlands. This includes as well programmers for open and distance learning, as well as programmers for non-traditional students from different age groups, combining working and studying. Universities must move away from classroom teaching to consolidated groups of students, which has become the most common type of university teaching in a time of democratization and rapidly growing numbers of students. Instead, the universities must create a learning environment that challenges and optimizes the opportunities for individual study paths. This not only suggests the addition of some student counselors; it asks for a complete re-thinking of the internal organization of the university. The old model of faculties and departments is no longer appropriate to cope with these new challenges. There is a need for a clear matrix structure of disciplines on the one side and study and research programmers on the other, with clear assignment of tasks and responsibilities.

10. It is, in particular, important to strengthen research management in universities. The traditional structure of faculties and departments is not adequate anymore in a time in which the investments in top research have become so high, and partnerships with other research institutes and strategic alliances with industry so important. Just to separate research from universities, however, is not the best solution: research groups need a continuous influx of young, creative researchers, whereas faculties need the motivating impulses of the best researchers in their study programmers. The matrix structure mentioned in the previous point seems an adequate solution to contribute both to flexibility in the use of human resources and to continuous change in internal structures.

11. For the functioning of any governance system in universities, talent scouting among the academic staff is essential. It is also crucial that preparing young staff for administrative positions in the university should become a regular part of staff development programs. This should include internationalization, in the sense of learning from practice in other countries. Systematic talent scouting, staff development and internationalization may, after all, matter most when it comes to improving governance.

CHAPTER 12

Three Successful Modes of Research Governance: Lessons from the Past, Issues of the Present, Implications for the Future

Robert C. Dynes, Sharon E. R. Franks, Charles F. Kennel

INTRODUCTION

In a rapidly changing intellectual environment in which research is growing increasingly specialized while cross-disciplinary collaboration is opening new pathways to understanding, research institutions grapple with an array of internal and external challenges. Boundaries that once separated traditional academic fields have become less distinct, and multi-disciplinary research now spans the continuum from basic science to applied research. These changes, along with dramatic acceleration in the pace of research, have prompted us to examine the internal governance structures of three outstanding research organizations and ask: How will the decision-making procedures that have contributed to the success of these organizations evolve to respond to future challenges?

Leaders of research institutions, relying on input from their scientific associates, are charged with making decisions about issues as diverse as resource allocation and fundraising, hiring and promotion, apportionment of physical space, and, in the case of academic organizations, recruitment and education of students. The processes by which these decisions are made, as well as the decisions themselves, can influence fiscal prosperity, scientific productivity within the institution, and morale of the faculty and research staff.

We begin with a look at the internal structure and management of two top-ranked organizations at the University of California San Diego (UCSD): Scripps Institution of Oceanography (SIO) and the Graduate Program in

Neurosciences (GPN). As a counterpoint to the academic environment, we consider the configuration and leadership of the Physical Sciences Research Laboratory (PSRL) of Bell Laboratories Lucent Technologies in Murray Hill, New Jersey. Our goals are to identify internal management practices, both formal and informal, that contribute to research excellence, and to highlight creative approaches that hold promise for responding to future reconfigurations in the research environment.

The three organizations share a number of fundamental characteristics: size, scientific focus, and reputation for excellence. Each is larger than a traditional academic department, the size of which typically reflects teaching requirements. Each comprises a number of divisions or programs that function semi-independently and present governance challenges. Each relies on a balance of formal and informal decision-making procedures. All are scientific enterprises in which individual productivity is a prerequisite for institutional success. The two university entities, SIO and GPN, have as a second primary mission the education of graduate students. Both were rated number one in their fields by the National Academy of Sciences' National Research Council (Goldberger *et al.*, 1995). Bell Labs' PSRL, a model of private sector research, was selected for this discussion on the basis of its recognized success and familiarity to one of us (RCD).

It is not surprising that these highly regarded organizations have in common certain structural and management features that support their prosperity. More intriguing, however, is the noteworthy differences among the organizations. The complexity of the internal structure and governance system ranges from relatively straightforward in the case of PSRL, to moderately multifarious within GPN, to comparatively enigmatic at SIO. The degree of direct influence exerted by the leader(s) is strongest within PSRL and comparatively circumspect within SIO and GPN. Strategies for recruiting new personnel vary significantly among the three groups. A well-developed system of active recruiting at PSRL and an innovative advertising strategy used by the principal department of GPN contrast with SIO's reliance on its reputation of excellence to attract outstanding candidates. Specific examples will illustrate how aspects of each organization's structure and management contribute to, or in some cases detract from, the goal of promoting continued success in the research arena.

Interviews with faculty, researchers, and administrative leaders at the three organizations shed light on internal structure and policies that contribute to the success of these groups. Those interviewed were forthcoming with constructive criticism as well as praise for their particular organization's structure and decision-making practices. Their insights, opinions, and concerns reveal key elements of successful internal management.

BACKGROUND

Each of the three organizations has a peculiar internal structure and governance that reflect its size, composition, purpose, and, in two of the three cases, position within the university infrastructure.

Scripps Institution of Oceanography (SIO)

Scripps Institution of Oceanography has been a multidisciplinary academic organization since its inception nearly a century ago. With its amalgamation of strengths and weaknesses, SIO may serve as an interesting model for other growing organizations that are becoming increasingly interdisciplinary. The institution now employs some 1,700 people, including 90 faculty, 100 researchers, and 170 graduate students, who work in more than two dozen buildings on the roughly one-half square mile seaside La Jolla campus. Research in the ocean, earth and atmospheric sciences, as well as graduate education are primary missions of the Institution.

The peculiarities of SIO's flexible academic personnel structure, which distinguish it as a non-traditional constituent of the university, can be simplified by a two-component model: 1) faculty (professors) of the SIO Department who teach, conduct research, and vote in the University's strong Academic Senate; and 2) researchers who are members of SIO and employees of UCSD but who do not engage in the organizations' governance via the Academic Senate. Since many faculty members also hold research appointments, and some researchers are actively involved in the guidance of graduate students, the distinction between faculty and researcher is not as sharp as the simple model might lead one to believe. But the reality of the separation bears conspicuously on decision-making practices within SIO, and consequently affects perceptions of hierarchy among individuals and groups. On the other hand, the administration has steadfastly held to the principle (and practice) of maintaining equity between faculty and researchers by maintaining equivalent salary scales. This required substantial effort on the part of the administration.

This brings us to the sub-divisional structure at SIO, which, layered upon the complexity of the faculty/researcher dichotomy, makes for an institutional structure that frequently bewilders insiders as well as outside observers. Academicians (faculty and researchers) are grouped into twelve research divisions and their equivalents (Organized Research Units). The number of academics in each research division ranges from a half-dozen to more than three dozen, and some individuals are affiliated with more than one research division. The SIO director appoints research division directors who typically serve in this capacity for five years. Independent of the system of research divisions are the eight curricular groups into which SIO faculty partition themselves. Curricular groups concern themselves with graduate student recruiting, admitting, teaching, and supervision, among other issues relevant to the faculty, and are the rough equivalents of academic departments within UCSD. According to their status as faculty or researcher, and via their participation in research divisions, curricular groups, and institutional and *ad hoc* committees, scientists can participate extensively in decision-making about hiring, promotion, graduate education, design of new physical space, and more recently, fundraising.

The research and teaching functions at SIO maintain an uneasy distance from each other. They are not combined in departments as in most research universities, nor are they separated as at many institutions in continental Europe. This partial decoupling of research and curricular decision-making processes has both benefits and drawbacks. It allows interdisciplinary research to flourish, but weakens formal graduate teaching and curriculum design.

Historically, SIO has relied on strong directors; the Director also serves as a UCSD Dean and Vice Chancellor. As a university division, SIO thrives on a blend of faculty self-governance and directorial initiative. For an academic unit, the Director/Dean/Vice Chancellor holds an extraordinary concentration of formal power. This concentration of power can enable unconventional, often multi-disciplinary innovation. At the same time, the Director ignores faculty views at his extreme risk.

There is a strong tradition of "shared governance" in the University of California, in which the administration and the faculty govern together. Throughout the entire University of California system, the Academic Senate is strong, and SIO and UCSD follow well-defined administrative procedures that govern how decisions are made. The faculty arm of the governance, the academic assembly, holds primary responsibility for curriculum and student admissions, while the remainder is under the purview of the administration. In practice, the faculty and the academic assembly are an integral part of the advice to the administration. SIO strongly follows these principles of shared governance.

Graduate Program in Neurosciences (GPN)

In contrast to SIO, the GPN is not an academic division or department of UCSD; rather, it is a highly regarded, cross-departmental, multi-institution, integrated program focused on graduate student training in the field of brain research. The relatively youthful field of neuroscience comprises specialties as diverse as physiology, anatomy, pharmacology, chemistry, biology, psychiatry, and cognitive sciences. The GPN brings together more than 120 faculty members supervising some 70 graduate students. Faculty hold appointments in a dozen academic departments and the School of Medicine at UCSD, and a number of affiliated, neighboring institutes, including The Salk Institute, the Scripps Research Institute, SIO, the UCSD Medical Center, and the Veterans

Administration Medical Center.

Under the leadership of a program chairman, GPN faculty make decisions about the content and structure of the graduate program. It is important to note that the only real power of the GPN chairman is controlling access to bright graduate students. Matters such as hiring, promoting, and resource allocation are handled not within the GPN, but within the university departments and affiliated organizations in which faculty are appointed. Unencumbered by the requirement to deal with such issues, the GPN is more comparable to a curricular group within SIO than to the Institution as a whole.

Faculty members affiliated with the GPN describe its leadership as a collective effort and characterize the program as relatively flexible and unstructured. One individual suggested that part of the GPN's success may be rooted in its youth and the absence of long-standing traditions and traditionalists. As within SIO, a lack of rigidity and blend of self-organization and effective leadership provide fertile ground for GPN scholars and entrepreneurs to take initiative. On the other hand, the lack of structure presents few clear pathways to success.

Bell Laboratories' Physical Science Research Laboratory (PSRL)

Bell Labs' PSRL includes approximately 150 scientists, including 30 post-doctoral researchers. Supervised by a director who reports to a company vice-president, nine department heads and five technical managers oversee research conducted by the technical staff. In contrast to SIO and GPN, PSRL does not concern itself with graduate training, except in a few isolated cases; however, it must deal with an array of business issues less relevant to the two academic organizations. While self-governance and shared governance figure prominently within academia, PSRL's industrial orientation relies much more heavily on a strong hierarchical system in which it is always clear who makes management decisions. It should not be inferred from this statement that the research environment lacks intellectual freedom, or that scientists' views are unimportant in management decisions—on the contrary, researchers enjoy the support of the company in pursuing their scientific and technological interests. Managers, themselves scientists, recognize and encourage staff members' intellectual pursuits.

While it is more generally the case that management decisions are made within the hierarchy of the administration, staff scientists clearly can strongly influence research directions. An administration of good scientists recognizes good ideas that "bubble up", and it is perceived that a good first line manager is one who can recognize these good ideas and facilitate them, while all the while being aware of the corporate mission.

While less formally empowered than their university counterparts, Bell Labs' staff advisory organizations report to the senior management on issues ranging from science to technology to staff morale. These organizations do not have the power of the academic assembly but do carry influence on decisions. At Bell Labs, an effective administration usually has a strong "kitchen cabinet" of staff.

Overriding this organization is the company mission, for which the Director is responsible. It is his job to justify the research on the basis of the long term mission.

Hiring and Promoting the Best and the Brightest

Attracting and keeping outstanding scientists is the highest priority for both academic and private-sector research organizations. We look at how SIO and PSRL, as well as UCSD's Neuroscience Department, in which nearly a third of GPN faculty hold appointments, have been successful in hiring the best and the brightest scientists. In all three organizations, maintenance of high standards is practically accomplished by hiring, promoting, and releasing. Within the university, Academic Senate procedures uphold high standards. Strong institutional reputation, the presence of a world-class professional community that includes young creative thinkers, commitment to active recruiting, and willingness to let individual talent rather than scientific specialty frequently drive hiring decisions are among the factors that contribute to these organizations' successes.

Success breeds success. Organizations that enjoy reputations of scientific excellence attract outstanding researchers. For several decades the GPN has produced accomplished young researchers, whose achievements continue to reflect well on the UCSD program and its faculty. Likewise, for nearly a century SIO graduates have gone on to become world leaders in the oceanographic community. Bell Labs PSRL though not directly involved in graduate education very actively supports post-doctoral research and has been instrumental in launching the careers of many young scientists. The very presence of bright young scientists at these institutions, as well as the respectability their continued career success conveys on the programs responsible for their training, draws outstanding researchers. Many successful scientists throughout the world have passed through these institutions and their careers have benefited, while in return they have contributed to the intellectual fervor during their stay.

Consider the GPN that does not itself hire or promote faculty. Interestingly, this loose program is a salient enticement to prospective faculty in many traditional university departments. Active, voluntary participation in the GPN entitles faculty to supervise the high-caliber graduate students that the program attracts. Since many of these students are funded by grants from the UCSD Medical School, The Salk Institute, the UCSD Office of Graduate

Studies and Research, and the National Institute of Health, the full burden of support for students does not fall to individual researchers as is the case in conventional departments. This mutually beneficial arrangement in which the interdisciplinary, inter-departmental GPN and the individual university departments are strengthened suggests that development of such cross-departmental graduate training programs is a worthwhile endeavor.

In addition to its valuable role in drawing outstanding faculty and students to UCSD, the GPN may represent a model of scholarly reform. A provocative statement made by a senior professor illustrates an intellectual advantage of the multi-disciplinary program. In explaining that the GPN is not overly subject to the parochialism of any individual department, he asserted that "departments are graveyards where faculty are buried." He went on to describe how peer evaluation, so critical to funding, publication, and promotion decisions, encourages stasis and narrow focus among academicians. There is little incentive in a traditional department to branch out, despite this professor's observation that so much "interesting stuff happens at the fringes or between fields." His answer to this dilemma is formation of institutes, labs and centers created explicitly to pursue research at the margins. A recent example illustrates the point: a chorus of researchers from across the UCSD campus and sister institutions, with the support of the UCSD administration, worked together to raise the funds to build a research grade FMRI (functional magnetic resonance imaging) facility that is now in the planning stages. This leading edge laboratory will surely serve as a recruiting tool.

As we think about how the presence of bright, capable students enhances the research environment, it is also worth contemplating the merit of hiring junior faculty and staff who infuse an institution with fresh ideas and creative vitality. Since young researchers cost less than their more senior colleagues, it would seem that adding to the entry-level ranks would be fiscally as well as scientifically attractive to a growing research organization. Indeed, the director of Bell Labs' PSRL related that of the three dozen people hired over the last two years, the vast majority are young scientists and engineers. A sizable flow of Bell Labs' research staff into product divisions as well as other institutions and corporations allows continual replenishment of young researchers. Within UCSD's Neuroscience Department, of the five FTE appointments made over the last three years, four were at the assistant professor level. These groups seem to be doing well in fortifying their ranks with young professionals.

Though young scientists are reasonably well represented in SIO's research series, there is a relative dearth of young (under 40 years of age) faculty. While the reasons for this are complex, it appears that a hesitancy to hire young faculty may be rooted in concerns about the Institution's ability to maintain sufficient and consistent quality control at the promotion and tenure stages. Nearly 90 percent of faculty who come up for tenure are awarded it. While the high tenuring percentage is typical of units at the University of California, the percentages at top-ranking private institutions in the US are typically much lower. With such a high percentage of faculty promoted to tenure this way, there is reluctance to hire young, unproved scientists. Several SIO faculty members suggested that resurrection of an institutional post-doctoral program could provide an effective funnel and filter for new hires.

It is clear that change is on the horizon, for SIO has recently moved to rejuvenate its faculty and research staff by hiring predominantly at the assistant level. The Director and faculty engaged in broad discussions concerning how as many as 9 faculty and 6 research positions should be utilized to foster the long-term intellectual vigor of the institution. While there was consensus on the commitment to hire young scientists, there were tensions concerning the relative merits of directing the search for candidates at individuals with expertise in specified areas, versus conducting broadly defined searches with the goal of attracting the very best scientists, irrespective of specialty. Ultimately, SIO decided to recruit in only four very broad areas. It took a year to consider the hundreds of applications received, but in the end SIO succeeded in landing its first choices for the six junior positions. Two of the successful candidates were geochemists, an area not recognized organizationally at SIO. This suggests that individual excellence was the most important consideration in the institution-wide faculty vote.

UCSD's Neurosciences Department, in which many GPN faculty hold appointments, conducts very broad searches, specifying as many as a half-dozen diverse areas in which they intend to hire. These position announcements have produced an extensive field of qualified applicants, from which outstanding candidates have been hired. Primary criteria in candidate selection have more to do with excellence of an individual's research than with her or his field of specialization. Recognizing that such a flexible approach might be serve SIO well in its goal of attracting the very best earth, ocean and atmospheric scientists, the Director has set in motion a novel process for stimulating faculty-wide discussions and potentially creating consensus on new directions and new hires. With this process underway, the cross-disciplinary discussions have generated a valuable exchange of ideas among colleagues.

Within a system of shared governance in a state-supported university, the university is obliged to adhere to public hiring regulations and procedures that can slow the process to a snail's pace, much to the frustration of prospective employers and employees. In the business world, such constraints are negligible. The PSRL Director, reporting to a Bell Labs' Vice President, can and does respond quickly in offering positions to outstanding job candidates. Offers can be made within a few days if the situation warrants it.

In contrast to the usual university course in which a position announcement is issued to identify candidates, hiring at PSRL relies extensively on active, personal recruitment by Bell Labs' scientists. Researchers assigned "prime recruiter" responsibilities regularly travel to major universities throughout the US and internationally to identify and follow the careers of outstanding graduate students whom they encourage to apply for post-doctoral and junior positions. Similarly, when appropriate, they encourage more experienced academic colleagues to join the Bell Labs research team. A close relationship between the prime recruiter and the university is maintained. Often the recruiter is a graduate of that institution and is in a good position to identify the best students.

Within the business community there is more latitude than within the university to offer fiscal and other incentives to top-notch prospective employees. Among the most alluring enticement an industrial lab can offer is freedom from the continual exigency of generating funding proposals, an often fruitless, energy-consuming activity that can be the bane of university researchers.

Turning briefly from the issue of hiring personnel to evaluating and rewarding employees' contributions, once again we note substantial differences between the academic and industrial approaches. The procedure by which academicians are promoted in the University of California is formal, involves numerous time-consuming steps, and requires considerable input from colleagues both within and outside of the institution. In contrast, PSRL conducts annual performance reviews for every member of its technical staff during an intensive one-week session. Department heads and technical managers together consider each individual's accomplishments during the previous year and over the preceding several years. Employees whose productivity is questionable are given assistance in resolving difficulties and ample opportunity to improve their performance. On average, fewer than one percent of employees leave the company as a result of their unsatisfactory performance. Following PSRL's performance review week, lab leaders conduct a strategy meeting during which they take a good hard look at what changes should be made to enhance individual and collective productivity. Compared to the academic system for faculty evaluation, the industrial model is more efficient, better streamlined, offers more constructive feedback to both employees and management, and allows more flexibility in performance-based rewards.

What can research university leaders learn by studying the hiring and promotion processes within an industrial research lab? The success of PSRL's recruiting suggests that using professional connections to stimulate interest in joining a research group can be an effective tool in attracting highly talented personnel. The model also suggests that it might behoove academic research institutions to streamline their hiring and promotion procedures to keep pace with their private sector counterparts. Finally, more extensive private or public endowment of academic research could significantly improve recruitment and scientific performance of top-notch university researchers.

While much of this discussion implies an advantage that a scientist at Bell Labs has over his or her academic colleagues, the independence of researchers at SIO and GPN counterbalances the advantages of Bell Labs discussed above. Scientists in the academic environment, while more heavily burdened with raising their own support, are much more independent in their choice of research direction. A faculty researcher doesn't have a "boss" in the same sense as a researcher at PSRL has. This independence results in a more individualistic and entrepreneurial style inside the organization.

FACILITATING INTERNAL COMMUNICATION

Assembling a team of brilliant scientists is a requirement in building an outstanding research institution; creating an environment in which these great minds can interact is the subsequent fundamental challenge. By no means is research excellence predicated on collaboration; many outstanding scientists do their best work independently. However, the ease with which members of a research organization can recognize colleagues with common interests and coordinate research initiatives is perhaps a measure of internal institutional synergy. Beyond building a sense of community, collaboration is increasingly essential in addressing multi-disciplinary scientific issues. With the current ease of global electronic communication, a scientist in California might find it as easy to exchange data (but not necessarily work) with a colleague in Tokyo as with a colleague in the lab down the hall. What can or should be done to facilitate communication and encourage collaboration among scientists within an institution?

When we posed this question to a dozen university professors and researchers, their initial responses amounted to a collective shrug of the shoulders. At SIO, most agreed that there is room for improvement in internal communication. They expressed concern, however, that the task is daunting at so large an institution where curricular and research groups are de-coupled and individuals are affiliated to varying degrees in multiple subdivisions that tend to view each other as competitors for resources rather than members of the same team. One associate professor bemoaned the weakness of internal communications within her research division of 40 people, and sighed that the climate at SIO can best be described as "every man for himself". Some roots of this divisiveness are no doubt historical in origin, and those gnarled fibers are resistant to extrication.

While the road to improved communications may be rough, members of the SIO community and outside institutional reviewers agree that the time has come to begin to pave the way. Whether or not the process will entail major structural changes remains to be seen. The goal will be to strike a balance between preserving the flexible, individualistic organization that fosters exciting science and an entrepreneurial spirit and promoting collaborations that foster interdisciplinary projects. Some tempering of overly assertive personalities that may threaten institutional cohesiveness may be required.

The Bell Labs organization is masterful at internal communications. One of the most important responsibilities of the first and second level administration is to bring together scientists with overlapping interests and complementary skills. Indeed, managers are measured and rewarded for these accomplishments. As a result of the annual performance review, each manager acquires a good sense of the interests, skills and accomplishments of every staff member. Much of the discussion of the performance evaluation is aimed at bringing scientists together on problems of interest.

Furthermore, seminars, journal clubs and focus groups are institutionalized. It is part of the culture to attend internal seminars in which debate, discussion and ideas abound. Scientists and managers routinely attend these regularly scheduled seminars. Everyone is expected to contribute periodically to these seminars; they are used in performance evaluations and rewards.

In thinking about how to facilitate internal communication at SIO, it may be worthwhile to analyze when and how scientists interact, and identify barriers to dialog. The most successful scientific collaborations are self-initiated. Commonly built on a history of mutual professional respect, these joint efforts arise almost spontaneously among scientists in the same or related fields. Opportunities to learn about the work of colleagues in other disciplines, however, may arise infrequently, limiting cross-disciplinary communication. Exacerbating this paucity of opportunity is a natural tendency to stick with the familiar rather than endeavor to understand, much less participate in fields in which we are less knowledgeable. On top of all this, spatially immaterial, but psychologically immense, geographical barriers to interaction inhibit communication.

In this era when ubiquitous access to electronic communication seems to shrink space and compress time, it might seem as if physical separation no longer presents a barrier to scientific communication and collaboration. Yet, somehow, the physical size and structure of a research organization do affect, either beneficially or deleteriously, the level and effectiveness of internal communication among individuals and groups. It is interesting to note that the perception of physical distance may be more important than true distance in shaping attitudes about the cohesiveness or fragmentation of the institution. It has been observed that, at Bell Labs, collaborations thrive over a range of about 100 meters on the same floor of a building and on adjacent floors. Farther away, interactions amongst colleagues decline dramatically. This could be regarded as a surprising result in this era of electronic communications, but it illustrates clearly how important personal interactions are.

Prior to exploring strategies aimed at forging ideational connections that transcend geographical impediments, we contrast perceptions of distance within two university organizations. At SIO, scientists work in more than two dozen buildings spread out over a seaside campus of less than one-half square mile. In some cases, the structures house scientists with similar research interests; others accommodate specialists in diverse fields. While the actual distances among buildings, offices, and people are not great, and the mild climate is conducive to walks and lunches outdoors, it is surprising how infrequently many scientists make the effort to visit their colleagues in nearby buildings. A perception among many at SIO, that the institution is a loose confederacy of individuals, is reinforced by the inscrutable internal structure described earlier.

Oddly enough, GPN faculty, who are spread out over a much larger physical area (on the order of 5 square miles) than SIO scientists, expressed a stronger sense of community and seemed less influenced by physical separation. Since it's unlikely that these individuals are far more physically fit than their SIO counterparts, we must look elsewhere to account for this observation. One tenable explanation is that the GPN faculty network is united by a more clearly defined sense of joint purpose. Graduate student training is the cardinal mandate of the GPN, whereas SIO scientists must interact with colleagues to contend with a dizzying array of issues. Dealing with more tractable tasks may create a situation where collegiality thrives and spatial separation does not seem to hinder cooperation.

Additional factors that come into play in fostering cohesiveness within the GPN involve the nature of neuroscience research and the structure of the student program. Many scientific problems involving brain structure and function require multiple techniques and instrumentation available only in particular laboratories. In the course of formulating and carrying out experiments, students are often the catalysts for the exchange of ideas among their faculty advisors. Students rotate among several laboratories during their first year and later are commonly co-advised by faculty from two or more different departments. Cross-pollination facilitated by student "bees" continues as students carry out their research. The role of students in catalyzing scientific exchanges among professors may be paralleled by Bell Labs managers who instigate and support collaboration among members of their staff.

One overriding contribution to communication and interaction is the interdisciplinary nature of all three institutions. No one investigator can have all the skills, equipment and expertise in his or her lab to remain at the edge of their discipline. Interactions then becomes the necessity in order to compete. If the quality of the investigators is such that being "second" is not good enough, the scientists will seek out knowledgeable collaborators and complementary techniques.

Let us turn now from observations about collegial interactions – or lack thereof – to viable suggestions for counteracting perceived geographical obstacles to communication, in effect, "extending the virtual corridor" as one SIO professor eloquently put it.

Seminars and Retreats

Institution-wide seminars can be effective in providing a non-intimidating forum in which to learn about colleagues' research. Incentive to attend and interact can be bolstered by concluding each seminar with light refreshments in an atmosphere conducive to conversation. SIO has recently begun to experiment once again with periodic institution-wide seminars presented by highly engaging faculty. Attendance by faculty at GPN weekly seminars is strong, and faculty attend mini-retreats – three times a year for three hours each – to promote internal communication. At Bell Labs, too, staff members present internal seminars that are highly stimulating, interactive, and well-attended.

Informal Social Events

Casual, social encounters present outstanding opportunities for researchers to exchange ideas and sow the seeds for more formal collaboration. Bringing together scientists to chat over coffee, lunch, or cocktails can stimulate exchanges that seldom occur in the course of more formal meetings and seminars where the pressure to impress one's peers is more intense. Introductions of unfamiliar or newly hired members of the organization are another important benefit of social gatherings. This is particularly important in larger institutions with many subdivisions where the natural encounter rates among individuals tends to be low. At SIO the Director hosts monthly coffee & bagel get-togethers in various locations on the SIO campus, and the Institution finds occasions for collective celebrations.

To encourage participation in informal social events and reinforce an institution's atmosphere of collegiality, directors might consider extending personal invitations to some of these events and perhaps limit the size of the groups to promote more personal interactions and draw out colleagues with a tendency toward shyness. To have one's presence personally requested is an honor and conveys an impression that the leader(s) of the institution value the invitee's contributions to the organization.

Encounters in the Course of Daily Activities

Where and when possible, shared facilities such as mailboxes, copy machines, fax machines, and even attractive break areas can be arranged to draw people out of their offices and labs, increasing the likelihood of casual encounters.

Many faculty members voiced their conviction that the most effective strategies for enhancing interactions among scientists involve uncontrived meetings in the course of everyday activities. Several enthusiastically echoed a desire that SIO establish an attractive centralized cafe or pub where scientists could gather informally. Already burdened with too many formal meetings, university researchers favor low-energy opportunities for dialog.

Introductions via Newsletters

Weekly newsletters announcing seminars and meetings might include a feature on a "colleague of the week". A brief summary of the individual's professional and personal interests could be accompanied by a photograph. Each year this practice would offer 52 opportunities to meet or learn more about colleagues in the organization. Such unceremonious introductions would make it easier for people to initiate conversations.

Benefits of the approaches described here may extend beyond sowing seeds for potentially fruitful scientific exchanges; improved communication can lead to better-informed decisions on matters of institutional importance as well as engender a stronger sense of community. It would not be at all surprising to find more formal institutional meetings infused with a new sense of civility and respect developed in a context of personal and professional familiarity. Heightened communication among individuals in different divisions could also be useful in resolving real or perceived differences in the way these groups function. Recognition of shared or overlapping interests among individuals and groups could facilitate the identification of joint funding opportunities and even potential new job candidates. Considering their low-cost and potential rewards, the approaches outlined here seem to be logical starting points in efforts to improve internal communication.

SUMMARIZING KEYS OF SUCCESS

Our examination of two academic organizations and one private industry research division reveals management practices that foster research excellence:

1. Whether management is strongly hierarchical or more loosely structured, ensuring that individual scientists participate in decision-making processes promotes effective leadership and contributes to the overall health of an organization.
2. Recruitment and promotion of bright, young scientists and/or students, who lead into new directions, challenge the establishment, and create headaches for administration, fosters research excellence. In turn, a reputation for research excellence is a factor in attracting and retaining the best scientists.

3. Hire the best people, placing less emphasis on specialty and more on individual talent. Employ active recruiting strategies, and strive to streamline hiring and promotion procedures.
4. Create an environment of collaboration and competition. Some internal competition is healthy, but it must be managed so that it is not destructive.
5. Mitigate geographic barriers to internal communication by facilitating informal as well as formal encounters among individuals. Students can be particularly effective in catalyzing scientific exchanges.

CONCLUSIONS

Perhaps the most striking observation is that, despite their differences, these organizations are all highly successful. None of the three is structured as a traditional academic department; all are larger than a typical university department, and seem more able to cope with the diverse demands of interdisciplinary research. Each has evolved its own approach to its internal structure and governance, which presumably responds to the particular challenges presented by its research goals and by its mission. One has to be very careful not to be overly prescriptive as to what constitutes success. Nonetheless, the clear thread that runs through all three institutions is that the quality and motivation of the scientists is the *sine qua non* of success.

REFERENCE

Goldberger, M. L., Maher, B. A., Flattau, P. E. (1995). *Research-Doctorate Programs in the United States: Continuity and Change*, National Academy Press, Washington D.C.

CHAPTER 13

An Agenda for the Governing Board

Harold M. Williams

This symposium addressed a very critical aspect of the future of the research university – governance. Without a clearer delineation of the responsibilities of boards, administrative leadership and faculty, leadership and decision making and the ability of the institution to address the future, responsibly and timely, is severely jeopardized.

Yet, throughout the symposium, I was discomforted by the lack of comment or discussion addressing the broadly based criticisms of higher education generally and the funding crisis facing public higher education, and the impact both are having on the future of the public research university. To address these issues, the following is a recommended agenda for governing boards and administrators concerned with the future of the public research university. While it relates particularly to the American situation, I believe much of it is relevant in other countries as well.

The issues do not lend themselves to simple solutions and some may be insoluble or just "too hot to handle." Individual institutions will respond differently— experimenting, innovating, and restructuring. But the collective response, I believe, will shape the future of the public research university. With certainty, it will be different than it is today.

The importance of the research university to a democratic society as educator and primary source of fundamental and applied research and public service has never been greater. However, the public research university faces unprecedented external pressures which can fundamentally alter its status, independence and ability to discharge its mission. Its quest for external funding makes it vulnerable to pressures from political forces, private donors, and private industry. The demand and expectation for access continues to grow far in excess of the resources available to accommodate it. Technology has the potential to reshape how and where learning occurs and research is pursued. Dissatisfaction with the emphasis on research at the expense of the quality of undergraduate education is growing. Private sector, for-profit enterprises are moving aggressively into higher education, using emerging technologies and addressing the need for life long learning and retraining. At the same time, the growth of knowledge will continue to exceed the available resources.

Yet the university appears to behave in the traditional fashion. The academy's inherent conservatism in addressing criticism or pressures for change is both a liability and a source of stability. Higher education as an institution responds to external pressures only slowly and then in an *ad hoc*, unorganized manner. The pattern appears to be to co-opt the critics, to ignore the complaints, to defuse the issue with bland reassurances that the situation is under control and ride it out as best one can with confidence that it will, eventually, go away. The objective: preserve the *status quo*, or at least modify it as little as possible. The positive of such an approach, of course, is the ability of higher education to insulate itself from the fad of the moment, as it sees itself responsible for protecting the essence and integrity of what the institution is all about and how it goes about fulfilling its institutional goals and obligations. At the same time, it constrains and neutralizes the ability of the institution to address major issues in a timely and optimal manner.

The crucial issue facing the public research university is the extent to which it will lead in shaping its own future, taking into account the external forces impacting it or, alternatively, whether it will be overtaken by those forces.

GOVERNANCE AND LEADERSHIP

The basic governance system of American higher education is sound in principle, with responsibility placed with an independent board of trustees.

Institutional leadership of the university has the responsibility to protect the academic principles that define and guide it and address the issues which will define its future. While shared governance may identify where the responsibility for a given decision may rest, the leadership responsibility remains with the board and the chief executive to assure that the critical issues are addressed comprehensively and timely.

Governing boards need to assure that university administrators exercise their authority and responsibility in this regard. Few university presidents appear to speak for the academic principles. Academic leadership tends to disappear in the process of deliberation. Shared governance has become so pervasive as to deny the concept of or erode much of the responsibility for academic leadership. Further, the time devoted to leading fund raising campaigns – now virtually continuous – distracts, or excuses, leadership from the responsibility for leading the institution.

Fund-raising underscores the troublesome "show me the money" attitude that increasingly pervades higher education and the research university – whether in its competition for public funding or in its capital campaigns. The direction of growth and the priorities of the institution are increasingly determined by those activities for which money can be raised. The tightness of public resources places the institutions under increasingly competitive market pressures to obtain resources. But market economy undermines intellectual independence. Leadership needs to be more deliberate than it appears to be in assuring that the quest for money does not distort the principles, direction and priorities of the institution or lead it in an unwise academic direction. What appear to be immediate opportunities may evolve into unwise long-term commitments. How will institutions of higher education protect and preserve their intellectual independence given the dependence on external resources i.e., government and the growing relationship to industry?

Leadership is made more difficult as the sense of institutional community has eroded. Administrators devote more and more time to fund-raising. Faculty are becoming increasingly independent of whatever institution with which they happen to be affiliated. Loyalty today tends to be more to the discipline and to other relationships external to the institution. The number of professors quitting the university to join computer or Internet ventures, or dividing their time between the two, or taking sabbaticals to work on high-tech ventures, raises questions about the depth of their engagement with the university. Faculty are also more responsive to recruitment offers from other universities of increased research funding and support. Hence their concern for the future of the institution and participation in its governance has diminished. Can this trend be reversed or does the concept or extent of shared governance need to be reconsidered?

Henry Rosovsky, in his final report as dean of the Faculty of Arts and Sciences (FAS) at Harvard wrote: "This brings me to the crux of the matter. FAS has become a society largely without rules, or to put it slightly differently, the tenured members of the faculty – frequently as *individuals* – make their own rules. Of course, there are a great many rules in any bureaucratic organization, but these largely concern less essential matters. When it concerns our more important obligations – faculty citizenship – neither rule nor custom is any longer compelling.

"To put it slightly differently, as a social organism, we operate without a written constitution and with very little common law. That is a poor combination, especially when there is no strong consensus concerning duties and standards of behavior." (Harvard Faculty of Arts and Sciences, Dean's Report, 1990-91, Cambridge: Harvard University)

ACCOUNTABILITY

The concept of accountability is difficult to argue against or to implement. Who should be accountable to whom and for what? At a minimum, there are widely held criticisms of the university that should be addressed. They undoubtedly impact adversely upon the image of the institution and the level of support for public funding. They go to the issue of whether the resources are being used wisely and whether leadership is holding itself and the faculty accountable for what they do.

We are a fractured society—critical, intolerant, lacking in community. In context, it is not surprising that higher education comes under criticism as well. But the fact that many of the criticisms have a basis in fact and are widely acknowledged—even by strong supporters—should be ringing alarm bells in the academy and its leadership.

Public financing of higher education has brought with it expectations that higher education be responsive to the inquiries, judgments and will of the public and its political representatives. These expectations have evolved over time to include criticisms of the institution and many of its activities. Higher education faces questions about its basic institutional purposes and goals, its policies on admissions and academic standards, controversy over undergraduate curricula and of quality of teaching, questions about academic culture, concern for costs continually rising beyond inflation, and accountability. As a consequence the institution of higher education is not held in the high regard it enjoyed in the past. These are concerns the governing body should address and to which it should respond publicly.

A report for the Education Commission of the States, entitled "Higher Education Agenda," stated the following:

"We sense a growing frustration – even anger – among many of the nation's governors, state legislators, and major corporate leaders that higher education is seemingly disengaged from the battle. Colleges and universities are perceived more often than not as the source of the problems rather than part of the solution. The issues raised are usually specific: lack of involvement in solutions to the problems of urban schools, failure to lead in the reform of teacher education, questions about faculty workload and productivity, and lack of commitment to teaching or the escalating and seemingly uncontrollable cost of a college education. But whatever the issue, the overall sense of many outside colleges and universities is either that dramatic action will be needed to shake higher education from its internal lethargy and focus, or that the system must be bypassed for other institutional forms and alternatives." (Education Commission of the States, "Higher Education Agenda," 17 November 1989)

What are the values of the public research university today that define the end in itself, not the university as an instrument of external ends? How does it measure up? What reforms must it undertake? How does it convince its constituents – boards, administration, faculty, legislators and public constituencies – to "buy in"? How are the complaints and criticisms of the public and its representatives to be answered?

The strengthening of the scholarly mission demands the willingness to focus on broad educational objectives, rigorous selection of priorities and understanding of and address to the university's internal weaknesses and failures. The demands on the institution and its opportunities will always exceed the resources available to respond. Its future will be determined by the choices it makes. It needs to be able to change and introduce new priorities and maintain the dynamism of the institution essentially without adequate additional financial resources. It needs to question existing premises and arrangements, evaluate, revise and/or eliminate existing processes and administrative structures. It needs to do new things and old things better with existing resources and eliminate or diminish some functions so others can be established or grow. It needs to reduce less useful areas in order to develop more useful ones.

The academy allocates additional resources reasonably well, but does not address resource reallocation decisions well. These circumstances place new pressures on the processes of governance and call for strengthening the decision making process – for the governing boards and administrators to be more proactive in addressing the issues and building consensus and for faculty to rise above parochial interests and to engage with the future of the institution.

FUNDING PUBLIC HIGHER EDUCATION

Access to public higher education in the United States has become a right rather than a privilege for every high school graduate capable of benefiting from it and at a cost that he or she could afford. Demand for access is growing due both to changing demographics and to the public perception that a college degree is essential for economic opportunity and upward mobility. In a shift attributed to the changing economy, higher education is increasingly seen as essential for access to the middle class. A college education has become as important as a high school diploma formerly was.

Public funding for higher education, however, does not correspond to the demands for access. It has been described as "boom or bust." It is not high in priority in relation to other demands on the public purse. Therefore, during economic recessions higher education tends to absorb disproportionate cuts in public funding, often accompanied by steep increases in tuition. To compensate, during economic prosperity higher education is often benefited disproportionately. However, over the long run, the percentage of government revenues devoted to higher education and per student funding have been shrinking.

Maintaining current quality and service levels for higher education will require either increasing taxes or favoring higher education over competing public service demands, such as elementary and secondary education, health, welfare and prisons. Neither is likely. It is likely that existing financing trends coupled with political and public demand for access will drive public policy on higher education. *The political and economic reality of public higher education is that access must be maintained and that education of at least present quality must continue to be delivered but at lower cost per student.*

This creates a situation which calls for a basic rethinking of the structure of public higher education generally and the role of the public research university specifically. It will not be solved by changes at the margin or by wishful thinking that political attitudes will change. Can both access and quality be maintained? Given priority for access, what will happen to quality? How can costs be contained?

Public higher education, and particularly the public research university, will not survive as it is merely because it should. It will not disappear, but the forces at work threaten to transform it so that at some point in the next half-century it may be recognizable in name only.

Many studies in the private sector demonstrate that the reputation of a product brand franchise can last much longer than the quality of the product justifies. There is a time lag between decline in the quality of a well-respected branded product and the public realization that the product is no longer what its reputation was based upon. The principle applies equally in the world of higher education. Erosion of quality is subtle and the realization that its product no longer lives up to its image may occur long after its current university and political leadership have retired without confronting the issue.

The pressures on access and quality do not have the same impact on the private institutions. Private research universities are not under public pressure to increase access. At the same time, their endowments have grown enormously. In the past year alone, many private university endowments have grown by 30 to 40 percent, and as much as 60%. Not concerned with increasing access, they can direct their expanding resources to improve quality. The ability of the public research university to compete is eroding. For example, the April 22, 2000 issue of *The Economist*, page 24, reports on a study by Ting Alexander, an economist at the University of Illinois, to the effect that the salary gap between full professors at the country's best private universities and its best public ones has grown from $1,300 in 1980 to $21,700 in 1998. They can offer larger research budgets, smaller teaching loads and tuition reciprocity programs, which Alexander characterizes as "a quarter of a million-dollar jackpot if you have three children." The article goes on to conclude that the nation's public universities are at risk of becoming training grounds for private universities with bigger checkbooks. Given the pressures for access and limited public funding, can the public research university any longer realistically aspire to compete with the private research universities? Is this a conclusion for which the public governing and funding bodies are prepared to accept responsibility?

EDUCATION FOR WHAT?

Historically, the central purpose of higher education has been the development of responsible citizens rather than training students for jobs. Isn't it time for higher education, including the research university, to re-examine its commitment to that purpose? What remains of general or liberal learning in the modern university? Are we educating citizens, potential leaders, and people with the ability to question and discern, or are we training a work force? What is the appropriate trade-off between professional preparation engaged in chiefly with a view towards primarily extrinsic considerations and a liberal arts education pursued first and foremost for its own intrinsic value? Undergraduates should have a broad learning experience in addition to their specialization. But it seems that the pressure towards the latter is increasing.

If the universities have no independent mission of their own other than the training of individuals for jobs, then they should not be surprised that they are treated like any other supplier of a service.

Renewing the institutional commitment to meaningful undergraduate teaching and learning would require a fundamental shift in resource allocation. It would also increase interest in exploring pedagogy and the use of technology. Can this be accomplished without a thorough re-examination of the academic culture as a whole, i.e. of the institutional environment?

TEACHING

The unity of teaching and research, a fundamental principle of the research university has lost its equilibrium.

Allegations are broad based that teaching as an activity is seriously undervalued, that undergraduate instruction and student mentoring are neglected as a priority or consigned to the hands of graduate students to an unacceptable extent and that professors have forsaken their classroom obligations for other pursuits, particularly research and published scholarship.

There are many students, parents and legislators, probably an overwhelming majority, who value institutions of higher learning not for their outreach and service functions or even for their research mission, but for the teaching they are capable of supplying. As consumers they will expect and demand improvement.

Is there a choice? Is the concept of a four-year undergraduate education on a residential campus, with graduate education in various academic disciplines and professions and faculty devoted to teaching research and service any longer a fit and will it meet with the needs and expectations of the various constituencies? Why should the research university engage in undergraduate general education? Why not begin in the upper division or possibly only at graduate level and professional schools? Can research institutions be economically viable without the undergraduate infrastructure?

To the extent that new, primarily for profit, providers of higher education focused only on teaching, erode the university's role of job training, what will happen to government and private support of research and service? For, regardless of how universities allocate costs internally, it is teaching that provides its largest revenue source and infrastructure, which in turn underwrites much of the research and service.

TENURE

What could be more detrimental to effective teaching than its order of priority in the attainment of tenure and promotion? Can teaching be improved without addressing the absolute job security provided by faculty tenure? Does tenure serve the best interests of the institution? If not, how might it be modified? While academic freedom is clearly a right, should academic tenure be of the same stature? While it is defended as a protection of academic freedom and a guarantee of independence, being permanent and without limit of time gives it a different quality. Upon grant, it is or should be recognition of competitive excellence. Unlike the right to academic freedom, however, shouldn't academic tenure continually be justified and sustained? Shouldn't it be a privilege rather than a right? Shouldn't it carry with it a special obligation to perform as a trusted professional and at a level that reflects continued competitive excellence not only in research but in teaching and service as well? Academic tenure should not be a form of security of employment similar to civil service. The expectations and obligations that come with a tenured appointment are greater than those that come with bureaucratic employment. Given federal legislation ending mandatory retirement, tenure truly guarantees faculty members the right to lifelong employment subject to very minimum standards of performance. Further, given the increasing mobility of faculty, tenure lacks a reciprocal commitment to the institution to justify it.

Recognizing the distinction between academic freedom and tenure may help focus attention on how academic freedom, which depends on institutional autonomy, can be protected when the institution is so vulnerable to the market economy.

RESEARCH

The research university is where society still turns for the solution to its problems and the address to its needs. This is where science, technology and modern medicine are created. Is higher education's research effort sufficient in the face of contemporary problems? Is investment in research at current levels sufficient to sustain the intellectual momentum of the research university? A strong case can be made for answering both questions in the negative. If so, what are the consequences?

Where might additional research resources be obtained and at what cost? The freedom of the university from market constraints has supported the kind of open-ended basic research that led to some of the most important discoveries in history. The university researchers should have the freedom to explore ideas that have no obvious or immediate commercial value. It seems it can only continue if universities maintain a degree of independence from the marketplace—a difficult thing to do in an age of dwindling public support for higher education. How can academic freedom and the integrity of university research be preserved in the context of the need for greater research funding and of increasing connectedness with industry and of proprietary research and faculty entrepreneurship?

SERVICE

Critics argue that the academy as a whole has grown too insular and removed from the actual circumstances of modern life and, therefore, is failing to discharge its service mission in a meaningful way.

Have higher education research and service efforts sufficiently addressed contemporary problems of our society? For example, what have graduate schools of education of the research universities contributed to address, ameliorate, and solve the current crisis in the quality of teaching? It has taken a national teachers' union in a recent statement to urge the strengthening of the standards for selection of potential teachers and the rigor of their content training. While it has not been the role of the research university to produce the majority of teachers for the public schools, they are looked to for the quality of research that would influence and guide the decision making process that results in student achievement. Yet, whatever the issue, whether it be the quality and content of pre-service training standards, student assessment, evaluation of teaching, or pedagogy, schools of education individually and collectively have had little positive impact on the most important issue confronting American society today. Indeed, their lack of impact, itself an indictment, can easily lead one to the conclusion that they share responsibility for the problem.

DOCTORAL EDUCATION

Does doctoral education need to be restructured? Most PhDs do not make their careers in research universities, yet their training is geared toward such positions. There are arguments within the academy that the apprenticeship model is outmoded. Graduate students feel exploited as teaching assistants and are trained for jobs at research universities that are few and far between. Teaching institutions find it difficult to hire new PhDs who actually know how to teach. Business leaders complain that many new PhDs cannot communicate and don't know how to apply theory to real world problems. It is argued that while we may have an oversupply of PhDs for the academy, we do not have an oversupply of PhDs for society, but that means that the training needs to be different. The challenges facing doctoral education in the sciences differ from the humanities and social sciences. In the sciences, how is the academy going to compete and hold the best and the brightest who are increasingly choosing industry?

INFORMATION TECHNOLOGY

Dr. Neil Rudenstein, president of Harvard University, has said he believes that the information technology revolution and globalization of the economy herald a tectonic shift in academia, akin to the switch from small colleges to large research universities at the turn of the century and the vastly expanded access to higher education after World War II. "The totality of the institution will be a different configuration," he said (New York Times, May 23, 2000), Whether or not one agrees, is this not an issue that should be closely examined and considered on an ongoing basis at the institutional level?

As new technologies spread into society and as demand for higher education becomes more global, how much of what the public research university does, or should do, can be served by it in the traditional model? As publishing, broadcasting, telecommunications and education merge, private sector organizations will create new educational programs and means of disseminating knowledge to ever-larger audiences at ever decreasing costs.

Institutional commitment tends to be inadequate to explore intelligently, and by application and experimentation, the impact of information technology – even on such immediately apparent possibilities as the extent to which it can enhance learning, embrace developments in pedagogy, promote access, economize on resources, make the very best scholar teachers more available, accelerate the time to graduation, make classes available at times and locations more convenient to the working student, etc. The concern that campuses would no longer exist, that student interaction within class and otherwise would be eliminated and that the costs and demands on faculty time would be greater impede reasoned exploration and experimentation. With few exceptions, whatever progress is being made is the product of individual creative faculty, rather than of institutional leadership, support and priority. Organized efforts to experiment, build on successes and learn from experience are developing much more rapidly in the private sector, which is offering degree programs and responding to the growing demand for lifelong learning and retraining.

CONCLUSION

The issues described are on the minds of many, both within the public research university and within the larger universe concerned with its future. They need to be addressed at the institutional level. While individual institutions may reach different conclusions on individual issues, I have confidence in the collective judgment, assuming that the issues are addressed objectively and in time.

APPENDIX

The Glion Declaration 2000

APPENDIX

The Glion Declaration 2000
University Governance at the Crossroads

Frank H. T. Rhodes
On behalf of the Glion Colloquium

The editors stress that the structures, missions and challenges of Western European and American universities have much in common. But there also exist significant differences, one relating to governing boards. In the United States, these boards fulfill important functions. But, in Western Europe, they do not exist at all, or only in a weaker form. Some European countries have boards similar to the American boards, but with less or little decision power. Others have no board or a board without authority; they have instead "participation councils", where the different internal stakeholders are represented. Moreover, some of the roles exercised by American boards are played by the State.

This declaration is influenced somewhat by the American environment characterized by powerful boards. However, the editors are convinced that the thoughts expressed about the role of boards are of interest to readers in Europe, because the development whereby boards take over some of the power to support and/or monitor the action of the Rector, Vice-Chancellor or President traditionally invested in the State is there gaining support.

The Glion Declaration of 1998 called for the reaffirmation of the social compact between society and its universities, so as to enable them to make their fullest contribution to the changing needs of the larger global community. It also urged universities to a new rededication to effective teaching, creative scholarship and research and the development of new and expanded partnerships in the public service. The signatories to the Glion Declaration, joined by a number of additional colleagues, met again in Del Mar, California, from January 5-9, 2000 to consider the governance of universities in Europe and the United States, and especially its relationship to their institutional well-being and effective performance.

THE DISTINCTIVE ROLE OF THE RESEARCH UNIVERSITIES

In both Western Europe and in the United States, there exists a number of distinctive universities, sometimes referred to as major research universities, that educate a substantial portion of those earning first professional degrees and the vast majority of those earning the Ph.D. and advanced professional degrees, that perform most of the basic research, and play a major role in technical development and public service. They do not stand alone in this. We recognize their heavy dependence on all other educational institutions —primary, secondary and tertiary —and applaud their efforts to increase cooperation with and provide added support for these and other institutions.

Universities are communities of enquiry, discovery and learning, created and supported by society, with the conviction that the growth and diffusion of knowledge not only enrich personal experience, but also serve the public good and advance human well-being. The university learning community—now enlarged by the steady growth in outreach of its activities beyond the campus, by growing participation in traditional courses and programs and by the worldwide explosion in all forms of distance learning—must assume an expanded role, undertake new tasks and accept added responsibility in a society where a global economy, growing competition and rapid technological change make it increasingly dependent on knowledge as a basic economic capital. Even as we applaud the readiness of the university to embrace this larger role, we note that it imposes new strains on long-established values and long-standing practices and produces added tensions in traditional patterns of institutional governance and management. It is to these challenges that we now address ourselves.

INSTITUTIONAL VALUES: FREEDOM AND RESPONSIBILITY

The effectiveness of the university over a period of more than nine hundred years has been dependent on the maintenance of a judicious balance between freedom and responsibility: this balance has involved institutional autonomy, allowing freedom of enquiry, expression and teaching, on the one hand, and, on the other, self-regulation, educational integrity, scholarly impartiality and professional responsibility. It is this balance which has served as the basis for the social compact, in which society supports the university, financially and in granting a remarkable degree of institutional autonomy and academic freedom, with the understanding that both its resources and its freedom will be used responsibly to serve the public interest.

This mixture of freedom and responsibility has served both society and the university well, but we now see it under growing strain, from both internal changes and external forces. In the United States, for example, the desire to encourage student achievement has seen the traditional commitment to educational integrity weakened in some institutions by widespread grade inflation; greater commitment to research has led in some places to inattention to undergraduate teaching and the subordination of advising and mentoring; a desire to recognize the interests of a wider public has sometimes led to partisanship within the classroom and the rise of "political correctness," while, perhaps from a sense of civic concern, scholarly impartiality has been weakened, in some cases, by advocacy, thinly disguised as scholarship. In several European countries, reduced funding has produced so great an increase in teaching loads as to diminish the effectiveness of some research programs. In identifying these issues, we mean neither to exaggerate their particular impact, nor to suggest that they are ubiquitous, or that collectively they represent a crisis in the affairs of the university. But, they do exist and, unless they are addressed, they could become serious challenges to the norms of impartial scholarship, true freedom of expression and full and fair enquiry that have long been promoted by the university.

Other challenges to these norms and values come from the commendable efforts universities are making to extend their outreach and enlarge their public service. In their attempts to cooperate with industry, universities wrestle with demands for restrictive corporate contracts and exclusive partnerships. In an attempt to increase sources of support for their traditional teaching responsibilities, some universities have experimented with the creation of separate for-profit companies, seeking to benefit from everything from distance learning to athletics, to technology transfer. In their efforts to better serve the public, universities have undertaken the sponsorship and management of community enterprises, such as schools, environmental initiatives and health care organizations, sometimes in alliances with public agencies, or other groups. All of these pose unfamiliar challenges to traditional campus norms and values, even as they seek to extend the effectiveness of the university's services and increase the usefulness of its activities. Paradoxically, each new initiative to increase the inclusiveness and extend the usefulness of the university poses challenges to familiar styles of governance and management and traditional values and raises difficult questions of institutional responsibility.

We should be neither surprised nor dismayed at these internal and external stresses, for the history of universities is rich in comparable examples, from the development of the curriculum and the nature of oversight of student conduct to the growth of scholarly enquiry and applied research. But history also reveals that the cherished values of the university—integrity, excellence, community, openness, respect, civility, freedom, responsibility, impartiality, tolerance—all exercised within an autonomous community of learning, are not items of intellectual adornment or personal convenience but are a means to an end, the essential requirements for the effective pursuit of knowledge. These values are, however, neither an excuse for inaction nor an alternative to appropriate accountability. They are the lifeblood of the institution. Developed and refined over centuries, contested within and tested from without, they have proved the essential means not only for effective learning and discovery, but also for its wise and humane application to human needs. It is these values that must continue to be prized and preserved and the principal responsibility for this rests with the board members, officers and faculty of each university. How these values are reflected and embodied in the life and work of the university will, no doubt, vary from institution to institution. That they should be reflected, is everybody's business. This is no casual obligation, but a responsibility of surpassing importance, for without respect for these values, there can be no university worth the name. In fact, in those countries where these values have been neglected or suppressed, universities have become places of political turmoil, pedestrian training, or dogmatic propaganda. We call on our colleagues to reaffirm and reassert these ancient values and to embrace them in every aspect of the life of their institutions.

INSTITUTIONAL AUTONOMY AND GOVERNANCE

Just as individual freedom has emerged as an essential means for the effective pursuit of knowledge, so also has institutional autonomy developed over centuries as the most effective means of harnessing knowledge to the public good. The means to achieve this autonomy differ from country to country and, in some cases, from institution to institution. In general, public universities, both in the United States and, to a lesser degree, in Western Europe, are governed by boards with substantial public representation, with a membership achieved either by constitutional, governmental or gubernatorial appointment or by election. In some cases, as in American public universities, the board has wide powers, appointing the president and granting tenure to faculty, for example, within a budget approved by the state legislature. In many European countries, in contrast, the university rector, or president, and the professors are formally appointed by the state, after nomination by the university, according to a procedure specific to each institution. In other European countries, some of the board's responsibilities are delegated to participating councils, composed of representatives of different stakeholders. In the quite different case of the private universities, which are found chiefly within the

United States, the board is typically self-appointed and is the final governing body for all decisions, though in practice many responsibilities are delegated to others.

We are concerned here with the broad principles of shared governance, between the board and/or council, the president and the campus stakeholders, especially the faculty. Because of the widespread existence of governing boards, and as many European universities which now lack them are in the process of developing them, we concentrate on the work of boards in the comments that follow.

The function of a governing board is always twofold: it serves, on the one hand, to ensure the public responsibility and accountability of the university and, on the other, to defend the autonomy and integrity of the institution against erosion or attack, both from without and within.

Because the governance of institutions of higher education has been entrusted to a designated group of public representatives, responsible for the oversight of its affairs and the integrity of its activities, the board has ultimate authority over and responsibility for all the activities of the university, though in practice it delegates much of its authority and support. In the United States, for example, the board annually confers upon the president the right to award degrees and delegates to the faculty the responsibility of developing the curriculum. This pattern of delegation and the tradition of shared governance it represents is never absolute; it may sometimes be subject to review and it may also involve some tensions. It is well, however, to minimize ambiguities and clarify the exact nature of delegation. Thus, typically, in the United States, for example, the responsibility for student admissions is delegated to the faculty and administration, but recent actions by the regents of some major state university systems have limited that responsibility. Similarly, the responsibility for curriculum requirements is substantially delegated to the faculty, but recent actions by the trustees of another major state university have eroded that particular responsibility.

The exact composition, role and responsibilities of governing boards differ from country to country. In the United Kingdom, an official guide to the conduct of board business has been published. We urge similar clarity in other cases.

We are persuaded that effective governance by the board, responsibly exercised, is just as vital to the performance and well being of the university as are the responsibility of the faculty and the effectiveness of the administration. We believe that a number of recent trends threaten to weaken this governance, especially within the public universities in the United States, where political influence and special interests sometimes compete with responsible governance.

EFFECTIVE TRUSTEESHIP: THE ROLE OF GOVERNING BOARDS

Just as we call on members of the faculty to play a responsible role in all their university activities, so we call on trustees and members of governing boards to exercise their fiduciary power in governance responsibly. At a minimum, this seems to call for:

- Reconsideration of the application of public meetings law requirements and a prudent evaluation of their benefits against the "tyrannies of transparency."
- Improved selection of trustees within constitutional categories, perhaps by the appointment of an independent screening board to provide impartial assessment.
- Reconsideration of board size (often now eight members in many public universities in the United States) in relation to function, with the possibility of increasing board size by adding additional independent members.
- Regular self-assessment of performance by the governing board.
- Development by boards of a code of conduct.
- Informed governance, based on adequate knowledge of the complexities of the institution. That, in turn, requires an adequate information base, involving not only statistical profiles and budgetary allocations, but also an understanding of the nature, quality and relationships of campus programs and activities.
- Appropriate delegation of some authority to other responsible groups and bodies (the president, the faculty and so on) with the understanding that explicit clarification of this delegation is likely to improve effectiveness, that decisions made by others under such delegated authority may sometimes be subject to board review and reconsideration, and that the board may not delegate its ultimate authority for the mission, integrity and financial viability of the institution.
- Recognition of the fact that board members, as citizen representatives, exercise not only institutional oversight, but also the responsibility to defend and promote the institution and nurture its values. Their loyalty to the larger public interest can be served only by their commitment to the institution as a whole, rather than to any constituency or special interest, whether internal or external. They should exhibit in their own conduct the high professional standards and impartiality they require from the faculty.
- Recognition and appreciation of the extraordinary variety, traditions and complexities of institutions of higher education, knowing that any general statement has exceptions and that no single pattern or style of governance can possibly be appropriate for all: nor can any

statement of principles be prescriptive. Nevertheless, because the board is responsible for the well being of all members of the institution and is the custodian of its resources, it has a particular responsibility for ensuring due process, orderly procedures and appropriate levels of decision-making and appeal. It will contribute to the harmony of the institution by requiring the development and application of these procedures.
- There is a world of difference between governance and management. Governance involves the responsibility for approving the mission and goals of the institution, the oversight of its resources, the approval of its policies and procedures, the appointment, review and support of its president, and an informed understanding of its programs and activities. Management, in contrast, involves the responsibility for the effective operation of the institution and the achievement of its goals, within the policies and procedures approved by the board, the effective use of its resources, the creative support and performance of teaching, research and service and maintenance of the highest standards of scholarly integrity and professional performance. The responsibility of the board is to govern, but not to manage.
- In American universities, the most important single responsibility of the board is the selection, appointment, periodic review and continuing support of the president. Candor, fairness, understanding and trust are essential ingredients in this critical relationship. The president, while performing at a satisfactory level, is entitled to the sustained support, candid advice and personal encouragement that the board is uniquely able to provide. That neither removes the need to question and to challenge, nor the obligation to understand the views of other interested parties, but the president has both a unique claim and a substantial need for the understanding and support of the board.

CAMPUS GOVERNANCE: THE ROLE AND RESPONSIBILITY OF THE FACUTLY

In urging greater attention to institutional values, we urge consideration of the following issues:
- We are particularly concerned that, in introducing newly appointed scholars to the professorial ranks and in preparing graduate students for scholarly careers, little or no attention is paid to the cultivation of scholarly values and professorial obligations. We urge faculties to address this lack.

- There exists at present a one-sided obligation in which the university is expected to provide tenure, compensation, professional support, technical services, facilities, equipment and the protection of academic freedom to the professorate, while the reciprocal obligations of the faculty member are nowhere specified. We believe a professional code of conduct would redress this imbalance and we urge the cooperative development and implementation of such a code by the administration and the faculty.
- We believe that the well being of a university requires responsible participation in matters of faculty governance and we urge the renewal of faculty interest in this important privilege. Such governance involves participation at all levels, including the department, the college or school and the institution. In Europe, where staff and students are part of the internal governing body, we urge the same responsible, informed involvement.
- We urge the principle of subsidiarity in campus governance, in which decisions are made at the lowest appropriate level of responsibility, so improving participation and understanding, and encouraging added responsiveness and accountability. We believe that, subject to the framework of the campus code, an aggrieved individual should generally have the right to appeal a particular decision to a level one step above the immediate supervisor.
- Not all "stakeholders" have an equal claim to participate in campus governance. For example, delegated authority from the board is never permanent. Nor do those with little experience and knowledge—students, for example—have equal claim to guide curriculum development as do those with substantial experience and knowledge—the faculty, for example. But, knowledge and experience are generally confined to particular areas of expertise. No faculty member and no board member, for example, can speak for the entire institution. Only the chairman of the board and the president can do so. Systems of campus governance should reflect these various levels of responsibility, avoiding burdensome proliferation of committees in favor of a streamlined governance system, with clear guidelines concerning the respective authority of each of its administrative officers and participating member-groups, and with definition of particular areas involving variously the right of information, consultation, consent or approval. Much of the present ineffectiveness of faculty governance and the cumbersome nature of decision-making reflects the confusion between the right of the faculty to be informed, their right to be consulted and their right to approve.
- The elaborate structure of campus governance and the labyrinth path by which consultations occur and decisions are generally made will

experience growing strain in the face of the increasing need for making difficult, and sometimes unpopular decisions, responding promptly to rapid changes and satisfying the burgeoning demands of government oversight and requirement. We are also concerned that because these structures and the notion of academic freedom have sometimes been used as an excuse for a failure to look critically at the performance of the university and the painful question of whether it practices the lofty values it proclaims, the public will become less tolerant of both the autonomy and the shared governance of our universities. If we wish external critics, of all persuasions, to respect the enormous importance of the research university and to recognize the need for latitude and freedom in the way it discharges its responsibilities to society, we need to respond to these concerns, to use our governance to address our own shortcomings effectively and to demonstrate that we are doing so.
- We believe effective governance requires shared goals and recognition of their achievement. We believe that faculty should be recognized and rewarded when they achieve professional success in their teaching or research, or display conspicuous devotion and commitment to their institution and its goals. This could be encouraged by designating some significant portion of the total annual faculty salary pool to be available as bonus payments to those faculty members whose performance has been outstanding.

THE ROLE OF THE PRESIDENT, VICE CHANCELLOR OR RECTOR

The essential link between the governing board and the institution it represents is the president, vice chancellor or rector. For convenience, we refer to this individual as the president. Without effective presidential leadership, no system of campus governance can be effective.
- It is the role of the president, not only to explain the role and concerns of the board to the campus community, but also to interpret for the board, the distinctive role and concerns of the faculty and other members of the campus community. The basis of this role is mutual respect and trust, without which no strong system of campus governance can develop.
- The president must lead. The president is far more than an intermediary between these groups. It is to the president that both the board and the campus look for leadership and direction. The president must supply that leadership, accepting the responsibilities and opportuni-

ties afforded by the office and delegated by the board. Presidential timidity and endless compromise are the enemies of effective campus governance. Nowhere is the need for presidential leadership greater than in leading the process of developing a statement of institutional mission, in consultation with the faculty and other stakeholders and subject to approval by the board. The president has a unique role in creating a sense of confidence and commitment among members of the campus community and in nurturing and promoting the values on which the well being of the institution depends.
- The judgment of the president is essential in achieving an effective balance between executive decision and campus and board approval, so assuring an appropriate role for each of the participants in the developing affairs of the university. Delegation, consultation, review and approval, should represent an orderly process, based on mutual understanding which pays due regard to the appropriate role and responsibilities of each of the several partners. This requires careful thought and planning of information flow, agenda preparation, consultation and cooperation.
- The president, as the duly appointed senior officer of the university, should enjoy the support and trust of the board. Proposals for action, carefully conceived, fully articulated and appropriately reviewed, both on campus and by the board, should be expected to find approval and support. While neither members of campus governance groups, nor members of the board, should ever regard their duties as mere formality or rubber-stamp action, an effective system of governance requires a clear working agreement on various areas of responsibility and the need for timely review and closure.

CONCLUSION

For over 900 years the university has supplied society with three vital commodities – shared experience, demonstrable knowledge and humanely used skills: these remain the business of the university, at once both its means and its products. Our successors in the new millennium will look back on a planet and a people whose condition will largely reflect how responsibly, intelligently and humanely we, the members of the universities, have cultivated them today and how wisely we have governed the remarkable institutions in which they are nurtured.

We believe that attention to the issues we have identified will strengthen the governance and thus improve the capacity of our universities to continue to play a beneficial role in society.

Réalisé en P.A.O. par STDI - Z.A. Route de Couterne - 53110 Lassay-les-Châteaux
Imprimé en France. - JOUVE, 18, rue Saint-Denis, 75001 PARIS
N° 292011C. - Dépôt légal : Mars 2001